Modern

BRIDAL PHOTOGRAPHY

TECHNIQUES

PORTRAITS FROM
BRETT FLORENS
TEACH YOU HOW

AMHERST MEDIA, INC. ■ BUFFALO, NY

About the Author

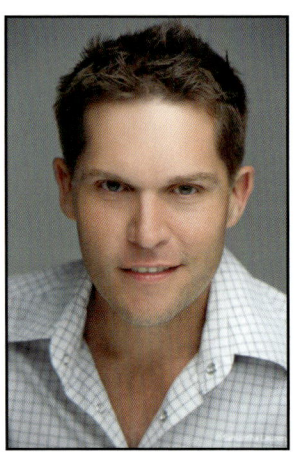

While fulfilling national service obligations in his native South Africa, Brett Florens launched his career in 1992 as a photojournalist. Since then, Brett's devotion to photography has taken him from covering police riot squads to a highly successful career as a wedding, commercial, and fashion photographer—with long-standing clients such as Wonderbra, Playtex, Quiksilver, and Roxy. Recently he received the distinction of being chosen as the representative Nikon Wedding Photographer, making him one of twelve photographers chosen worldwide as the best in their particular field. Brett is also the author of *Brett Florens' Guide to Photographing Weddings* (Amherst Media). He currently travels extensively, shooting and hosting professional seminars.

Acknowledgments

Thank you to Andrea Florens for her contributions to the editorial content of the book.

Published by:
Amherst Media, Inc.
P.O. Box 586
Buffalo, N.Y. 14226
Fax: 716-874-4508
www.AmherstMedia.com

Publisher: Craig Alesse
Senior Editor/Production Manager: Michelle Perkins
Assistant Editor: Barbara A. Lynch-Johnt
Editorial Assistance from: Sally Jarzab, John S. Loder, and Carey A. Miller
Business Manager: Adam Richards
Marketing, Sales, and Promotion Manager: Kate Neaverth
Warehouse and Fulfillment Manager: Roger Singo

ISBN-13: 978-1-60895-582-4
Library of Congress Control Number: 2012920994
10 9 8 7 6 5 4 3 2 1

Check out Amherst Media's blogs at: http://portrait-photographer.blogspot.com/
http://weddingphotographer-amherstmedia.blogspot.com/

TABLE OF CONTENTS

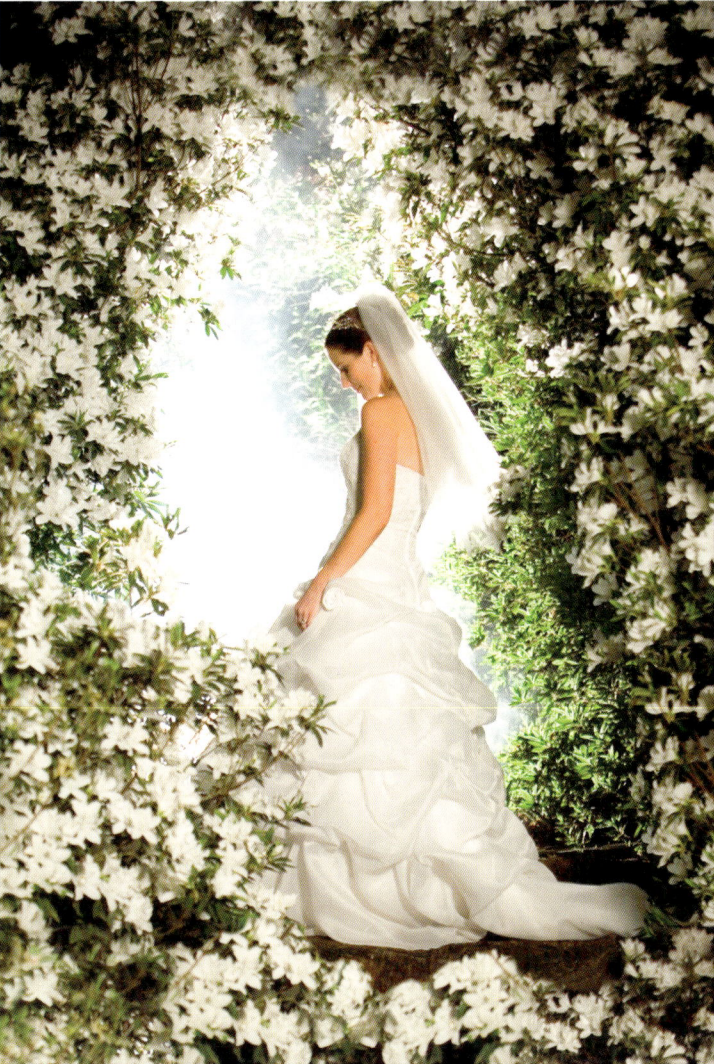

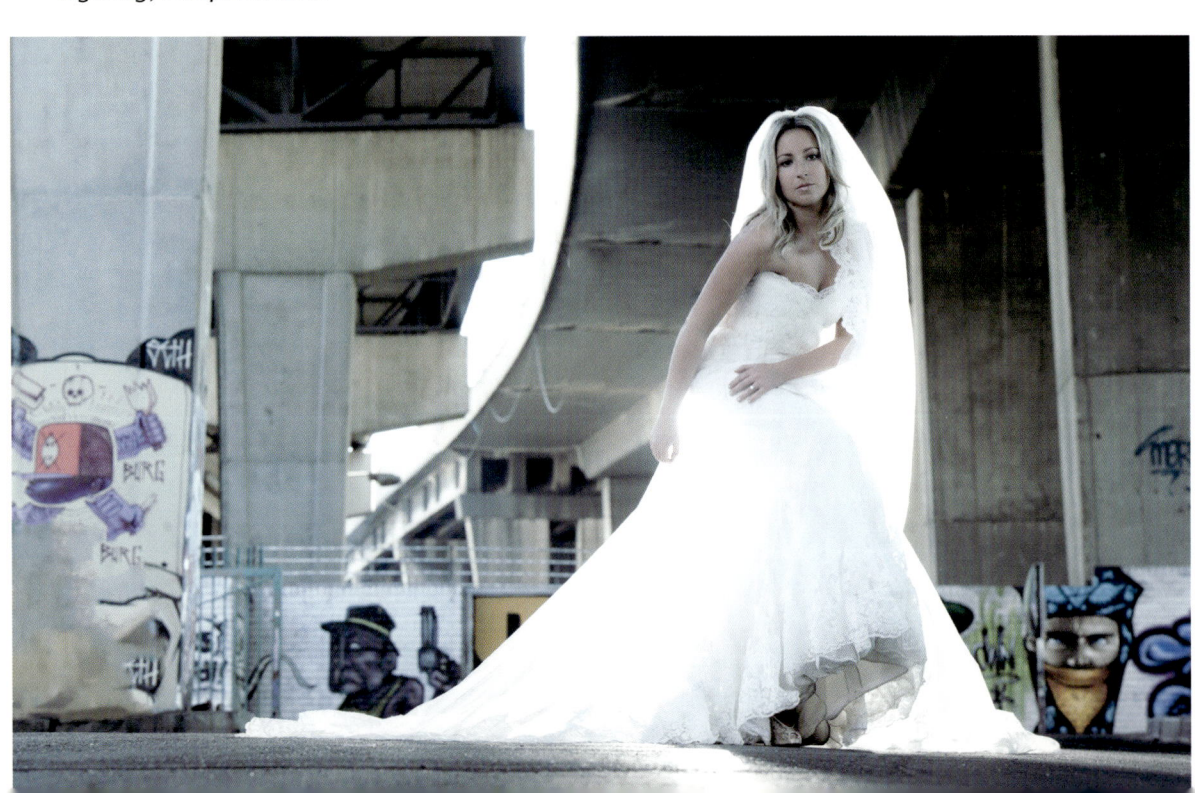

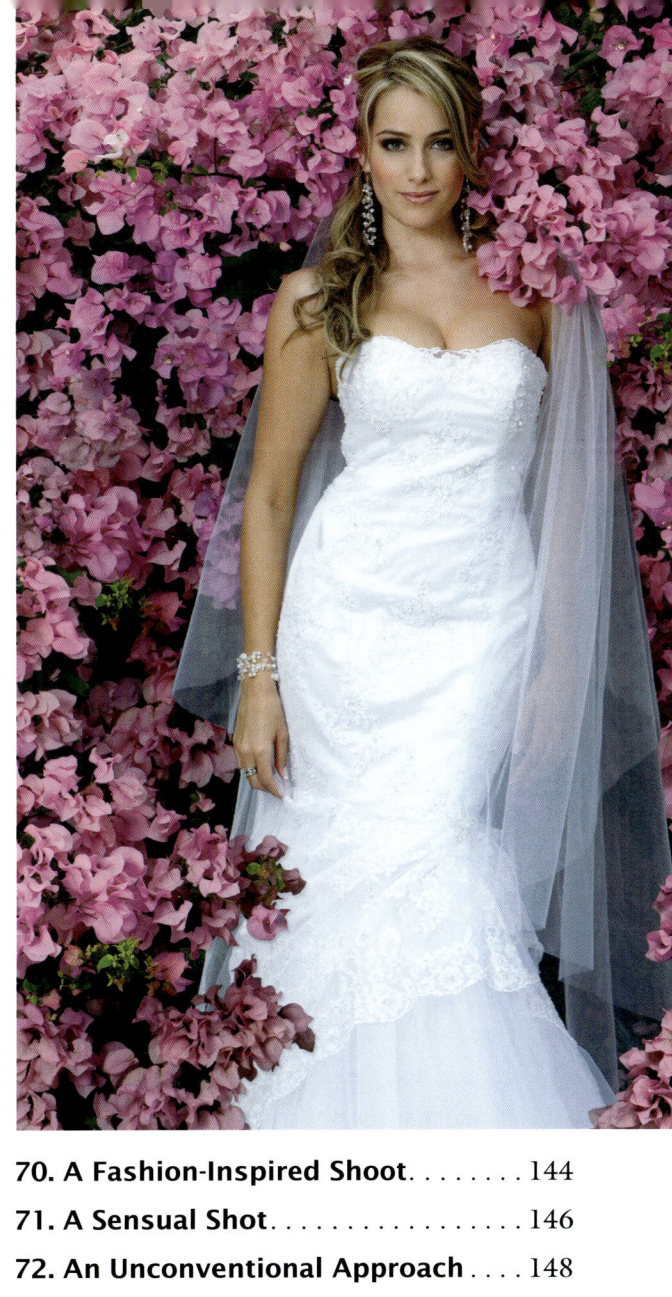

1. ESSENTIAL TOOLS

The 5-in-1 Reflector

There are a few tools that are practically obligatory in your kit. One of these is a reflector, which is used to bounce light into the shadow areas of a subject. There are a number of reflectors on the market, and the most convenient of these are the collapsible ones that fold up into an easily portable bag. The surface of these reflectors can be white, translucent, black (for subtractive lighting effects), silver foil, or gold foil. The silver and gold modifiers reflect more light than the white or translucent ones, and I find that the gold is particularly good for shading where a warm tone is needed. The 5-in-1 reflector is ideal in that it provides five surfaces and can reduce the contrast of an image in any available light situation.

This image was created with available light, using the white side of my collapsible 5-in-1 reflector. The light was coming from the bride's left side, and the reflector was able to fill in the light across the front of her face, creating a flattering image without sharp shadows.

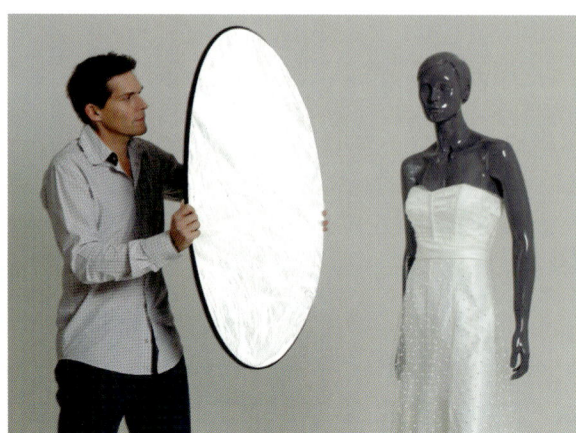

The reflector position.

The Setting and Pose

This image was created on the front porch of the bride's house. The bamboo roll-up blinds behind her served as a contemporary, organic background. The image was shot with a wide aperture of f/2.8. With a shallow depth of field, one is able to separate the subject from the background, creating a bit more of a 3-D image.

This classic pose is not difficult to emulate, and brides generally feel quite comfortable in it. Classic poses are also popular with parents and grandparents, and these tend to be the photographs that will be put in a picture frame upon the mantelpiece.

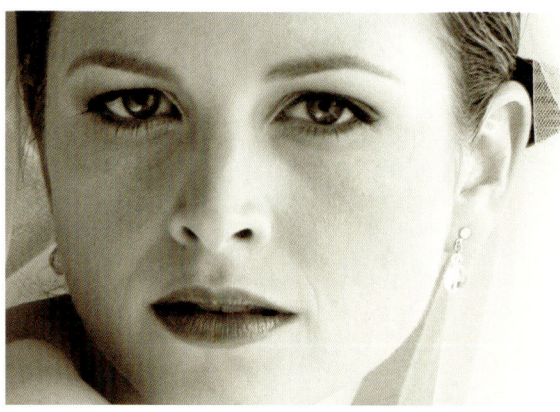

If you look closely, you can see the reflector in the highlight of the subject's eyes.

QUICK LOOK	
CAMERA	Nikon D3s
LENS	Nikkor 70–200mm f/2.8G ED VR II
MODE	A
ISO	400
SHUTTER	$^1/_{500}$
APERTURE	f/2.8
LIGHTING	Lastolite 5-in-1 collapsible reflector

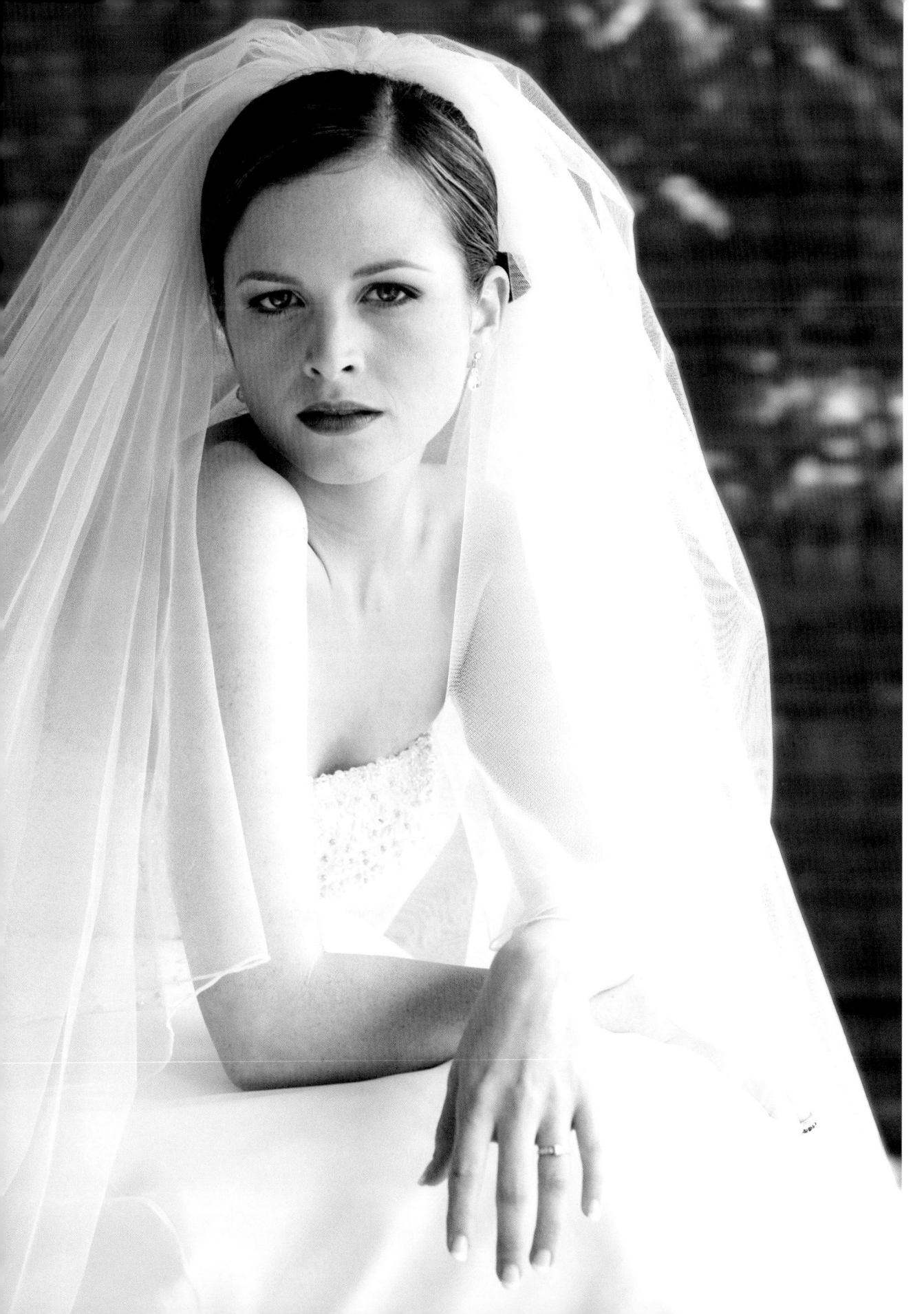

2. A CONTEMPORARY LOOK

The Appeal of Monochrome

Today, there's a trend to have unadulterated, clean lines with very little color, or a subtle monotone palette. There's a time and a place for everything, and classic bridal portraits full of color and radiance are still high in demand, but you'll often find that young brides are enamoured with these uncomplicated, contemporary shots.

Here, the pose is beautiful and subtle, giving the bride an innocent and demure look. The shutters in the background are very contemporary and quite Zen, adding to the power of the stark, clean image.

Camera Settings

This image was created by overriding the camera's matrix light metering system and over-

Had I not overexposed the image, it would have looked like this.

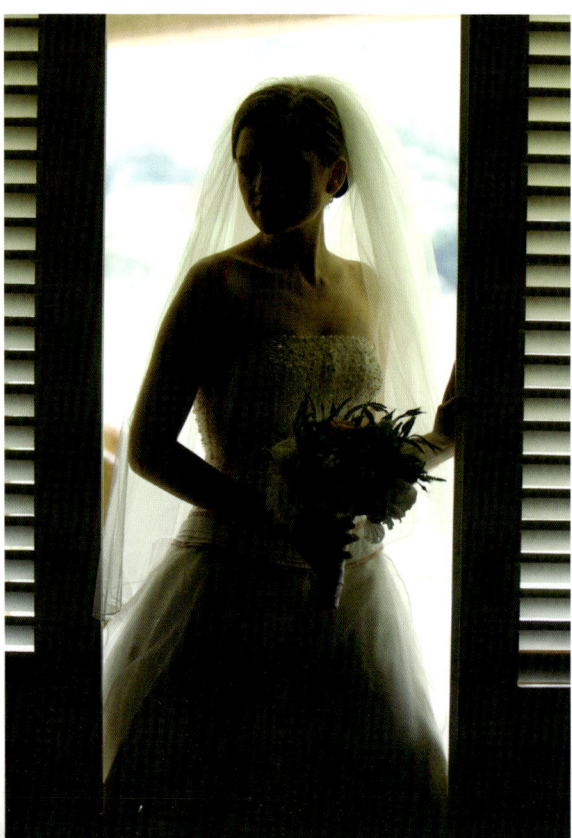

QUICK LOOK

CAMERA	Nikon D3s
LENS	Nikkor 70–200mm f/2.8G ED VR II
MODE	A
ISO	1000
SHUTTER	$^1/_{200}$ +2EV
APERTURE	f/2.8
LIGHTING	Available light only

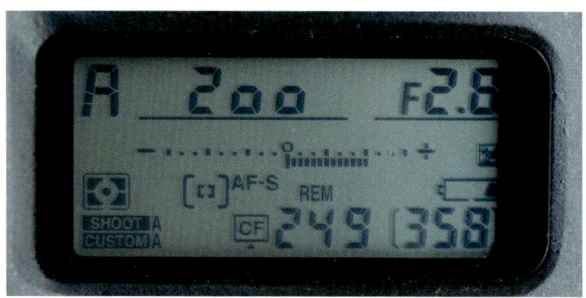

The exposure settings.

exposing the image by adjusting the EV (exposure value) setting. Because I was overexposing, it was possible that the shutter speed might decrease enough to record camera shake. To avoid this, I increased the ISO to 1000. I overexposed the image by 2 stops and basically elevated the midtones so that they became highlights. I elevated the shadows so that they became my midtones. The original highlights are blown out completely. It's a great technique to eliminate what is in the background so that you have a really clean image without distracting elements. If I had not chosen to increase the exposure, this would have been a silhouetted image. By understanding lighting, one can shoot images in areas where one would not otherwise be able to get a great shot, due either to the background details or the prevailing lighting conditions.

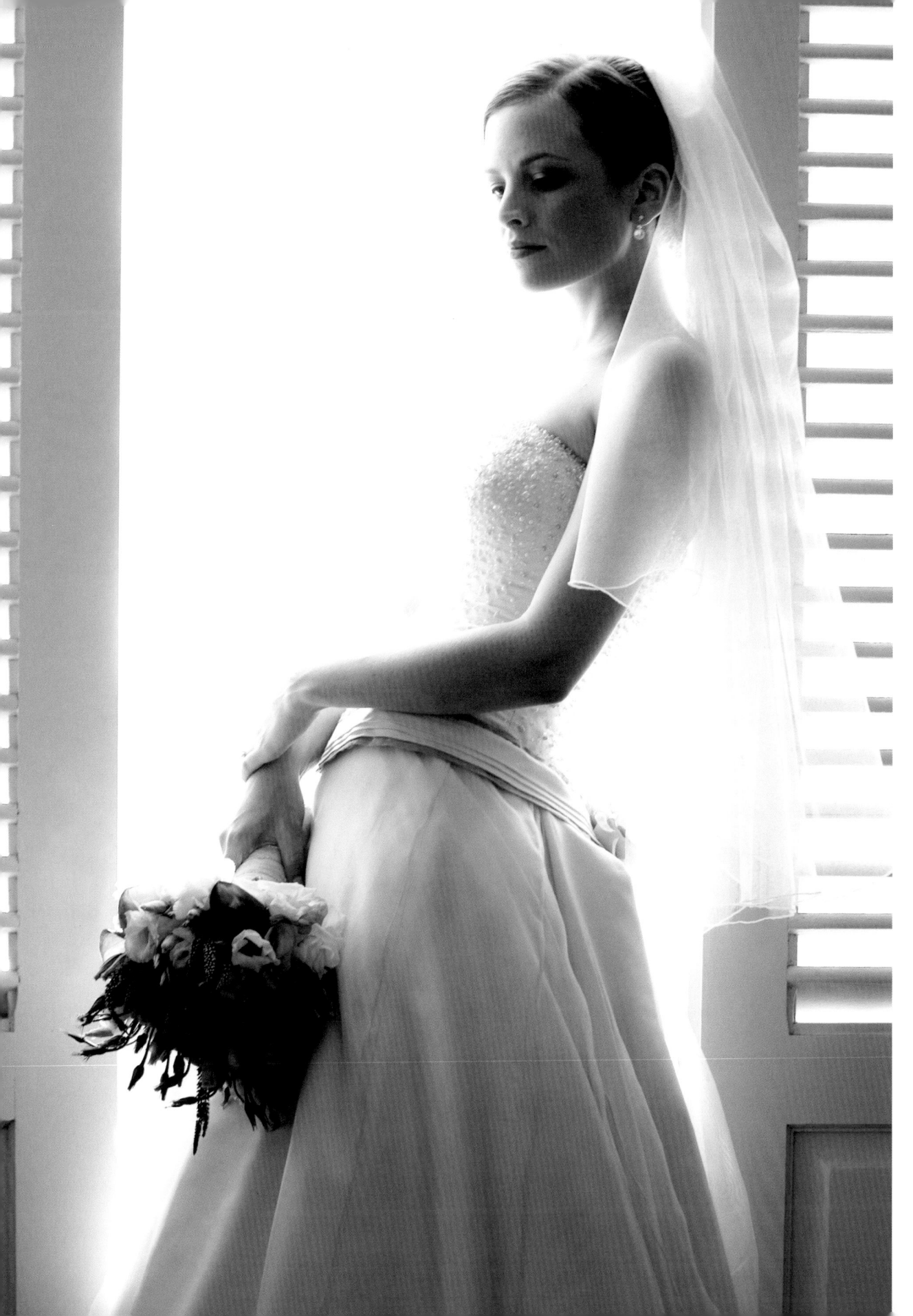

3. FROM CHAOS TO CALM

Preparing the Shooting Space

This image was shot in the doorway of the room in which the bride was getting ready. As a photographer, you often have to work to find an uncluttered spot to shoot in. The bride's room can be chaotic, especially if she has a number of bridesmaids! Sometimes I clear the bed of the bridal paraphernalia or move a chair from a well-lit corner of the room and take a painting off the wall. In this case, however, I asked the mother of the bride for a white double bedsheet, which I used as a backdrop. Two bridesmaids held either end of the sheet and stretched it behind the bride to create a studio- or stage-like feel.

The Pose and Lighting

The pose is graceful and elegant, almost balletic in feel, reminiscent of *Swan Lake* with the demure bowed head and soft, crossed hands. The full bridal dress and layers of tulle beneath add to the balletic characteristic. (Some dresses would not have lent themselves to this sort of pose.)

The light was fully frontal. I often find great light coming through a doorway; it can be both flat and flattering at the same time. I didn't use any light modification for this shot. The ambient light was enough for me to create the image I desired.

This was shot on f/2.8 so that the sheet is slightly out of focus in comparison to the bride.

Left: An alternate pose. **Right:** If you don't have a suitable fabric, you could use a Lastolite scrim.

> **QUICK LOOK**
>
> | | |
> |---|---|
> | **CAMERA** | Nikon D3s |
> | **LENS** | Nikkor 70–200mm f/2.8G ED VR II |
> | **MODE** | A |
> | **ISO** | 200 |
> | **SHUTTER** | $^1/_{250}$ |
> | **APERTURE** | f/2.8 |
> | **LIGHTING** | No manipulation or added artificial lighting. |

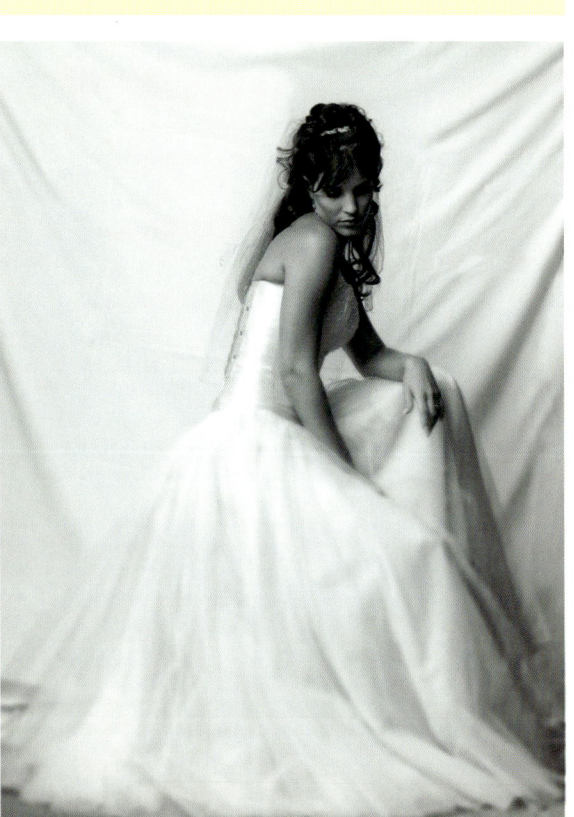

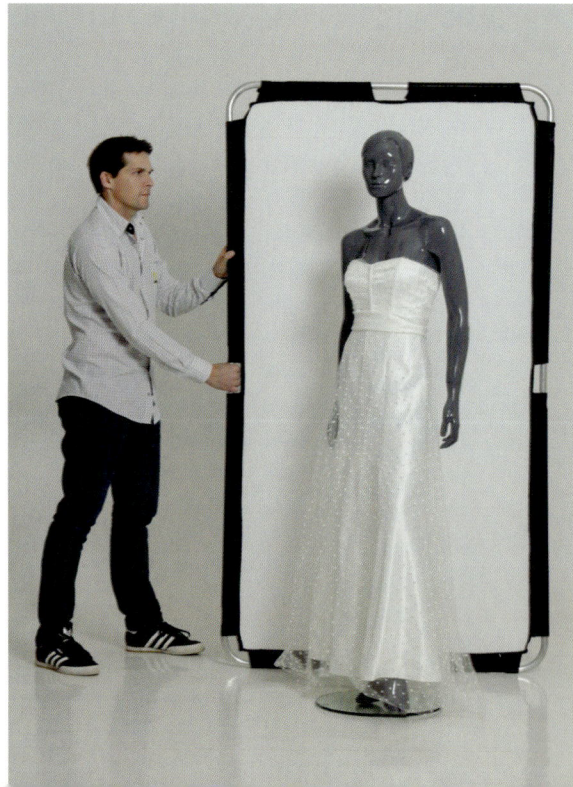

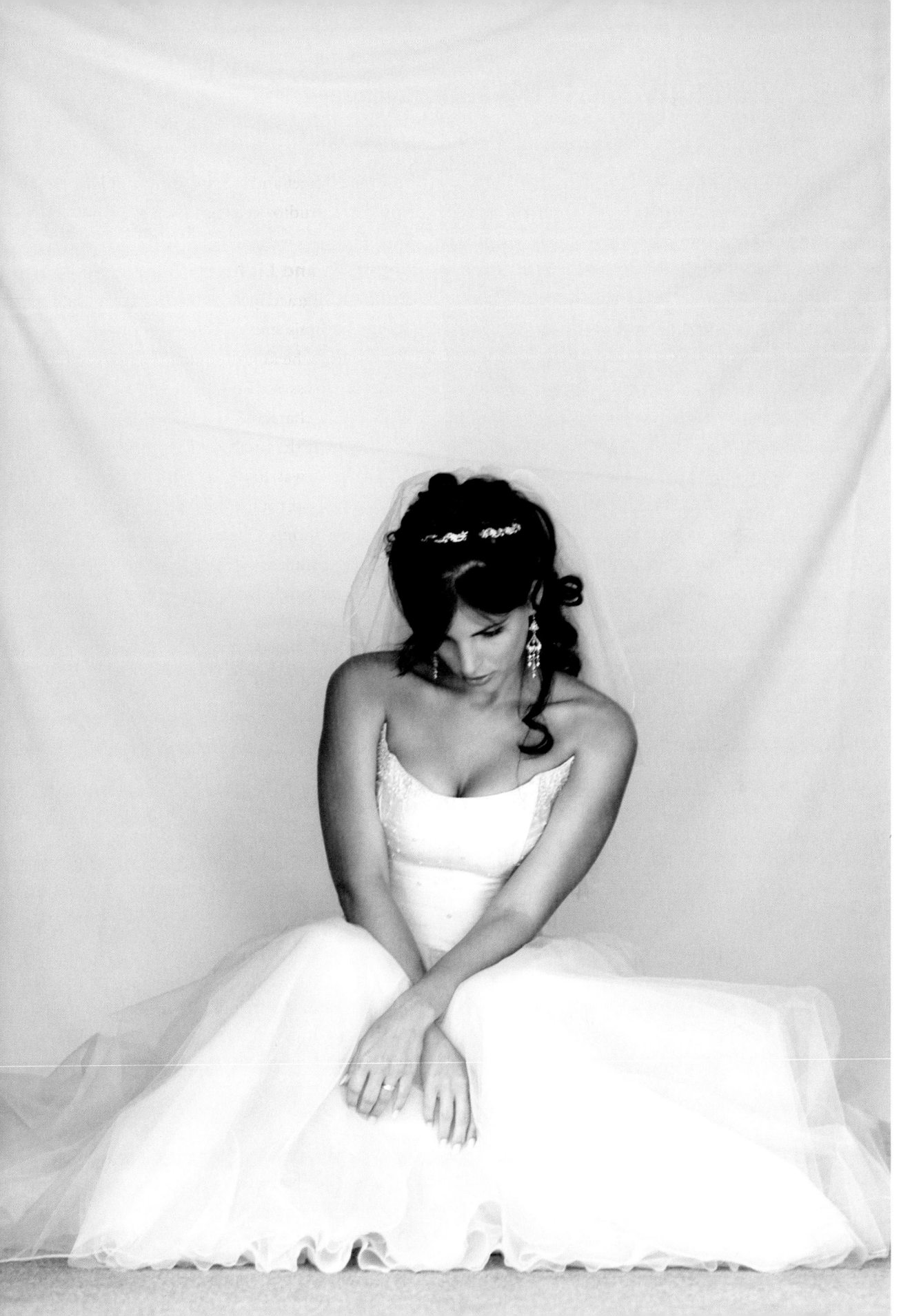

4. WINDOW LIGHT

Clean and Classic

For this classic portrait, I used available light to illuminate the bride. Beautiful soft window light came from her right side, and I used a 5-in-1 reflector on her left side to fill in the shadows.

I usually scout the venue where the bride is getting dressed for a spot near a window. The quality and direction of light are very important. Just be aware that you might need to turn off any artificial light in a room so that you don't have lights with conflicting color temperatures falling on your subject. When all of your lighting has a single color temperature, color management is easier. When working with window light, you can set your white balance to the shade preset; you'll get great skin tones and an accurate interpretation of the dress color.

Portrait Prep Work

In many cases, one might have to remove objects from the ideal shooting area, including pictures hung on the wall. This gives you the clean, uncluttered background you need when shooting a portrait of a bride.

This pose is classic, happy, and fresh, and the bride's eyes are nice and sharp. It's one that most parents of the bride would like to put in a frame. It's the type of "safe" pose that one should always shoot before moving on to more creative and experimental shots.

QUICK LOOK

CAMERA	Nikon D3s
LENS	Nikkor 70–200mm f/2.8G ED VR II
MODE	A
ISO	400
SHUTTER	$^1/_{250}$
APERTURE	f/2.8
LIGHTING	Lastolite 5-in-1 collapsible reflector

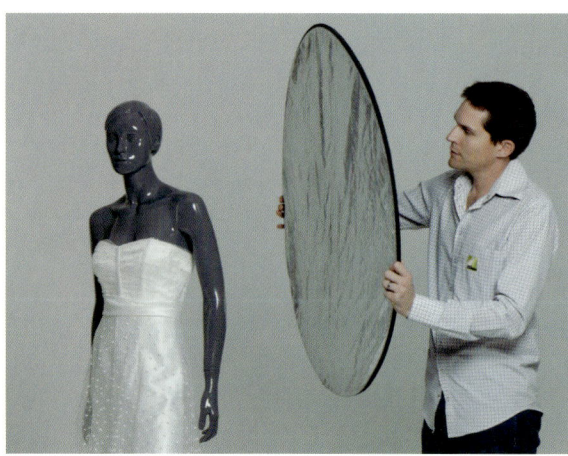

Left: An alternate shot from the session. **Above:** The reflector position.

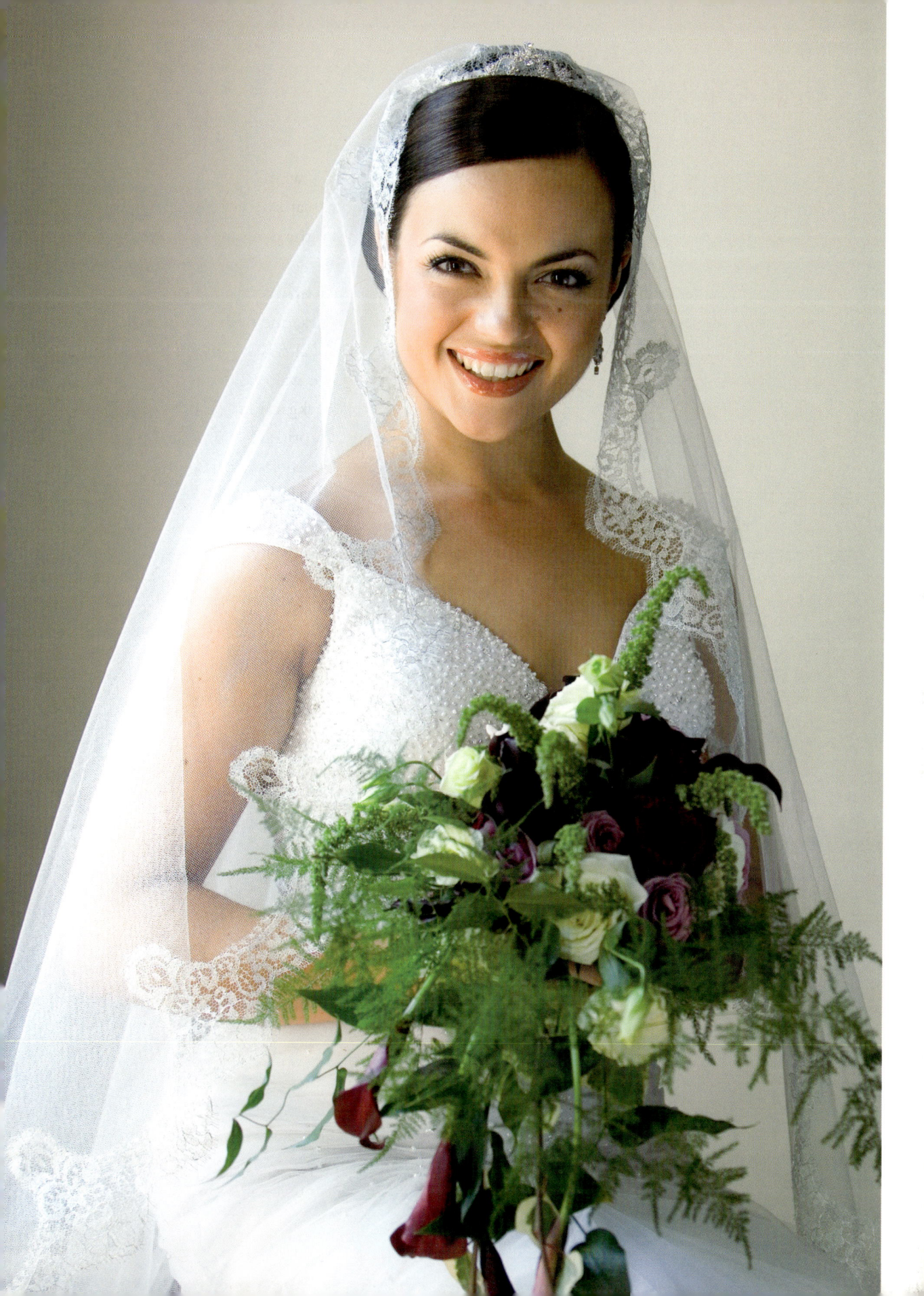

5. HIGH FASHION

Getting Inspired

Vogue, Harper's Bazaar, Elle, Cosmopolitan—when it comes to high-fashion magazines for women, the list is endless. I find them a constant source of inspiration, and these particular magazines are my greatest influence.

I photograph brides who generally come from an affluent background. These women read these magazines, and most are thrilled by the idea of becoming a supermodel for the day!

The lighting for this image came from strobes plus ambient lighting. Of course, having the sun directly behind the bride isn't traditionally associated with wedding photography, but in terms of shooting for the fashion industry, it's spot on. I added an Elinchrom 600w monolight with a silver umbrella to the bride's left.

Left: An alternate image from the session. **Right:** The position of the umbrella.

Showing Texture

This portrait was made in manual mode. I chose a shutter speed of $^1/_{200}$ second and an aperture of f/18. Without a flash in front of the subject, the background would have appeared underexposed. By positioning the flash to the left of the bride, rather than directly in front of her, I was able to bring out the texture of the dress. This is a practice often used in fashion photography to show the garments in their best light, so to speak.

Due to the nature of the image, I posed the bride in a stance typical of fashion models.

QUICK LOOK

CAMERA	Nikon D3s
LENS	Nikkor 70–200mm f/2.8G ED VR II
MODE	M
ISO	100
SHUTTER	$^1/_{200}$
APERTURE	f/18
LIGHTING	Elinchrom Style 600RX

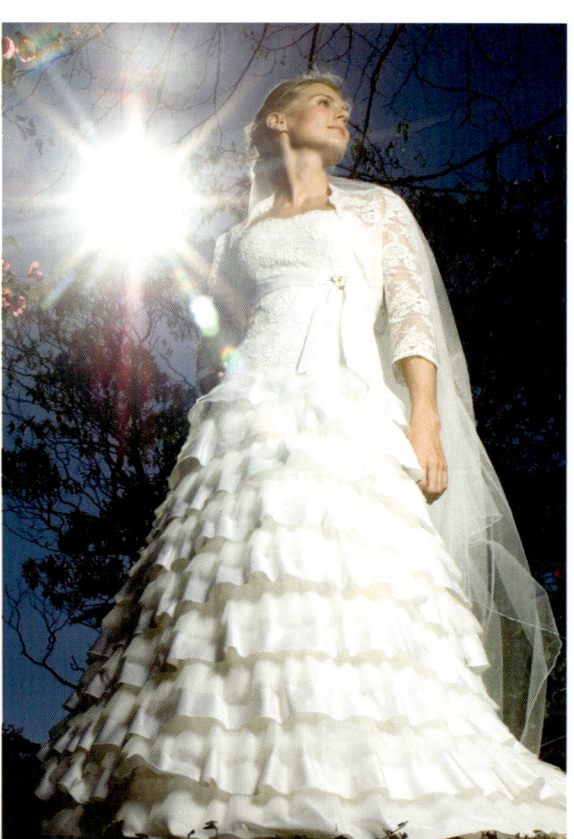

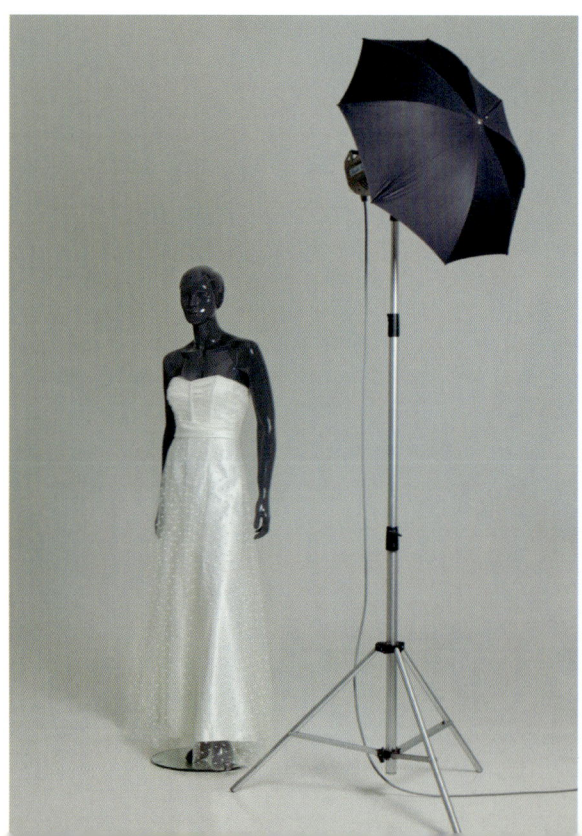

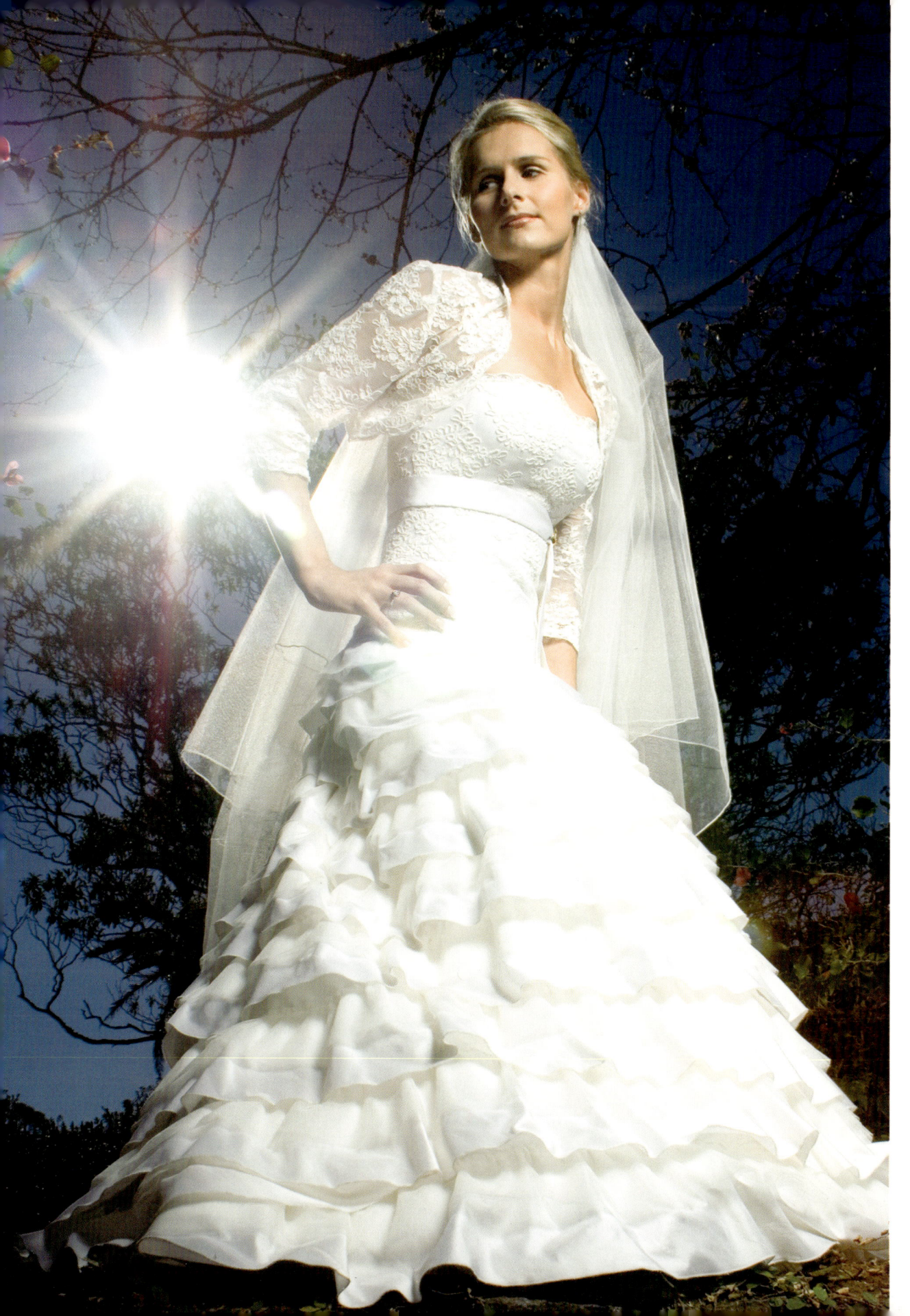

6. STUDIO LIGHTING OUTDOORS

Distinctive Images

Using studio lighting on location enhances the quality of one's images. Here, I used the Elinchrom Ranger RX, a portable battery-powered strobe with fantastic battery longevity. It's an indispensable part of my location lighting kit.

I used a white umbrella to modify the light for smooth, even illumination without hot spots. The sun was directly behind the bride, creating a gorgeous halo effect around her body.

I posed the bride on a small grassy hill and took the picture while lying on the slope below her. The unusually low vantage point, coupled with her high-fashion pose, made for a uniquely striking image.

The sky was rendered darker due to the studio lighting. I think the tone works quite well with the grass, and it creates a distinct frame around the upper third of the image.

Tell a Story

I love the way that the wide skirt of the bride's dress fills much of the photo and how the color and texture of the dark-green grass contrasts with the white gown. When you make a highly distinctive image like this, it is important that you shoot similar images, so that you can have complementary pictures for both sides of the pages in the album, thereby creating a story.

QUICK LOOK	
CAMERA	Nikon D3s
LENS	Nikkor 70–200mm f/2.8G ED VR II
MODE	M
ISO	100
SHUTTER	$^1/_{200}$
APERTURE	f/20
LIGHTING	Elinchrom Ranger RX

Left: An alternate shot from the session. **Right:** The umbrella position.

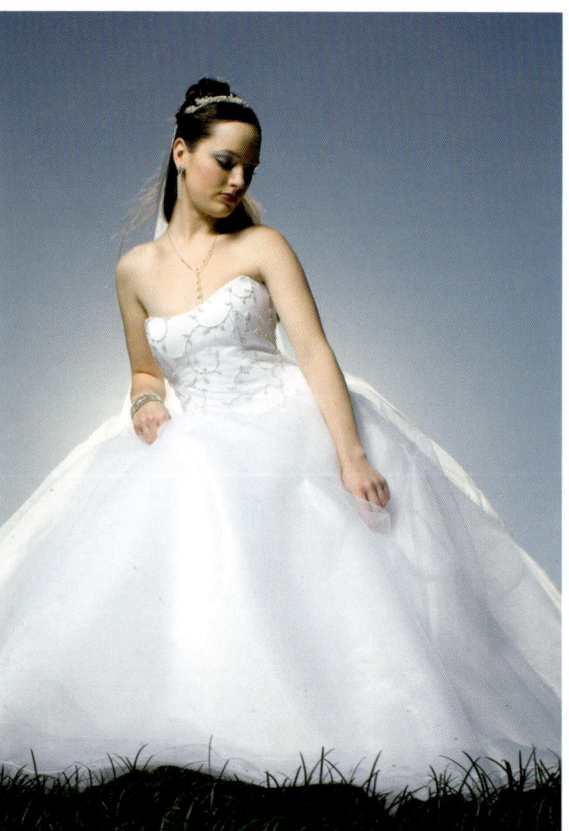

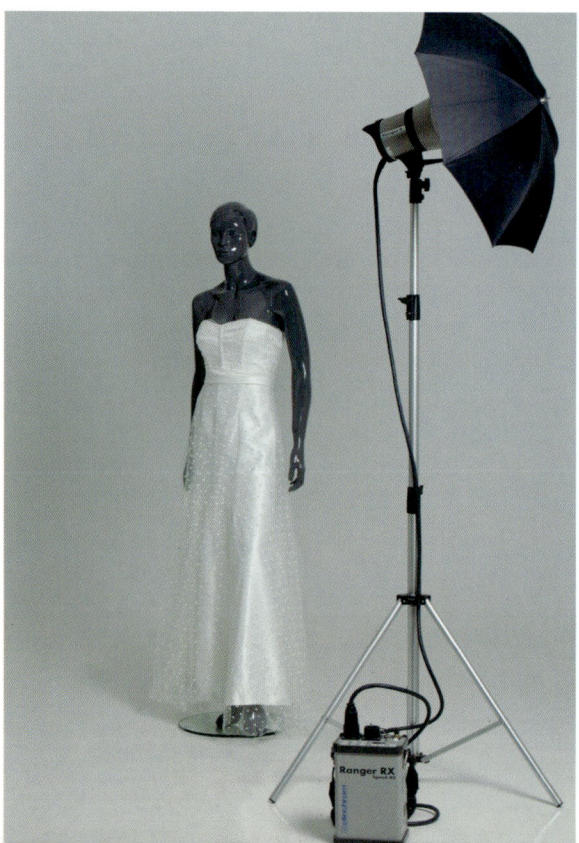

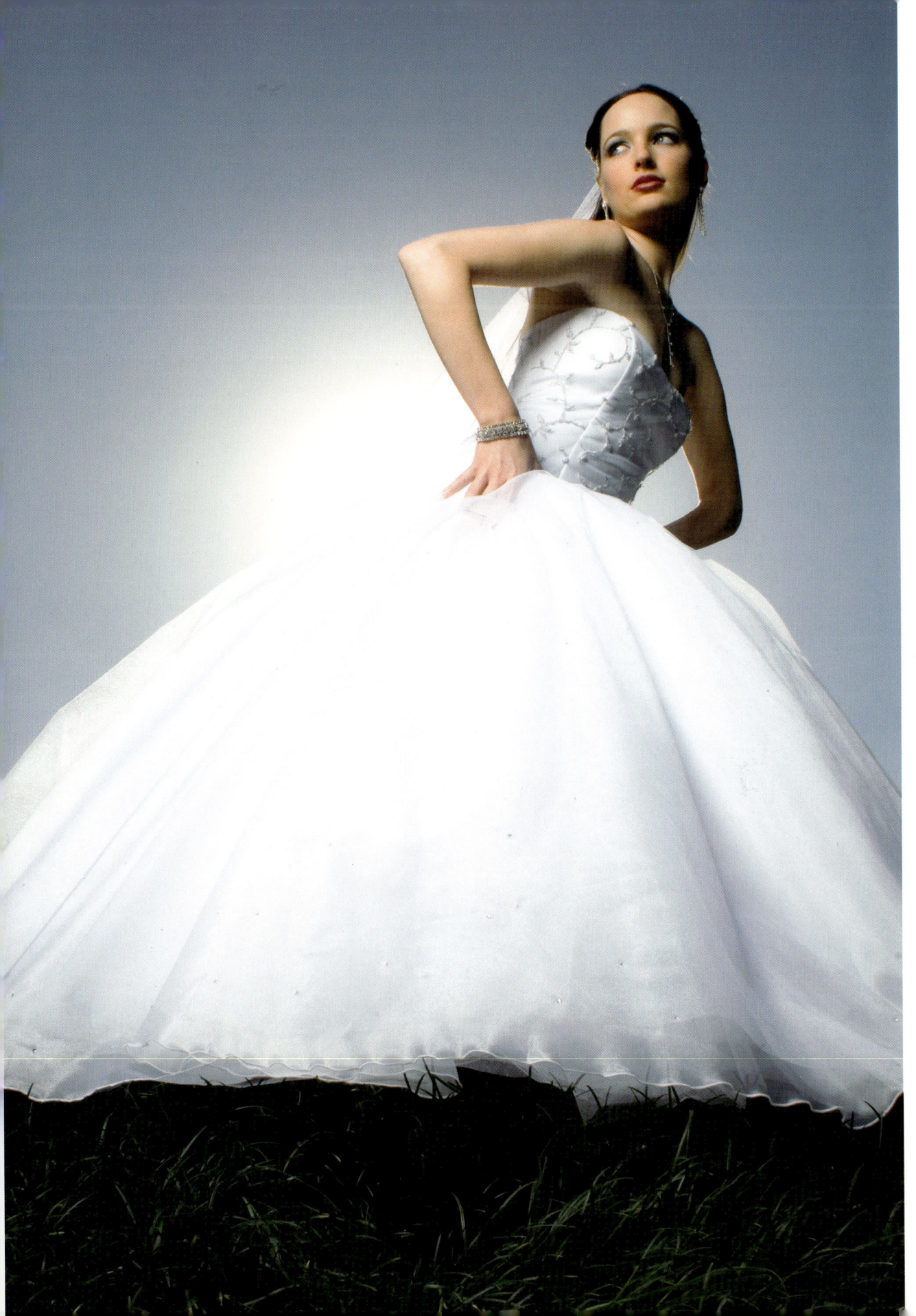

7. NIGHT MAGIC

Just before dessert, I often whisk the bride and groom off for a creative shoot in a quiet spot not too far from the reception. This location, a garden full of trees wrapped in fairy lights, was ideal.

Using a slow shutter speed, I was able to record the fairy lights in the exposure. I illuminated the bride from the front with my Elinchrom Ranger RX. The slow shutter speed meant movement could be captured, so I had my assistant toss the veil into the air, creating an ethereal backdrop. A smoke machined placed behind the bride created the impression of mist. I've since learned that throwing talc into the air is an inexpensive alternative.

There was no ambient light on the front of the bride, so even at a shutter speed of $^1/_2$ second, the bride's movement was frozen by the flash.

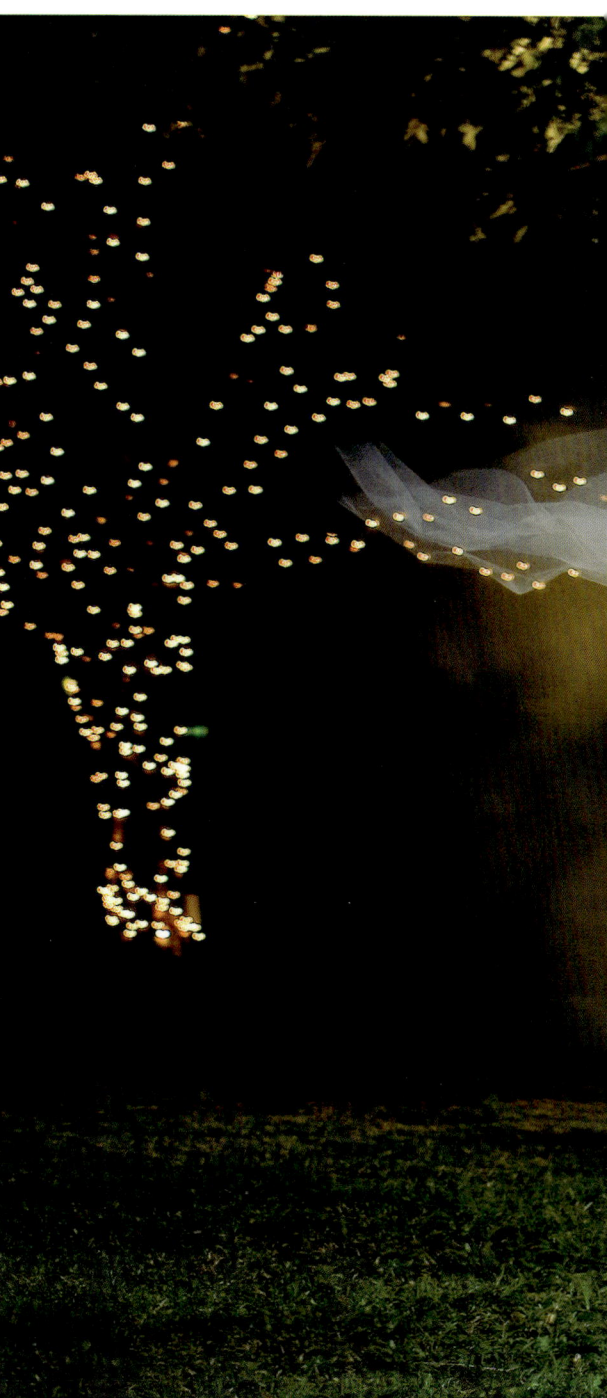

QUICK LOOK

CAMERA	Nikon D3s (mounted on tripod)
LENS	Nikkor 24–70mm f/2.8G ED
MODE	M
ISO	400
SHUTTER	$^1/_2$
APERTURE	f/5.6
LIGHTING	Elinchrom Ranger RX

The lighting setup.

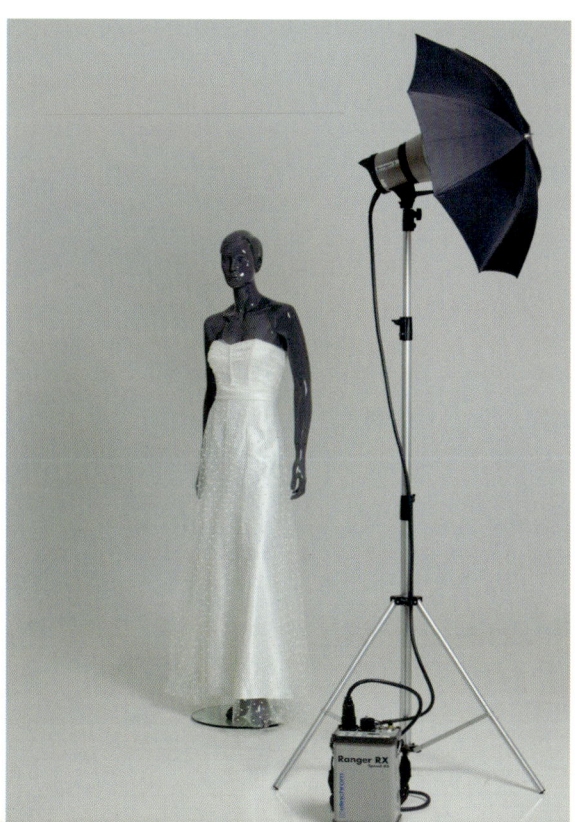

Here, you can see the smoke machine behind the bride. It was removed in postproduction.

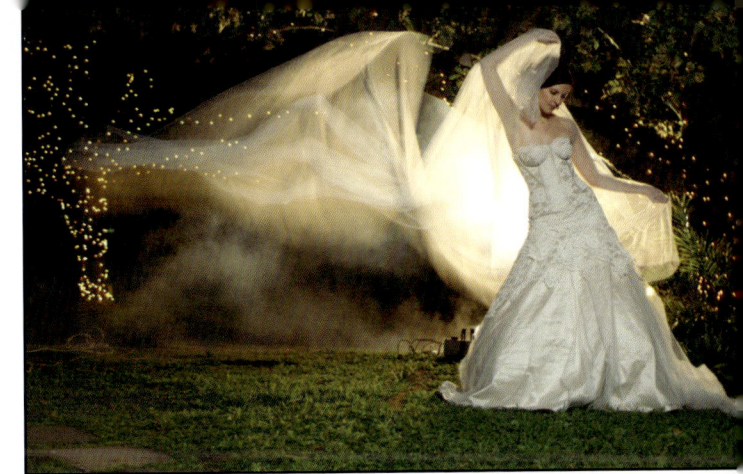

I had the bride almost emulating the arch of the tree on her left. She was positioned perfectly at the right-third portion of the image. Her veil and the "mist" moved into the black space between the fairy lights that are wrapped around the trees.

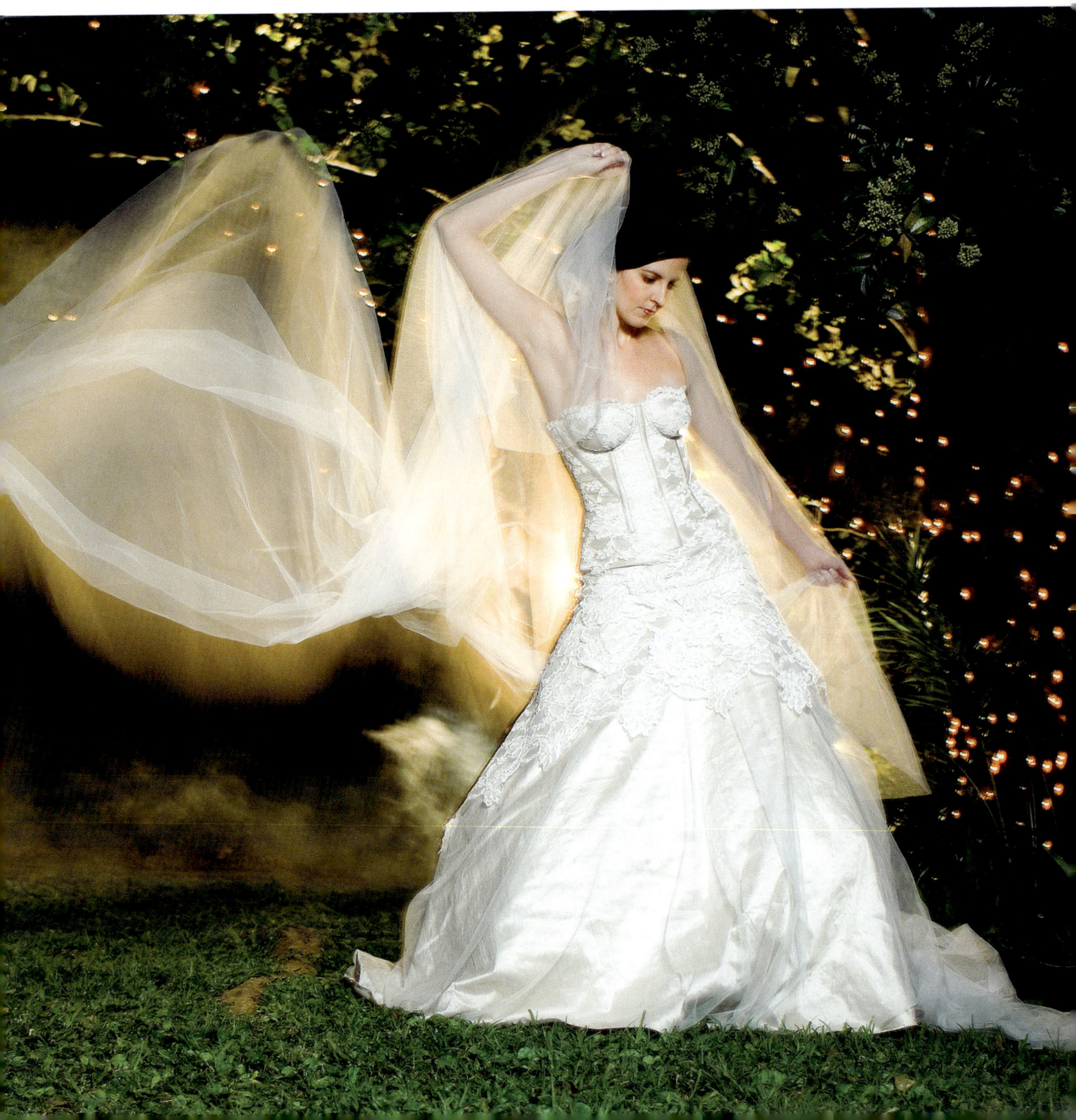

8. GARDEN VARIETY

Azaleas and a Beautiful Bride

This image was made during the reception, after the speeches were over and the guests were mingling. I'd found this stunning spot at the bottom of the garden, where a riot of azaleas were blooming around an archway at the top of three stone steps. I set up two portable strobe units, one at the base of the steps to the bride's left with a white umbrella (strobe A) and one at the top of the steps behind her shoulder (strobe B). The portable, battery-powered strobe system I use is the Elinchrom Ranger RX, which accepts two strobe heads. Since my strobes were placed far apart, I used my smaller Elinchrom Ranger RX Quadra power pack for strobe B. Strobe A was fired with a set of Pocket Wizards, and strobe B has a built-in photo-sensitive cell that fires the strobe at the same time as the front strobe.

Left: An alternate pose from the session. **Right:** The lighting setup.

Enter the Smoke Machine

I used a smoke machine to create the enchanted mist that surrounds the bride. I love the effect, but the setup was cumbersome (I needed many meters of extension cord). I've since found that talcum powder works just as well.

After checking the lighting and smoke machine with my assistant, we fetched the bride.

I cloned the azaleas at the bottom of the steps in postproduction, accentuating the magical quality of the image and creating the feeling that the bride is stepping into some mythical land through a florid tunnel.

QUICK LOOK	
CAMERA	Nikon D3s
LENS	Nikkor 70–200mm f/2.8G ED VR II
MODE	M
ISO	400
SHUTTER	$^1/_{125}$
APERTURE	f/8
LIGHTING	Elinchrom Ranger RX and Elinchrom Ranger RX Quadra

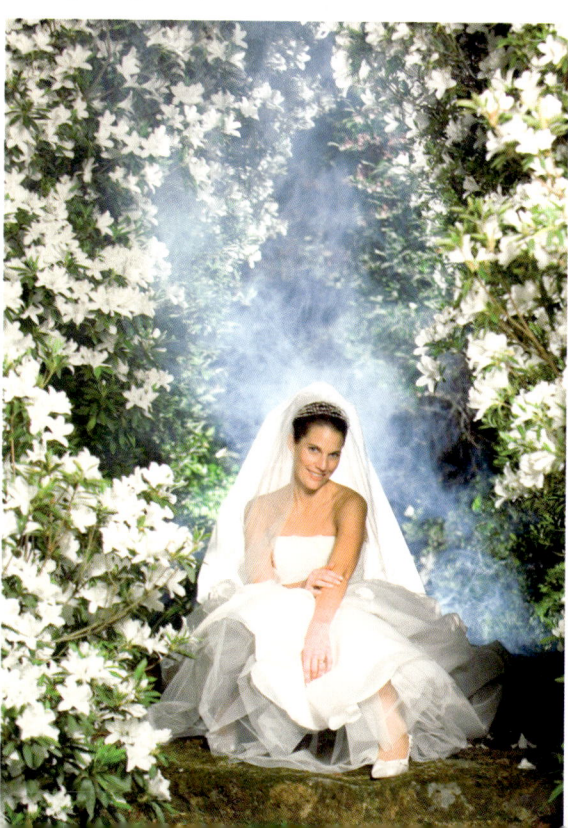

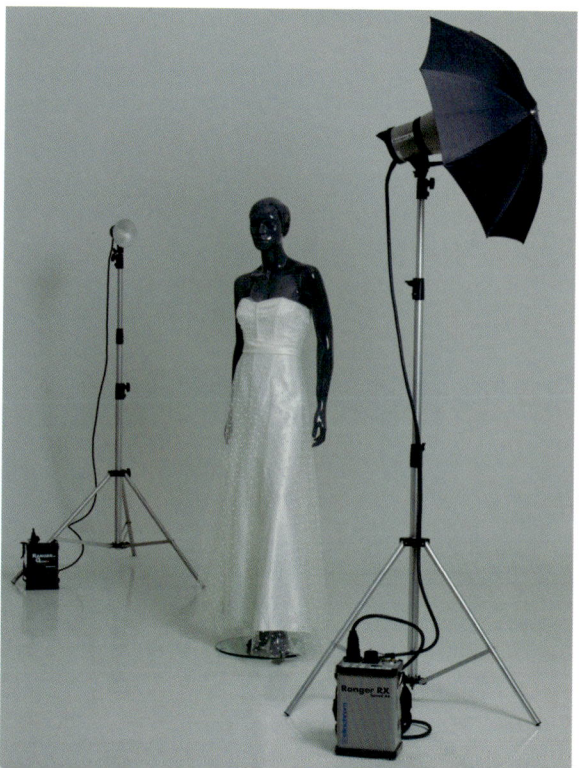

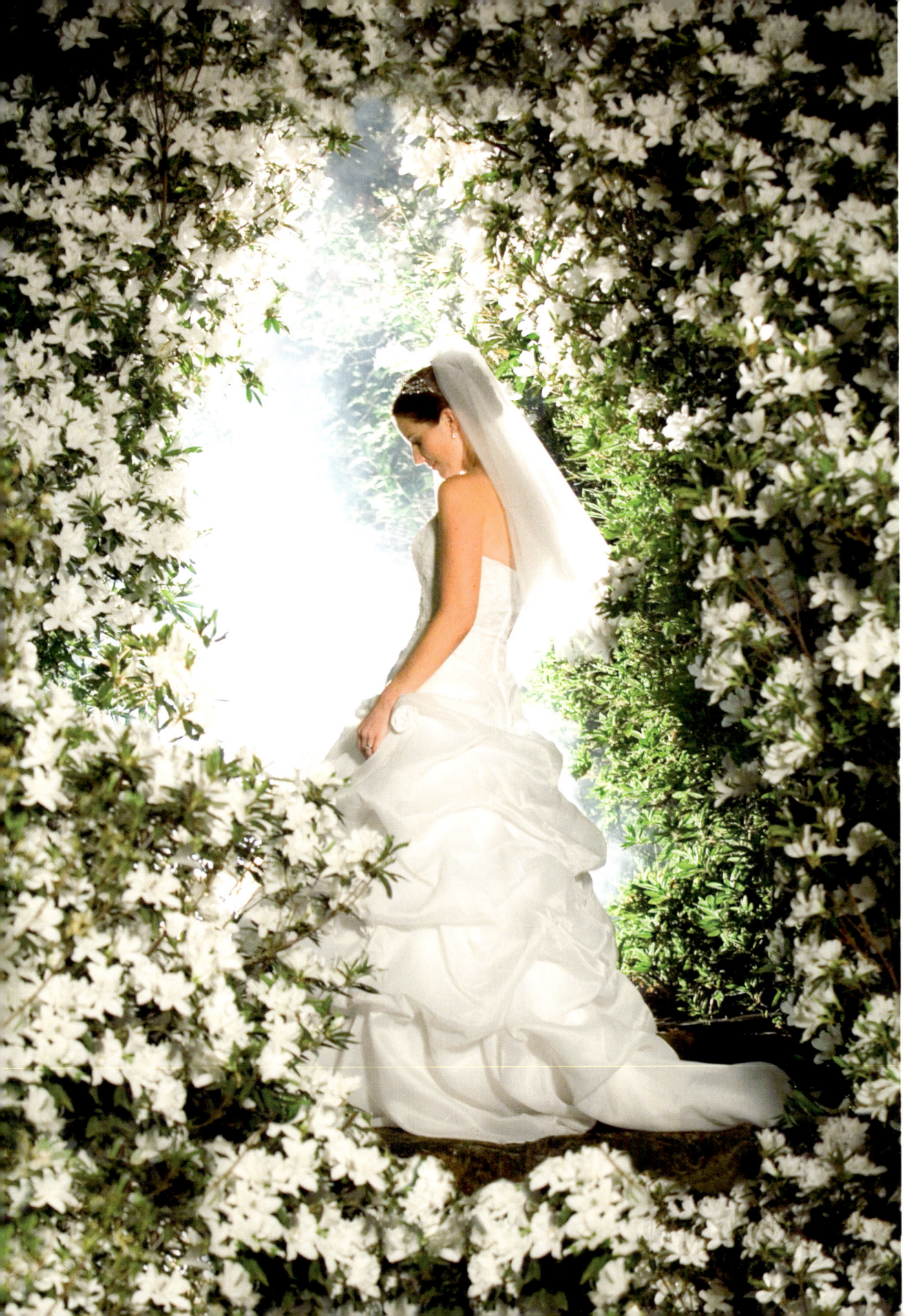

9. A MATTER OF PERSPECTIVE

Camera Height

Choosing an uncommon camera height allows me to capture images that are avant-garde and unique, and certainly on the fashion or editorial spectrum. Of course, fashion-type images won't suit every client, so you'll want to establish whether your bride will be comfortable with these poses during the pre-session consultation.

I took these images while lying at the bride's feet, with my camera pointed upward. Note the striking effect of the change of perspective. The skirt fills a good portion of the bottom of the frame, while the size of the torso and head are reduced. The details of the fabric are also beautifully obvious, while the sky and clouds above the subject loom overhead in a dramatic way.

The Lighting

I used my Elinchrom Ranger RX off camera in conjunction with the ambient light. I balanced the light in the background in order to make it less obvious that I shot with a strobe from the front. To do this, I reduced my shutter speed to $1/25$ second and shot with an aperture of f/20 on ISO 100. The flash brought out the fabric detail. This is the type of image that the designer or dressmaker would love to receive from you.

Left: An alternate shot from the session. **Right:** The umbrella placement.

QUICK LOOK

CAMERA	Nikon D3s
LENS	Nikkor 24–70mm f/2.8G ED
MODE	M
ISO	100
SHUTTER	$1/25$
APERTURE	f/20
LIGHTING	Elinchrom Ranger RX

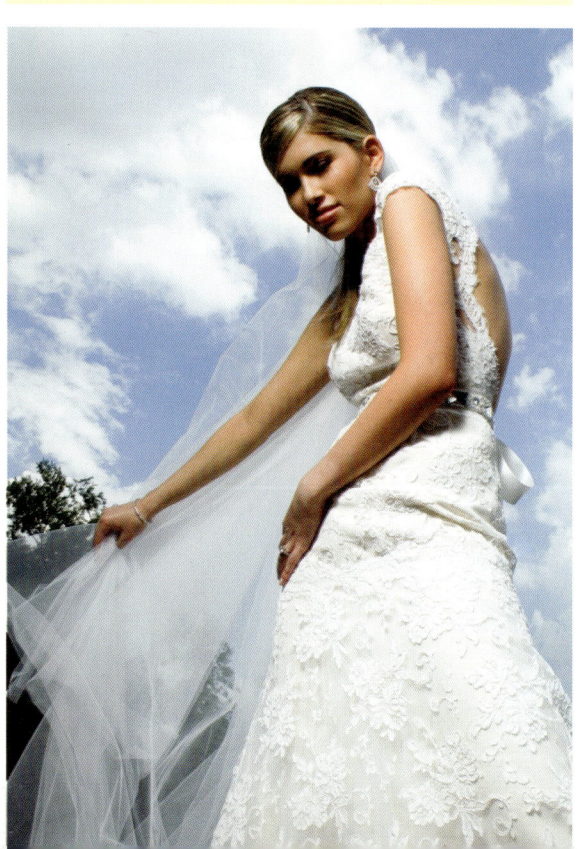

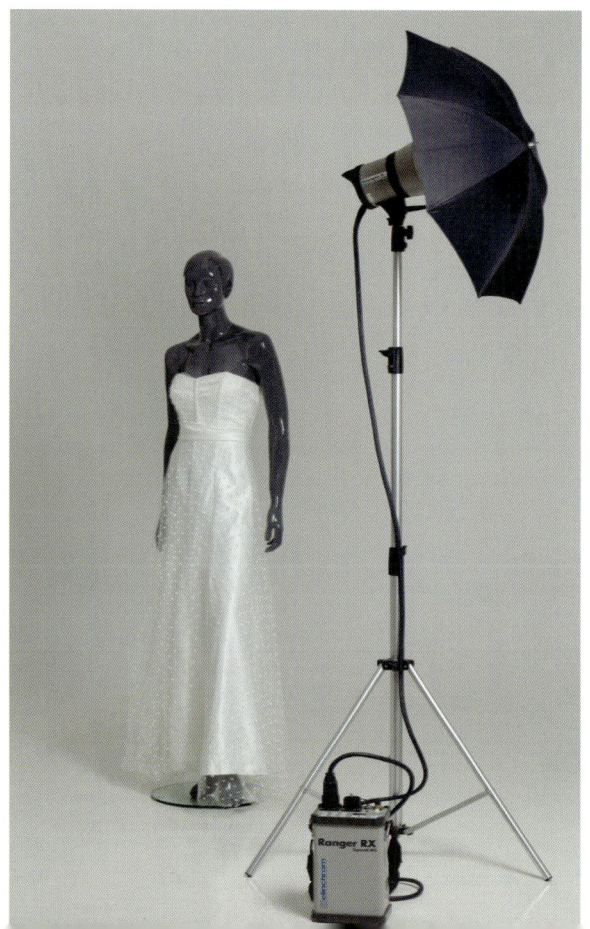

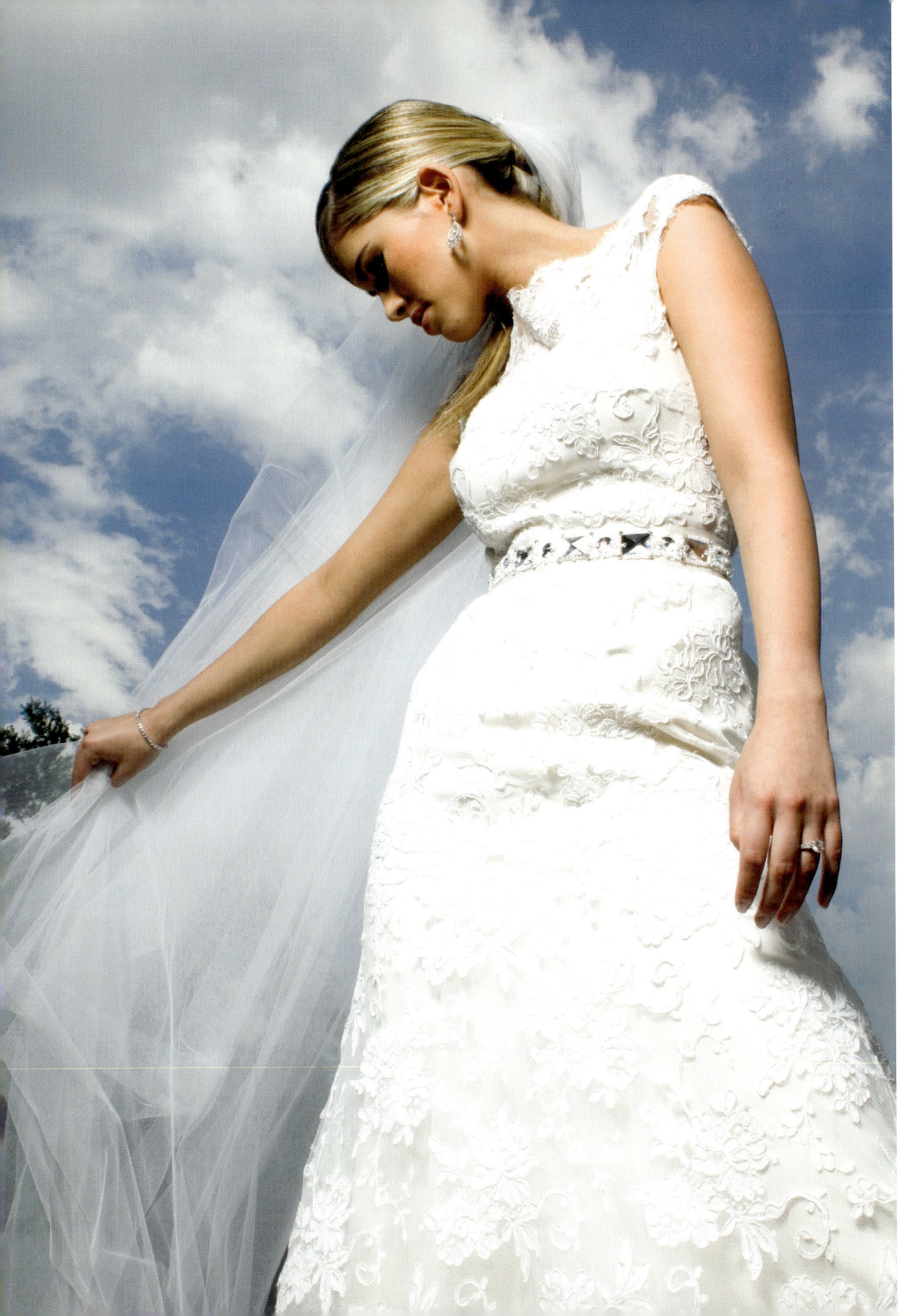

10. PURE ROMANCE

A Classic Presentation

I love posing my brides in high-fashion stances, but I also enjoy the more classic, formally posed bridal portraits. For this nighttime photograph, I wanted to capture the fresh beauty of the bride, and the gardens surrounding her venue seemed to have an incredible fairy-tale quality to them, with delicate cast-iron arches and gazebos, laced with jasmine creepers and overhanging branches.

Posing and Lighting

For a full-length shot, I positioned the bride just off-center to the arch and had her turn her body to the left. With her left shoulder angled slightly forward, one can see the detail on her bare-back dress. Her face is turned back toward the camera, and her front arm is classically relaxed by her side, so her wedding ring is clearly visible on her hand. Once again, I used my portable strobes with the Elinchrom Ranger RX. I placed my first off-camera strobe behind the bride to create beautiful rim lighting; the strobe also illuminated the foliage and arches surrounding her, giving me the wonderful backlight effect that I desired. With my second off-camera strobe, I used a 1x1-meter softbox. The front surface of this softbox is a double layer of translucent white nylon, while the sides are silver on the inside and black on the outside. The softbox is perfect when one needs a soft, diffused light on a very specific area. In this case, I positioned the softbox so that this flattering light could fall directly onto the bride.

QUICK LOOK	
CAMERA	Nikon D3s
LENS	Nikkor 70–200mm f/2.8G ED VR II
MODE	M
ISO	100
SHUTTER	$^1/_{25}$
APERTURE	f/8
LIGHTING	Elinchrom Ranger RX

Left: Using the same setup, the groom was added to the shot. **Below:** The two-light setup.

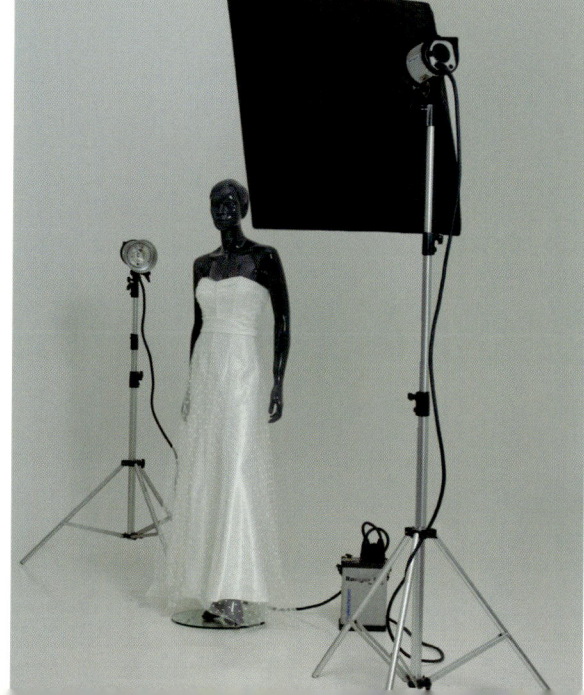

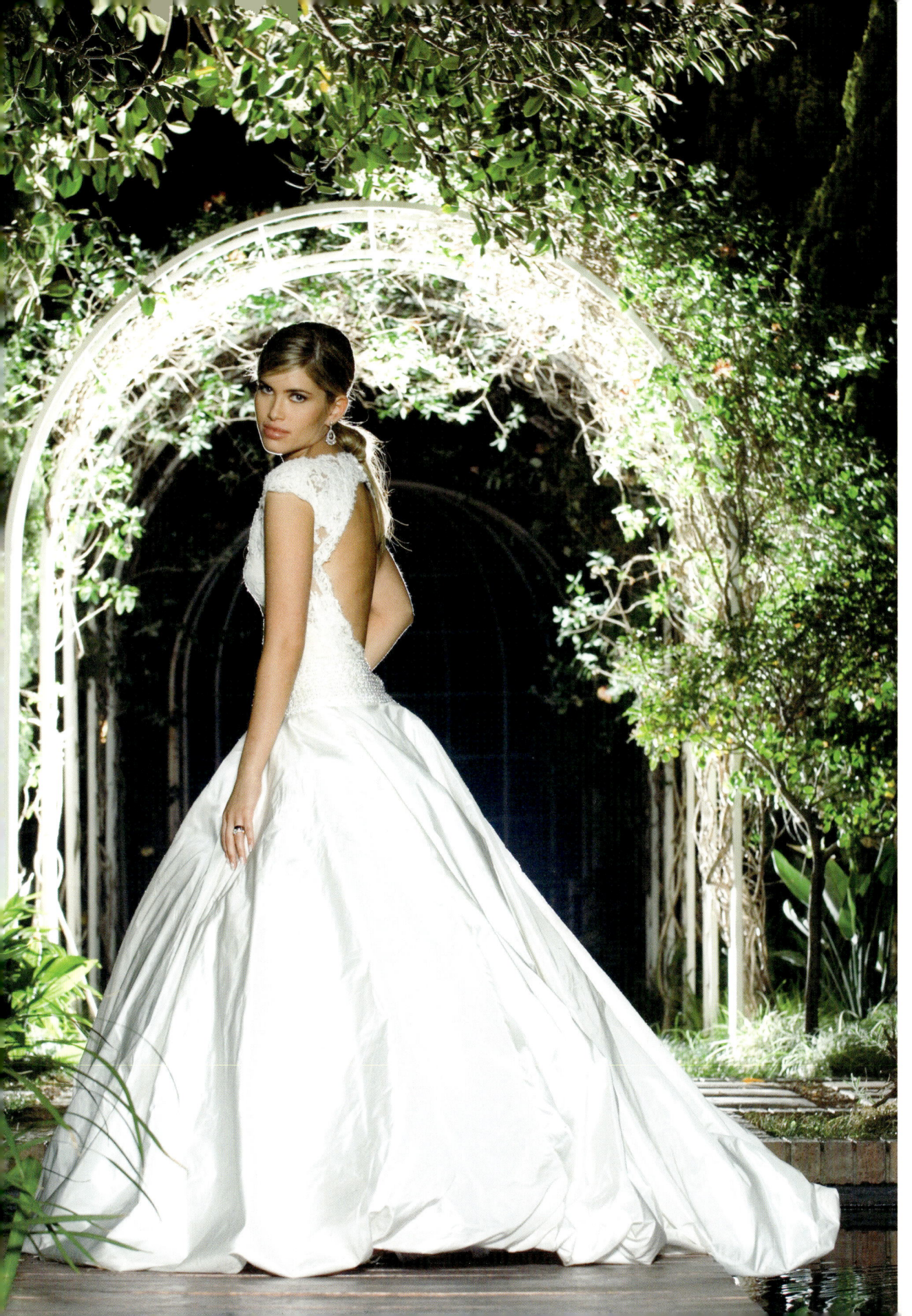

11. STRONG COMPOSITION

Three Variations

The many triangular shapes in this composition might not be immediately obvious to the viewer, but they offer a subliminal sense of equilibrium and peace. Notice how the eye is drawn up her arm to the hand, where she dangles her delicate necklace with its cross pendant. This becomes the main focal point of the picture, and the Christian cross speaks volumes about the importance of the commitment she is about to make when she says her vows in the church ceremony.

The image was made using only the available light that was pouring through the French doors. The light was beautiful, soft, and even, and it fell perfectly over the bride's striking features.

I had the bride kneel down near the wall. I asked the bridesmaids to leave her dress unbuttoned at the back, thereby exposing her bare back to the camera. We made sure that the dress was carefully tucked in so that it lay flat against her body and did not spoil the clean lines needed for the photograph.

The bare skin and pose lend a sensual, alluring look—an approach often used in perfume ads.

Postproduction

I converted the image from color to sepia to convey a feeling of peace and the significance of the ceremony. I de-saturated the sepia image slightly to enhance the sensuality.

QUICK LOOK

CAMERA	Nikon D3s
LENS	Nikkor 70–200mm f/2.8G ED VR II
MODE	A
ISO	800
SHUTTER	$^1/_{125}$
APERTURE	f/2.8
LIGHTING	Unmanipulated window/door light

Left and right: Two other posing variations.

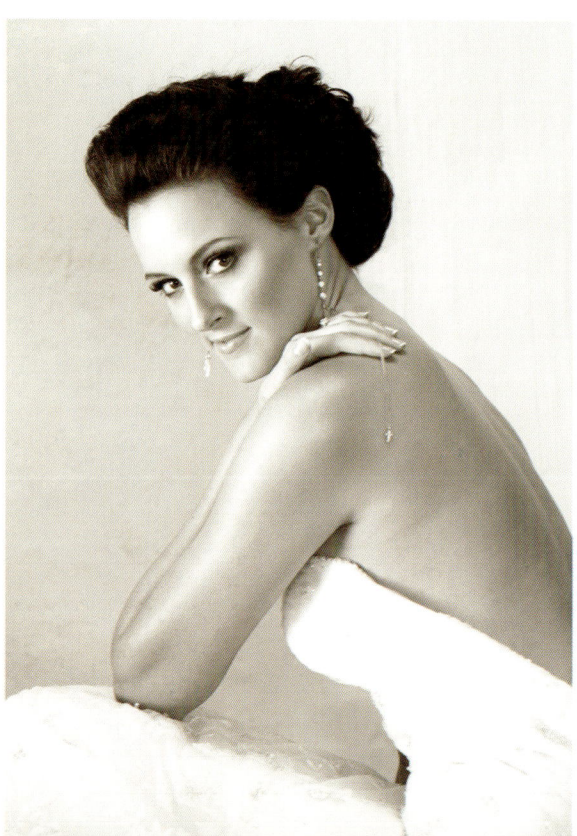
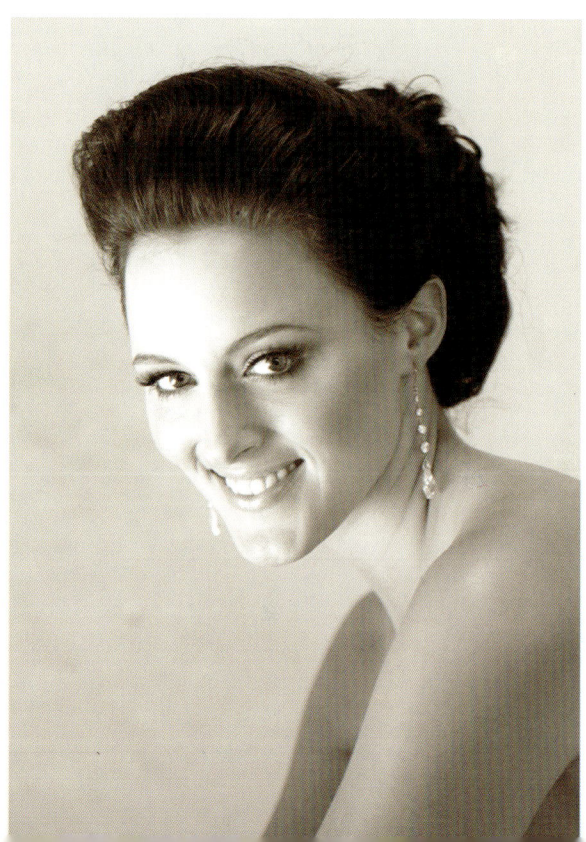

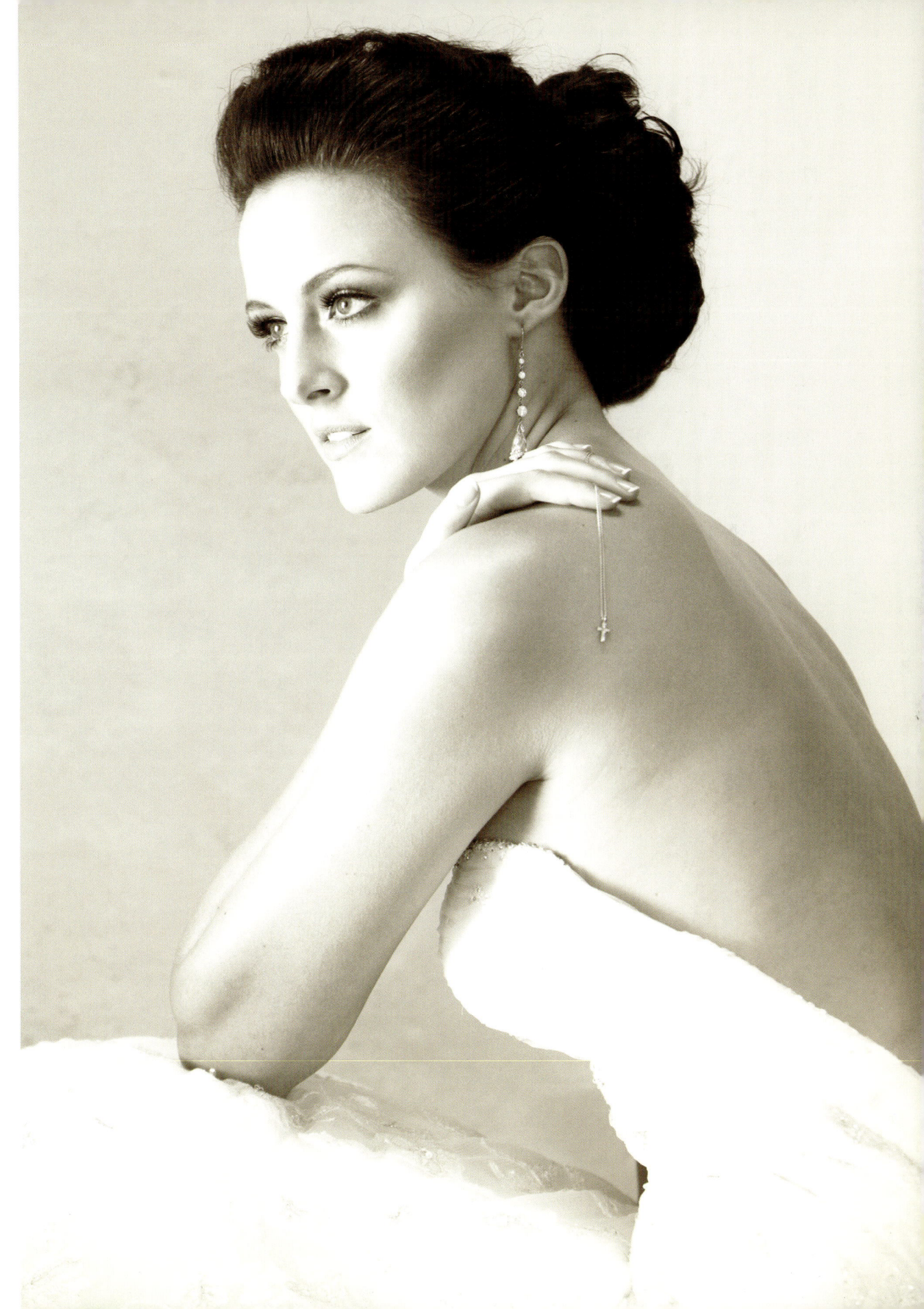

12. A POSE FOR THE PARENTS

Something for Everyone

Though the bride and groom are essentially the clients, the parents of the bride usually pay for the wedding. Given the generation gap, it's unlikely that they will all have the same taste in photography. So, while the bride and groom may like your avant-garde style or fly-on-the-wall photojournalistic approach, more often than not, the parents will want photos that are reminiscent of their own wedding album—that is to say, something far more classical and "safe." This is why I'm a big believer in mixing up the styles. The parents will love you and your album as long as they see some happy, traditional poses of their precious daughter. These are the shots that they will order as reprints and enlargements, ready for that gilded frame and the ideal spot in the living room. I encourage photographers to get these classic "money shots" out of the way before they start to experiment with their own style.

A Classic, Happy Look

This image is a perfect example of what I would call the happy, classic pose. I used a collapsible 5-in-1 reflector to bounce available light onto the bride's upper body. I had her cradle her bouquet and bring her shoulders forward slightly, creating a little bit of body shape and depth. I then made her laugh, which resulted in this very natural and jubilant smile, which also shows in her eyes. I chose a backdrop of leaves that was consistent in color and texture, avoiding a location in the garden that was too varied and busy.

QUICK LOOK	
CAMERA	Nikon D3s
LENS	Nikkor 70–200mm f/2.8G ED VR II
MODE	A
ISO	400
SHUTTER	$^1/_{125}$
APERTURE	f/2.8
LIGHTING	Latolite 5-in-1 collapsible reflector

Left: An alternate image from the session. **Below:** The reflector position.

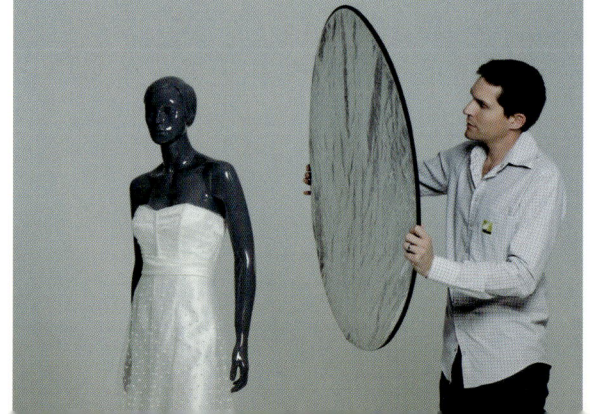

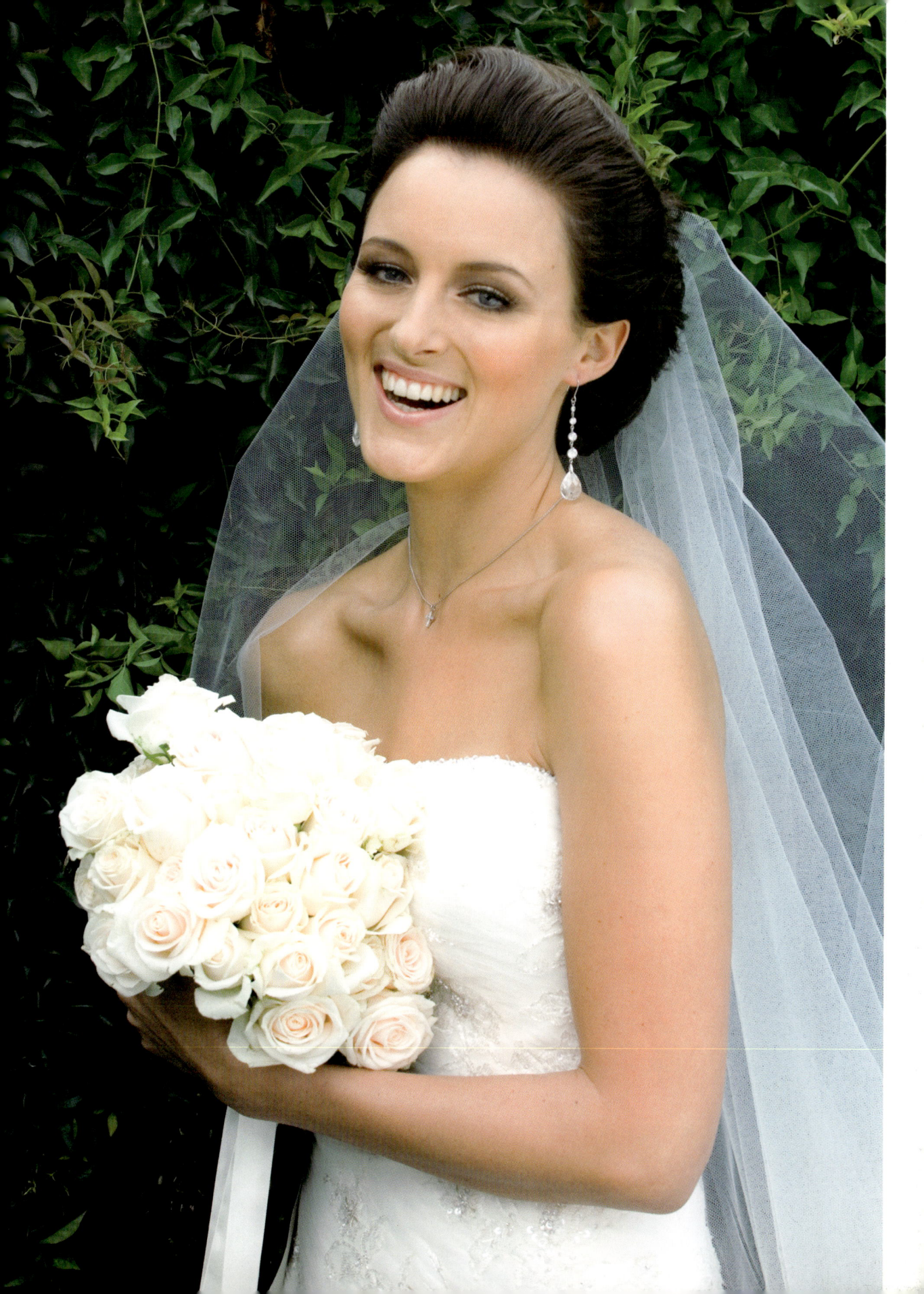

13. DRAMATIC NATURAL LIGHT

Backlighting for Impact

Working with lots of natural light can be tricky, but once you've learned how to compensate with your camera settings, dramatic natural light can be very effective.

This photo was shot in the middle of a forest, and there was a vast pool of light flooding in from a gap in the trees. I posed the bride in the midst of this pool of light, which resulted in a very backlit image. I love the way the light shines through the back of her hair and through the long veil, which is draped around her body. She is almost silhouetted due to the intense backlighting around the edge of her body. I didn't use any modifying tools; in fact, the white dress acted as a reflector, bouncing light onto her face.

Her pose is deliberately sexy, with the exposed leg and a bit of tension in her hand, which is grabbing and pulling up her dress. The position of her head and her expression are also sultry.

To ensure that I was exposing for her skin tone and to compensate for the sunlight illuminating her dress, I overexposed by $^2/_3$ stop.

Postproduction

I desaturated this image to enhance the sultry mysteriousness of the atmosphere.

Left: A lighting test shot. **Right:** An alternative pose.

QUICK LOOK

CAMERA	Nikon D3s
LENS	Nikkor 70–200mm f/2.8G ED VR II
MODE	A
ISO	640
SHUTTER	$^1/_{125}$ + $^2/_3$EV
APERTURE	f/5.6
LIGHTING	Unmodified available light only

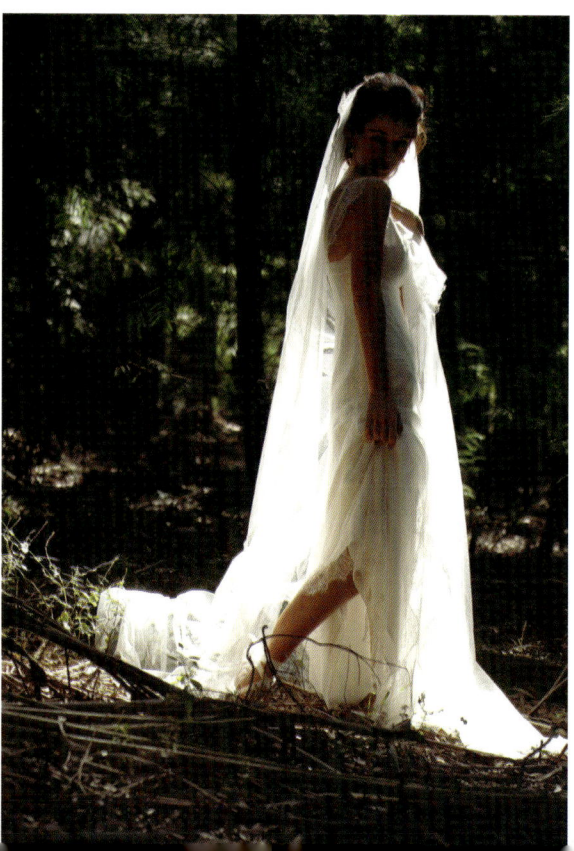

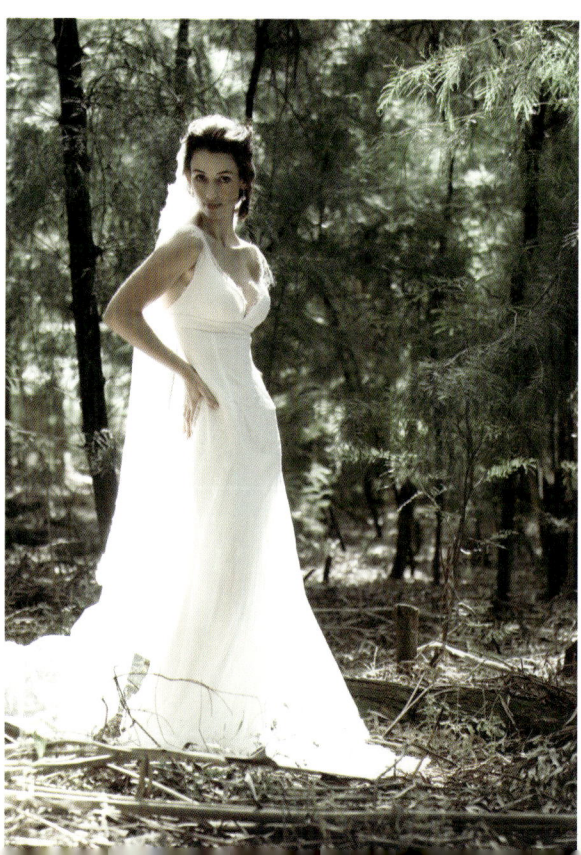

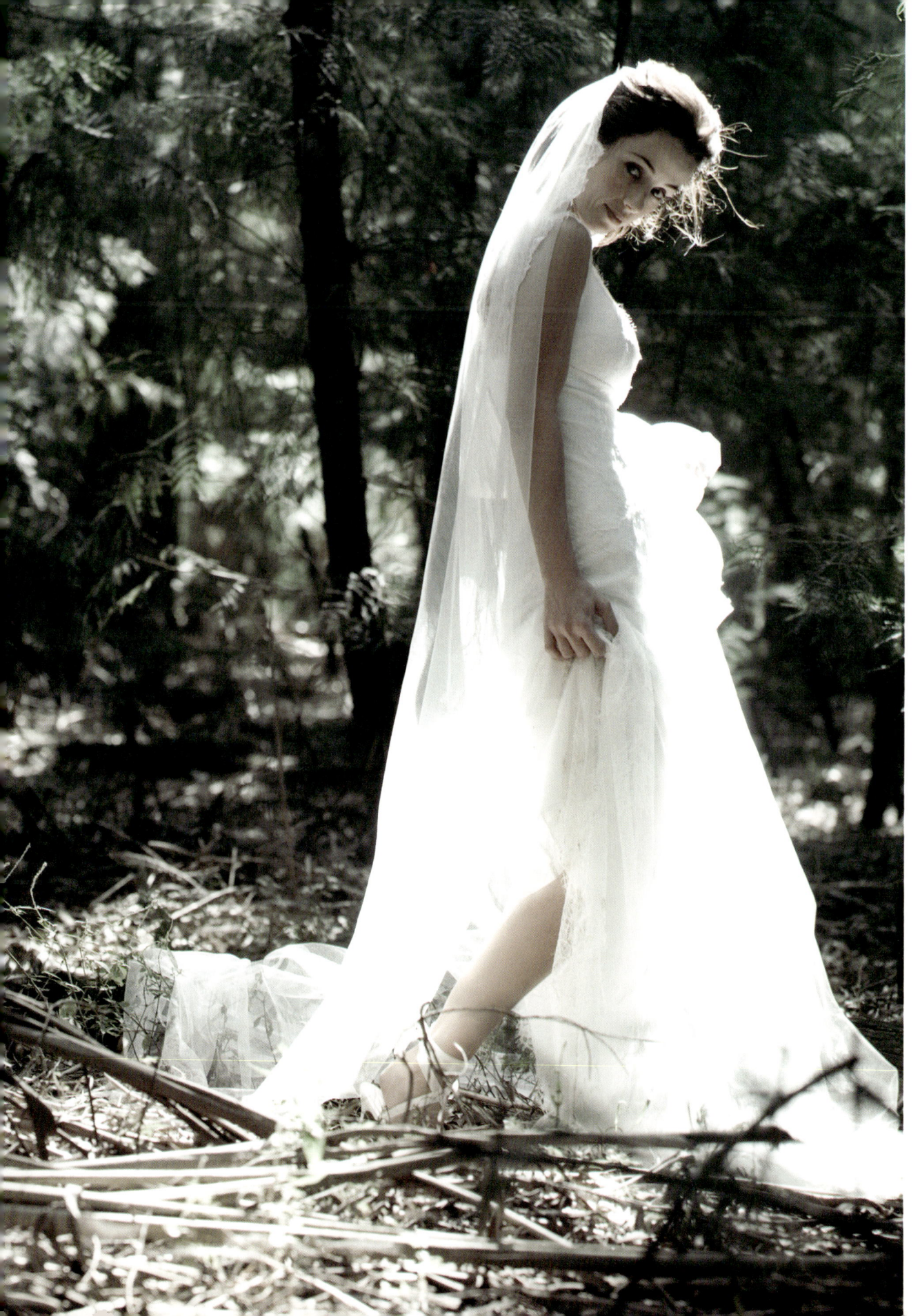

14. AN ELEGANT SEATED POSE

Emphasizing Her Curves

There are a couple of rules of thumb for posing a seated bride. First, she should always sit slightly forward in the chair, as sitting all the way back in the chair can potentially make her look stocky. Second, the chair should ideally be at an angle to the camera, and the bride should also twist her body slightly to accentuate her curves.

Top: An alternate image from the session.
Bottom: The position of the gold reflector.

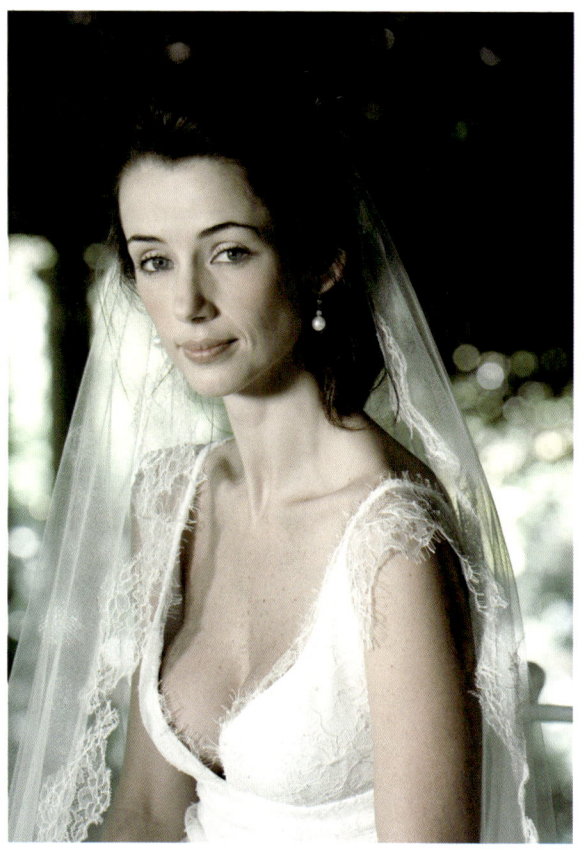

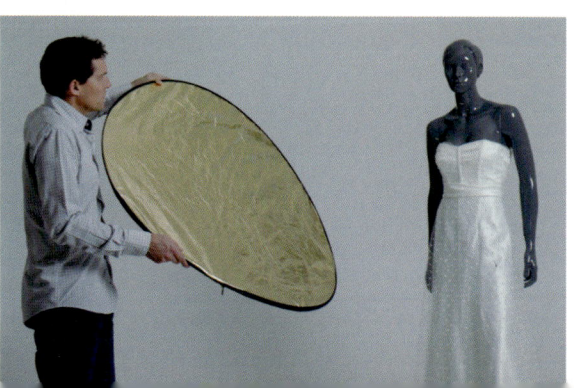

Lighting and Posing

I seated the bride in a wooded area with dappled light behind her. As she was completely in the shade, I had my assistant bounce strong afternoon sunlight onto her using the gold part of my 5-in-1 reflector to produce warm skin tones. This light, from the right side, was hard on her eyes, so I had her tilt her head down slightly toward her left shoulder. This resulted in a beautiful, classic feminine pose. I then asked her to lift her left arm up onto the chair, and the reflector spotlit her hand perfectly, showing off her engagement ring.

To move slightly away from what would have been a formal pose, I asked the bride to pigeon-toe her feet slightly and lift her dress just enough to expose her gorgeous satin-ribbon shoes. Now this classic pose has just enough of an edge to be laissez-faire.

Finishing Touches

The out-of-focus foliage helped me to separate my subject from the background. I desaturated the image in postproduction, as it was to be placed in an album with the image shown in the previous section, and I wanted a cohesive feel.

> **QUICK LOOK**
> | | |
> |---|---|
> | **CAMERA** | Nikon D3s |
> | **LENS** | Nikkor 70–200mm f/2.8G ED VR II |
> | **MODE** | A |
> | **ISO** | 800 |
> | **SHUTTER** | $^1/_{250}$ |
> | **APERTURE** | f/4 |
> | **LIGHTING** | Lastolite 5-in-1 collapsible reflector |

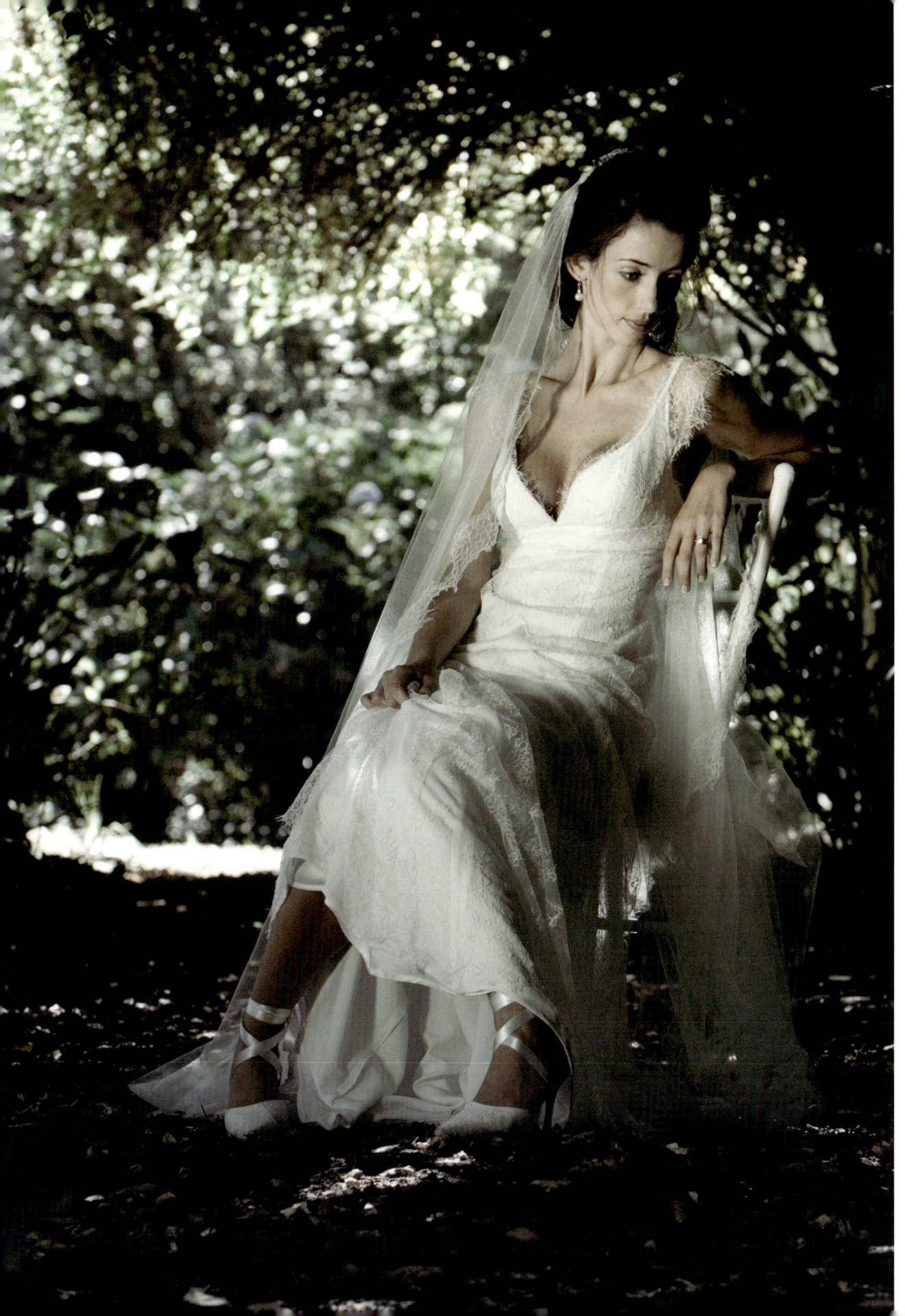

15. STAIRCASE PORTRAITS

Staircases offer a wealth of opportunities for great images—but the staircase need not be visible in the final picture, as you will see here.

For the image on the facing page, I stood a few steps above the bride, looking slightly down at her. There was a great deal of light that was flooding up the stairwell, coming predominantly from behind the bride. I love this backlighting. I find it extremely romantic, and I therefore feel it's very appropriate for brides.

My composition was serendipitous. I couldn't shoot her full-length because I would have pho-

tographed the stairs in the background, which for this shot I didn't want, so I crouched down as low as I could and only managed to get three-quarters of her into my frame. This worked well, and I was happy with the composition. The predominant negative space around her adds to the mystery and sense of solitude.

The bride's body shape creates a pose that is very introspective. It also shows off the bridal gown effectively, which would of course make the dress designer very happy too!

In postproduction, I desaturated the image to further add to the romance and to give a sense of mystery to the subject. Due to the fact that there was a lot of white in the image—both the walls and her dress—I had to overexpose the image by $1^2/_3$ stop.

QUICK LOOK

CAMERA	Nikon D3s
LENS	Nikkor 24–70mm f/2.8G ED
MODE	A
ISO	400
SHUTTER	$^1/_{320}$ +1$^2/_3$ EV
APERTURE	f/2.8
LIGHTING	No manipulation or additional artificial lighting

Left: An alternate image from the session. **Right:** The original image.

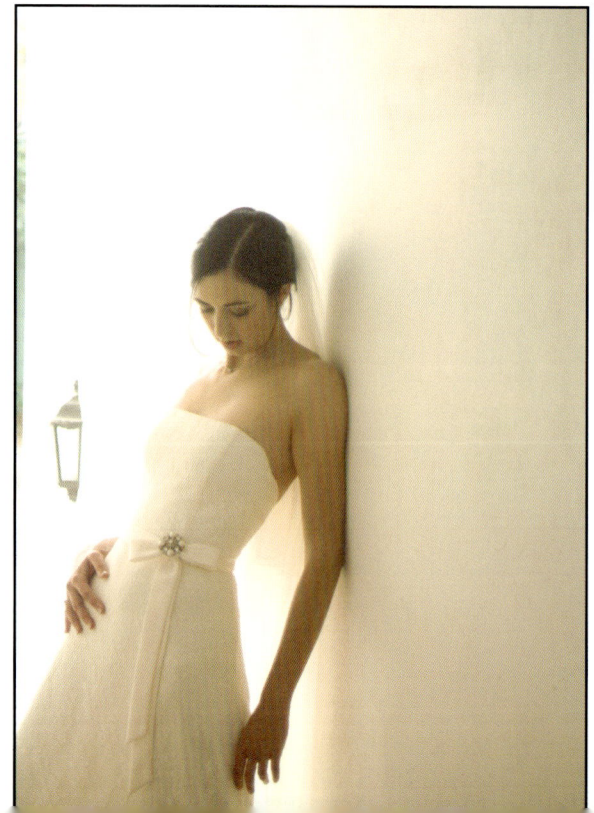

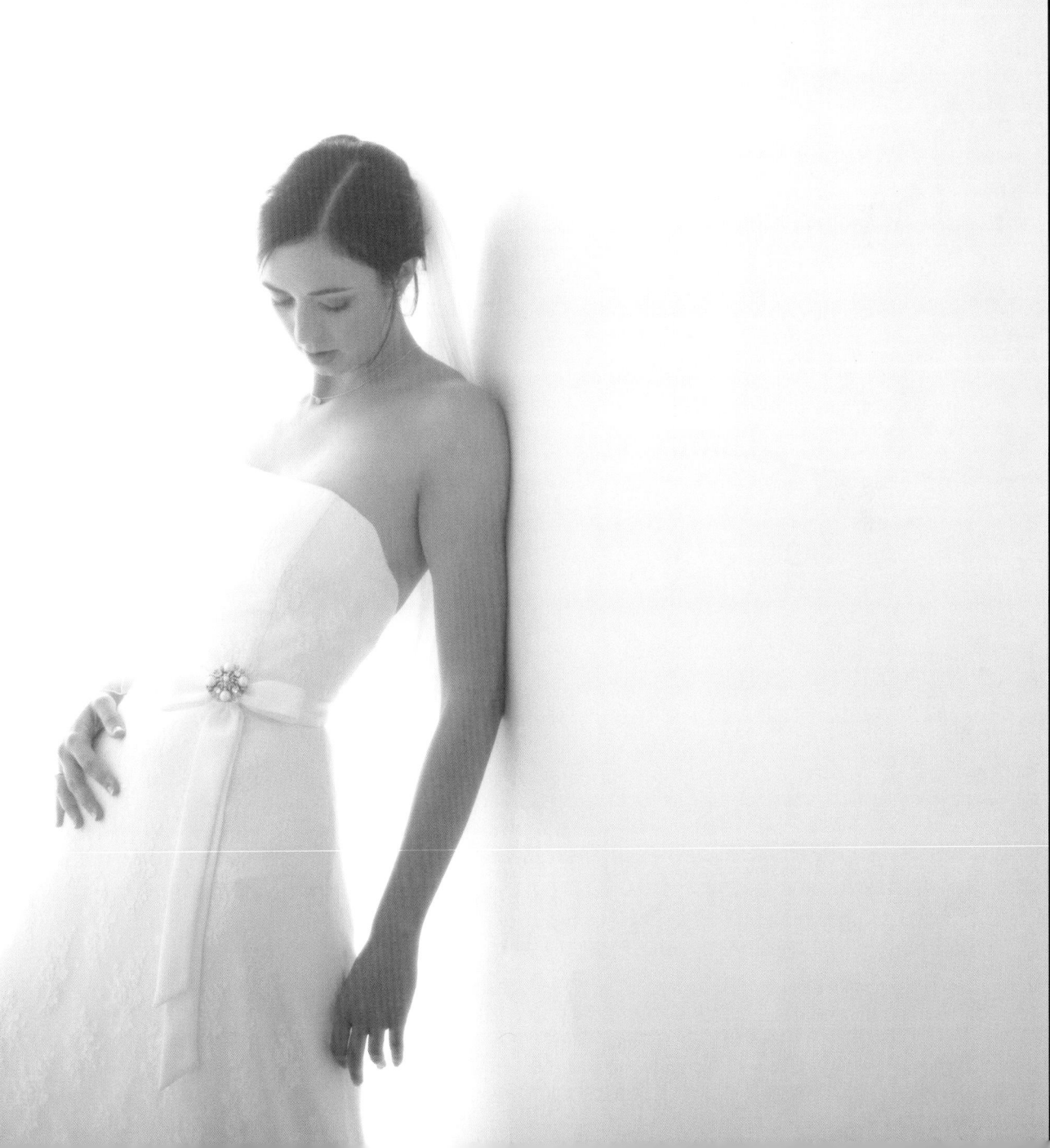

16. VIDEOGRAPHER'S LIGHT

Rain on the bride's wedding day can really dampen her spirits. Unfortunately, it's the one thing that none of us have any control over. When the weather is miserable, I make sure that I brighten the bride's mood by showing her some of the fantastic images that can be shot with the prevailing lighting and a little help from artificial light.

It's imperative that professional photographers learn how to shoot in every weather situation and under any lighting condition. For this image, I used the videographer's tungsten light, which was placed behind the bride on the floor. The bride was lit from the front by the available light coming through the doorway. I shot along the length of the passage, creating a framed look to the image. Behind the bride is the bathroom door; its lovely, dark natural wood framed the bride beautifully.

My white balance was set for the bride's dress. This made the tungsten light show up as a beautiful warm orange glow under her gown. The bride's pose is fashion-inspired. I love the quirky positioning of her feet and arms—they speak of a modern girl who is comfortable in her own skin!

I shot this with a 24–70mm lens due to my lack of space. When I showed the image to the bride, she was overjoyed, and the inclement weather no longer bothered her in the least.

QUICK LOOK

CAMERA	Nikon D3s
LENS	Nikkor 24–70mm f/2.8G ED
MODE	A
ISO	400
SHUTTER	$^1/_{30}$
APERTURE	f/2.8
LIGHTING	Videographer's tungsten light

Left: An alternate pose. **Right:** The position of the videographer's light.

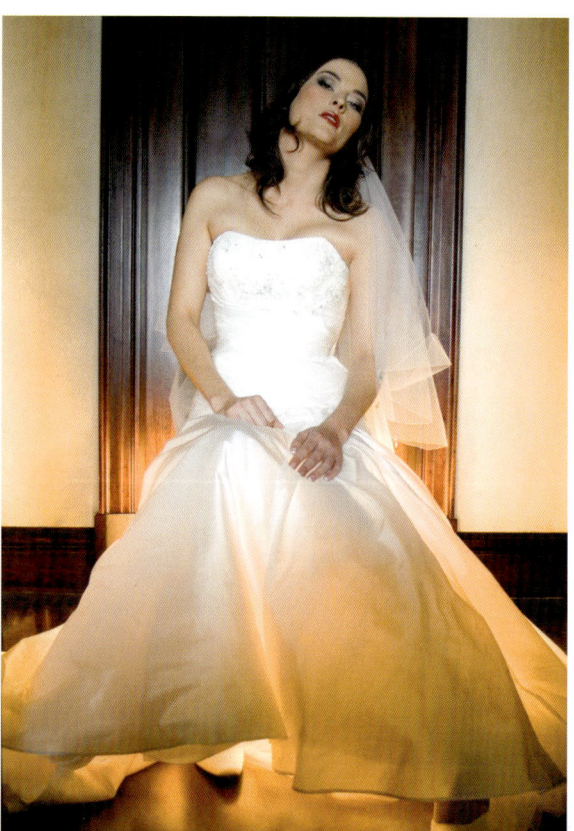

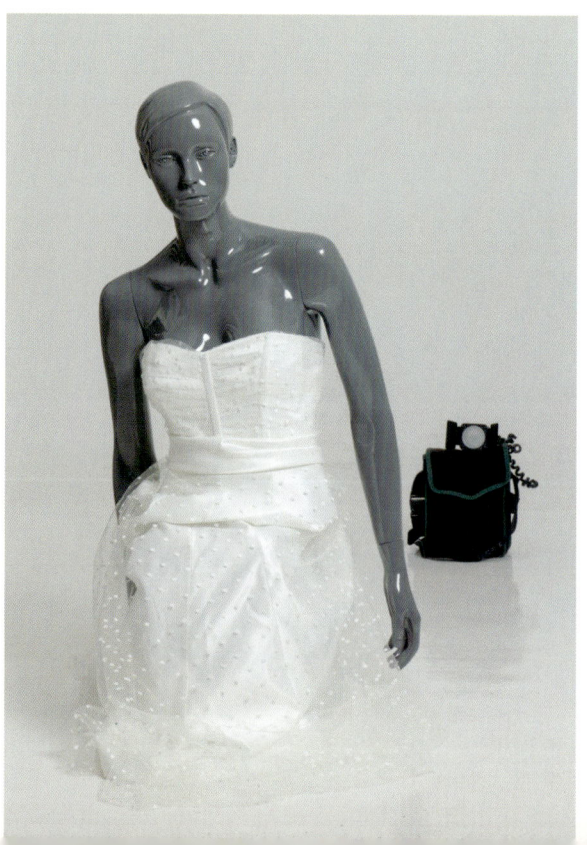

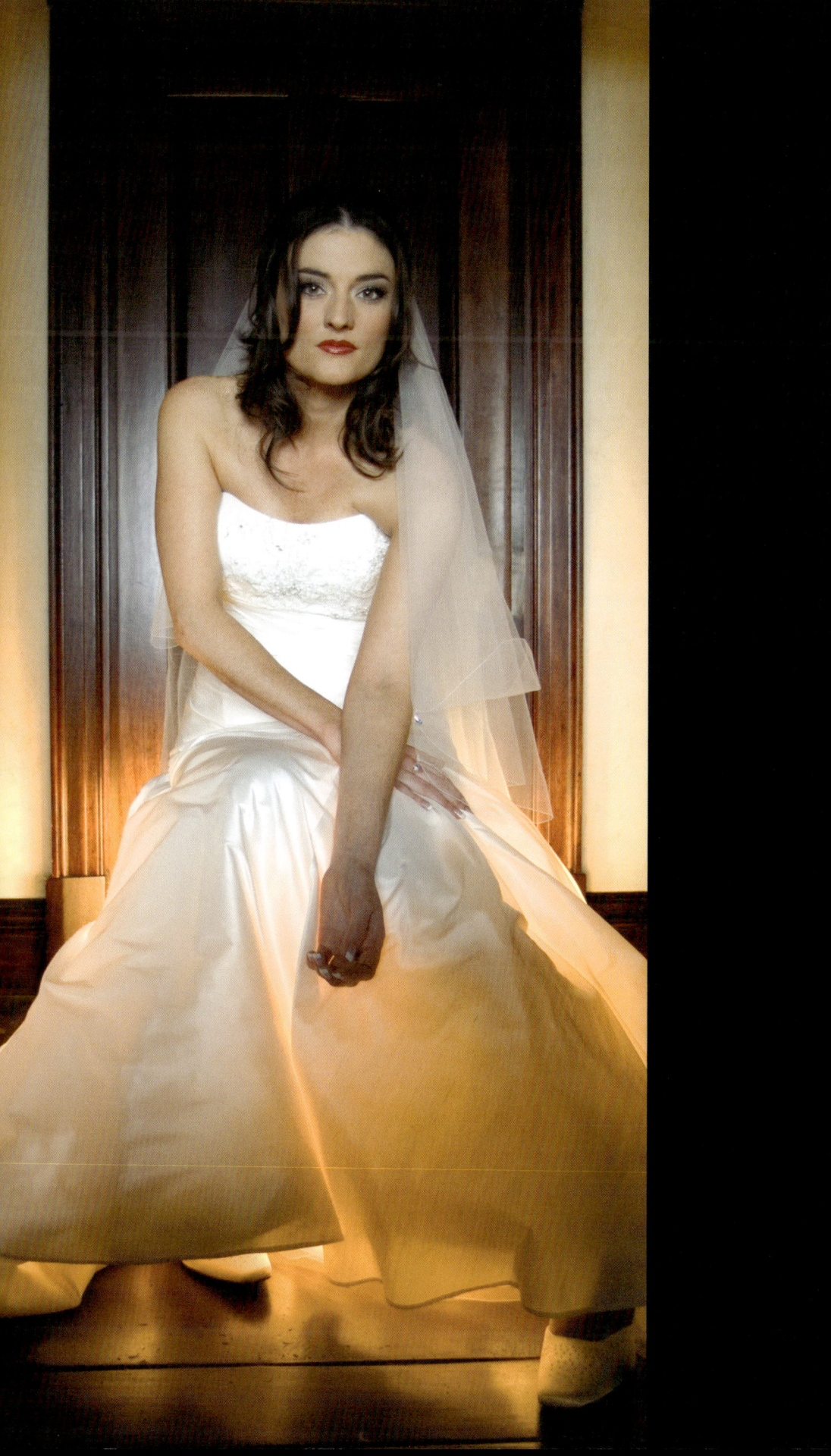

17. A FRESH TAKE ON A FAMILIAR POSE

The Veil Tunnel

There are certain poses that, as a wedding photographer, you are going to have to take year in, year out. It's not as boring as it sounds, as there are always a few variables within each pose. Enhancing a fairly standard head-and-shoulders pose of the bride can take just a little bit of thought and creativity.

By using the bridal veil as a "tunnel" between the bride and me, I add not only another dimension to this traditional wedding accessory, but also a sense of intimacy between the viewer of the photograph and the bride. The veil does have to

be very long, and I ask the help of either bridesmaids or my assistant, if he isn't holding the reflector, to hold the veil over my head and shoulders. This technique adds depth to the shot and creates a soft, romantic backdrop for the bride.

For this image, I positioned the bride, asking her to turn her body into a three-quarter pose and to raise her front shoulder ever so slightly—almost as if she's just taken a deep breath. This gives us the sense of excitement and anticipation that the bride is feeling at this stage of the day. Her arms are softly folded, and her bouquet is gently cradled in her arms.

The Lighting

My assistant held a 5-in-1 collapsible reflector. He used the tool's silver side to bounce the available light from the bride's left-hand side, thereby reducing the contrast on her face and body.

Left: An alternate pose. **Below:** The reflector position.

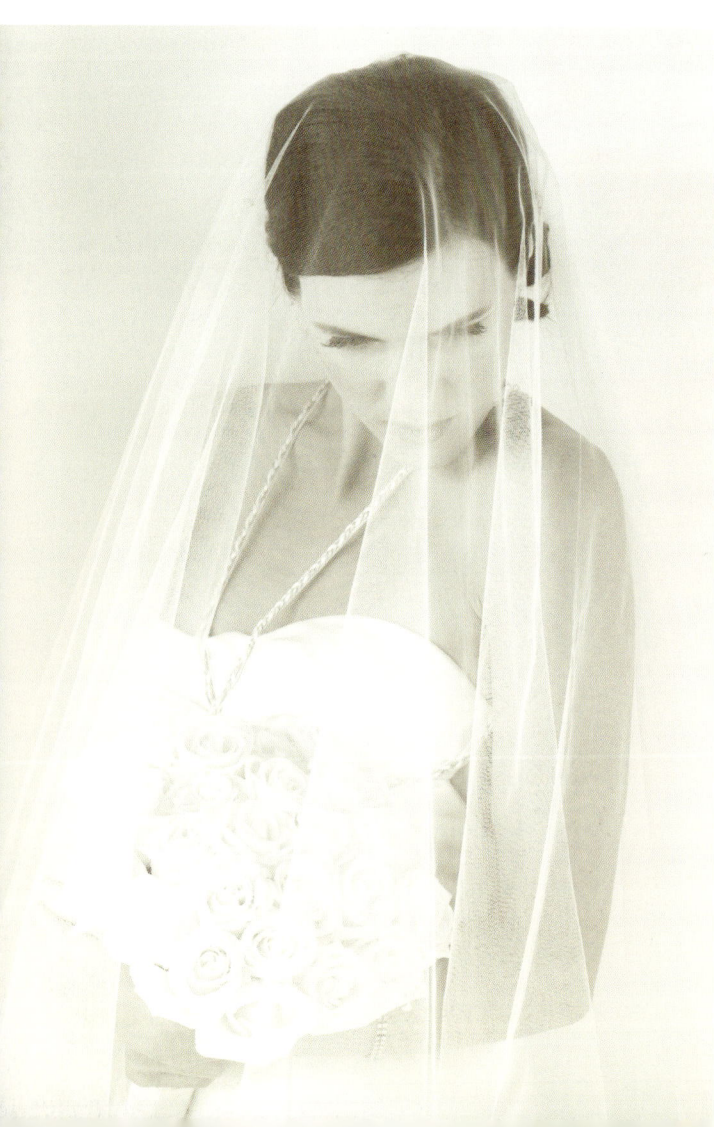

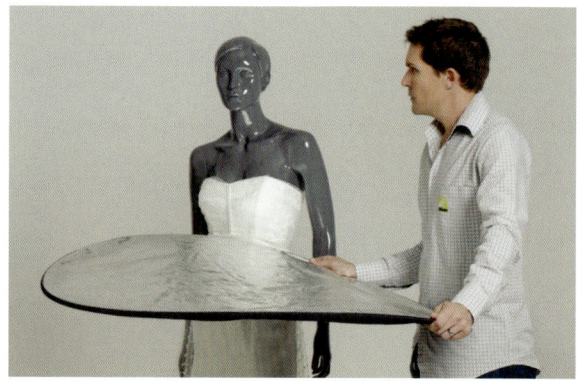

QUICK LOOK

CAMERA	Nikon D3s
LENS	Nikkor 70–200mm f/2.8G ED VR II
MODE	A
ISO	1000
SHUTTER	$^1/_{125}$
APERTURE	f/2.8
LIGHTING	Lastolite 5-in-1 collapsible reflector

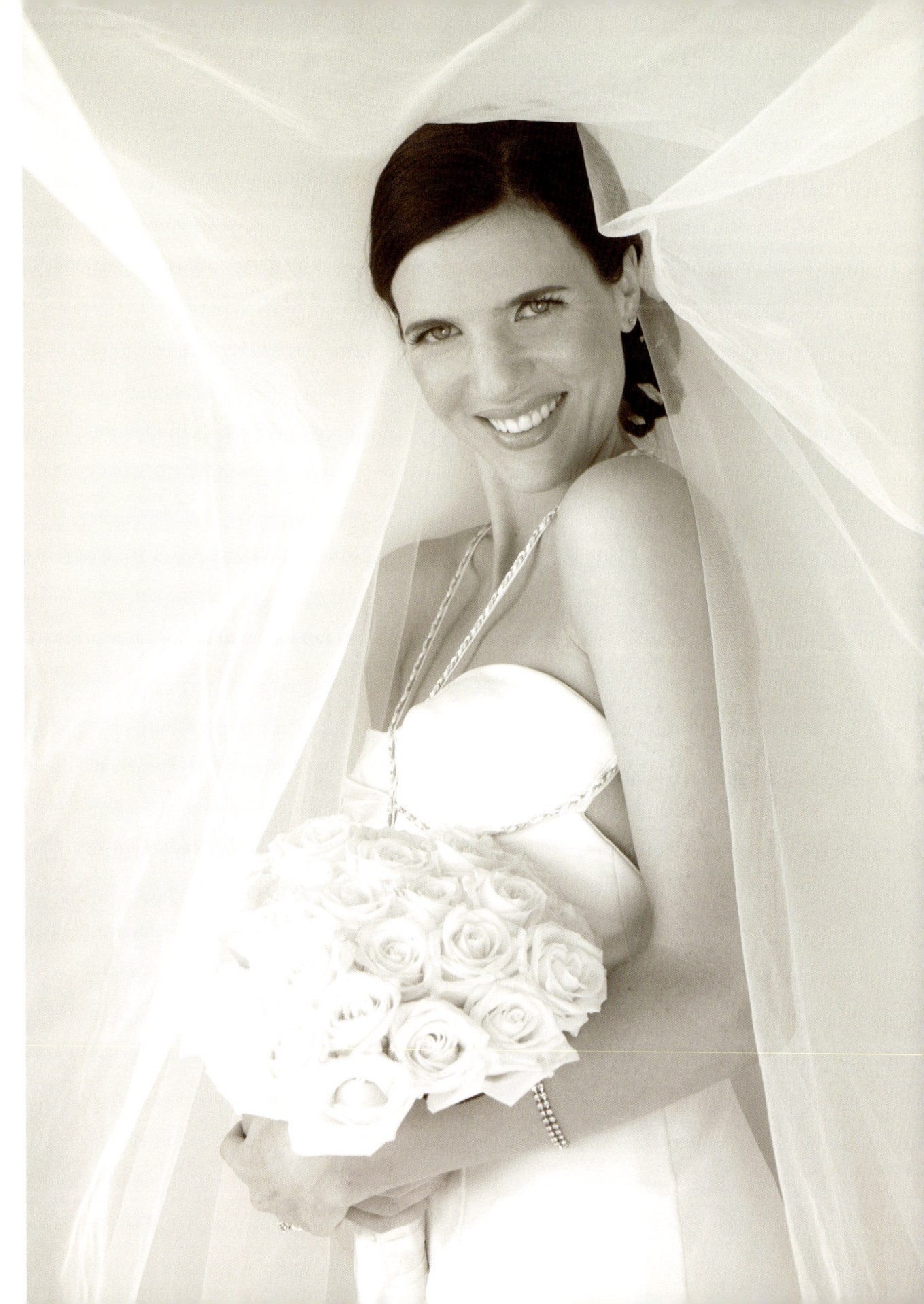

18. SUNSET SHOTS

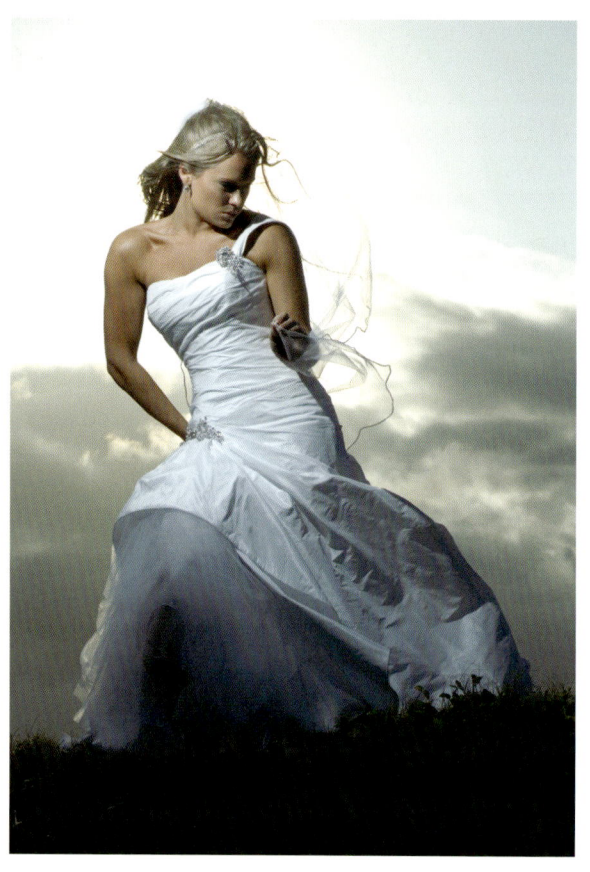

The Appeal of Sunsets

Sunset shots are always special in a wedding album. There's a sense of peace and warmth, a calm closing to a busy and exciting day. Sunset photographs are often about romance and serenity, but with artificial external lighting, one can change the mood as one desires.

A Theatrical Look

I opted to create an image with a powerful and theatrical feel. This portrait was shot with my Elinchrom Ranger RX. The off-camera strobe had no light modifier on it; there was simply a bare bulb, which offers up harsh shadows, but I wanted to create an intense light on the subject to match the intense glow of the setting sun.

I posed the bride so that she was facing the external strobe, and the flash created very flat, dramatic lighting on her face. The harsh artificial lighting also accentuated the folds and pleating in the dress, which added depth and character to the garment.

Although the external strobe was my primary light source for the bride, and without it she would have been in silhouette, it is interesting to note that the sunset was the primary light source for the clouds, which themselves were lit in a dramatic fashion.

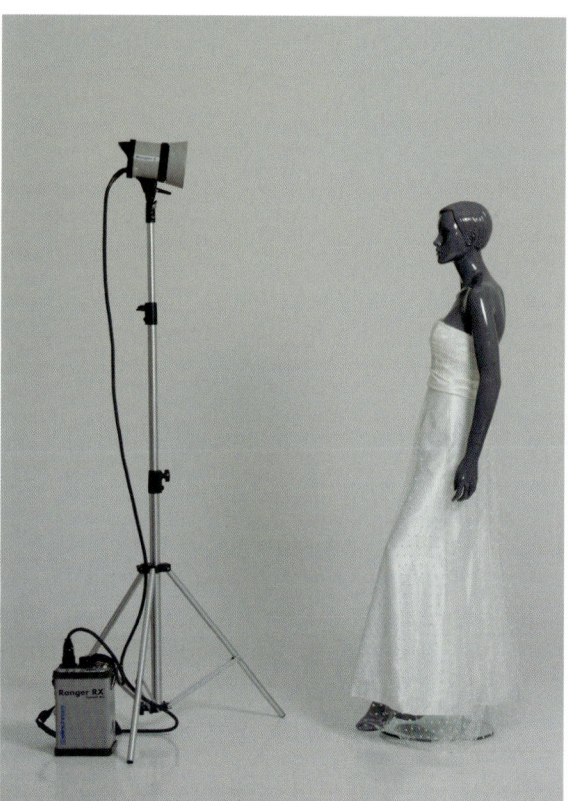

QUICK LOOK

CAMERA	Nikon D3s
LENS	Nikkor 70–200mm f/2.8G ED VR II
MODE	M
ISO	100
SHUTTER	$^1/_{250}$
APERTURE	f/22
LIGHTING	Elinchrom Ranger RX

Top: An alternate sunset shot.
Bottom: The position of the flash.

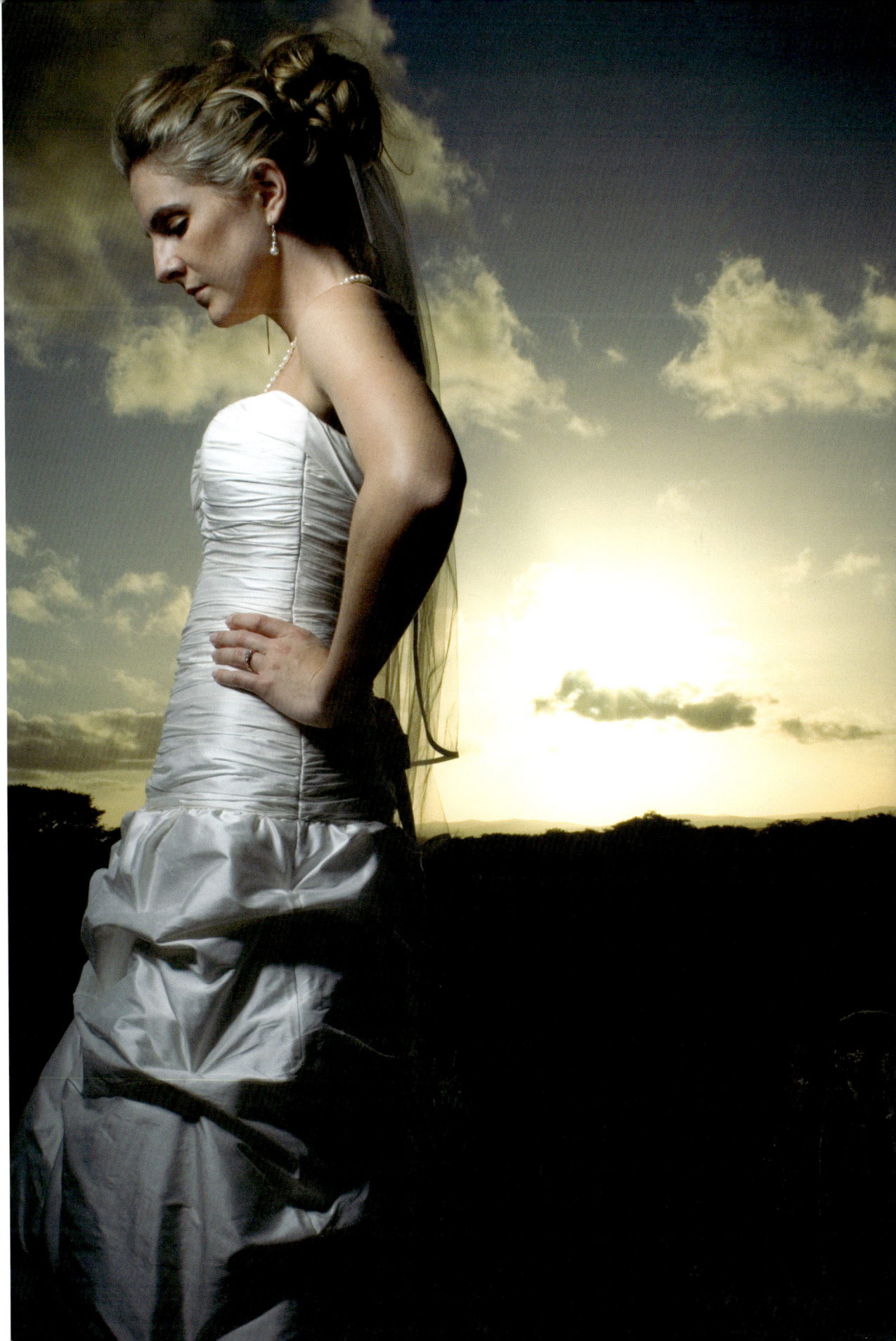

19. THE BEAUTY DISH

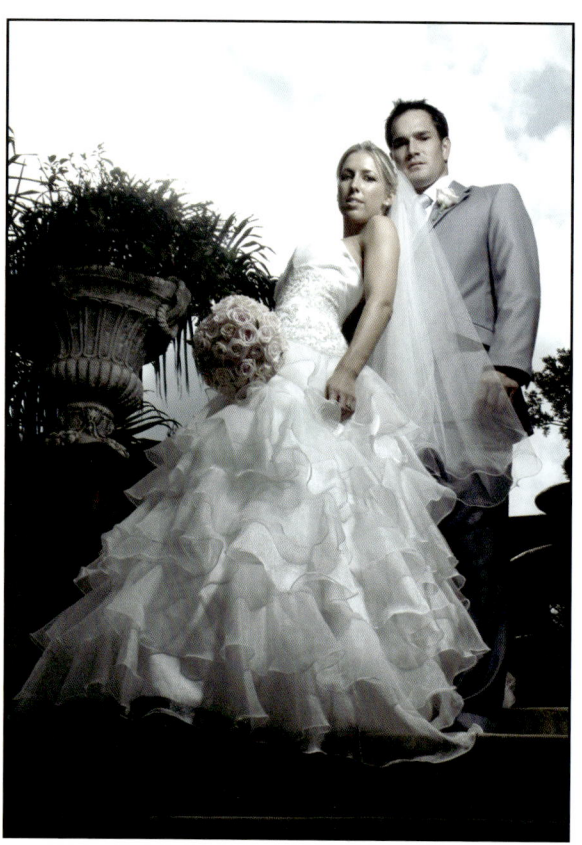

One of my favorite light modifiers is a beauty dish—a broad, shallow, dish-like reflector that emits a modestly soft light at portrait distances.

The light produced by a beauty dish is somewhat between that of a direct flash and a softbox. It gives the subject a wrap-around, contrasty look, which I love for its somewhat dramatic effect. My particular beauty dish is approximately 50cm in diameter. For this portrait, I used the dish with my Ranger RX external strobe.

This bride is a very confident, striking girl. She was excited about her photos and enjoyed posing like a fashion model. The image was shot fairly late in the afternoon on a day that was completely overcast, hence the lack of a dark-blue sky. The sun, however, still managed to make itself seen behind the cloud cover.

I posed the bride on the top of some garden steps and positioned the beauty dish to her left. I shot from three steps below. From that angle, the skirt of her dress, which was full of layered detail, became beautifully exaggerated. The beauty dish added to this effect, creating sculpted shadows and features on the garment and on the bride.

I desaturated this image in postproduction to further enhance the high-fashion feel.

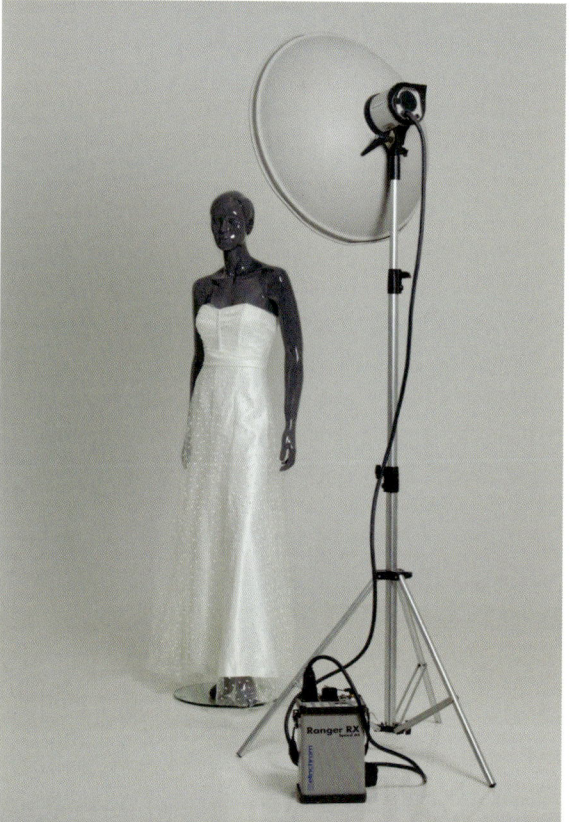

QUICK LOOK	
CAMERA	Nikon D3s
LENS	Nikkor 70–200mm f/2.8G ED VR II
MODE	M
ISO	100
SHUTTER	$^1/_{125}$
APERTURE	f/16
LIGHTING	Elinchrom Ranger RX

Top: With no change to the setup, the groom can be added to the bridal shot. **Bottom:** The position of the beauty dish.

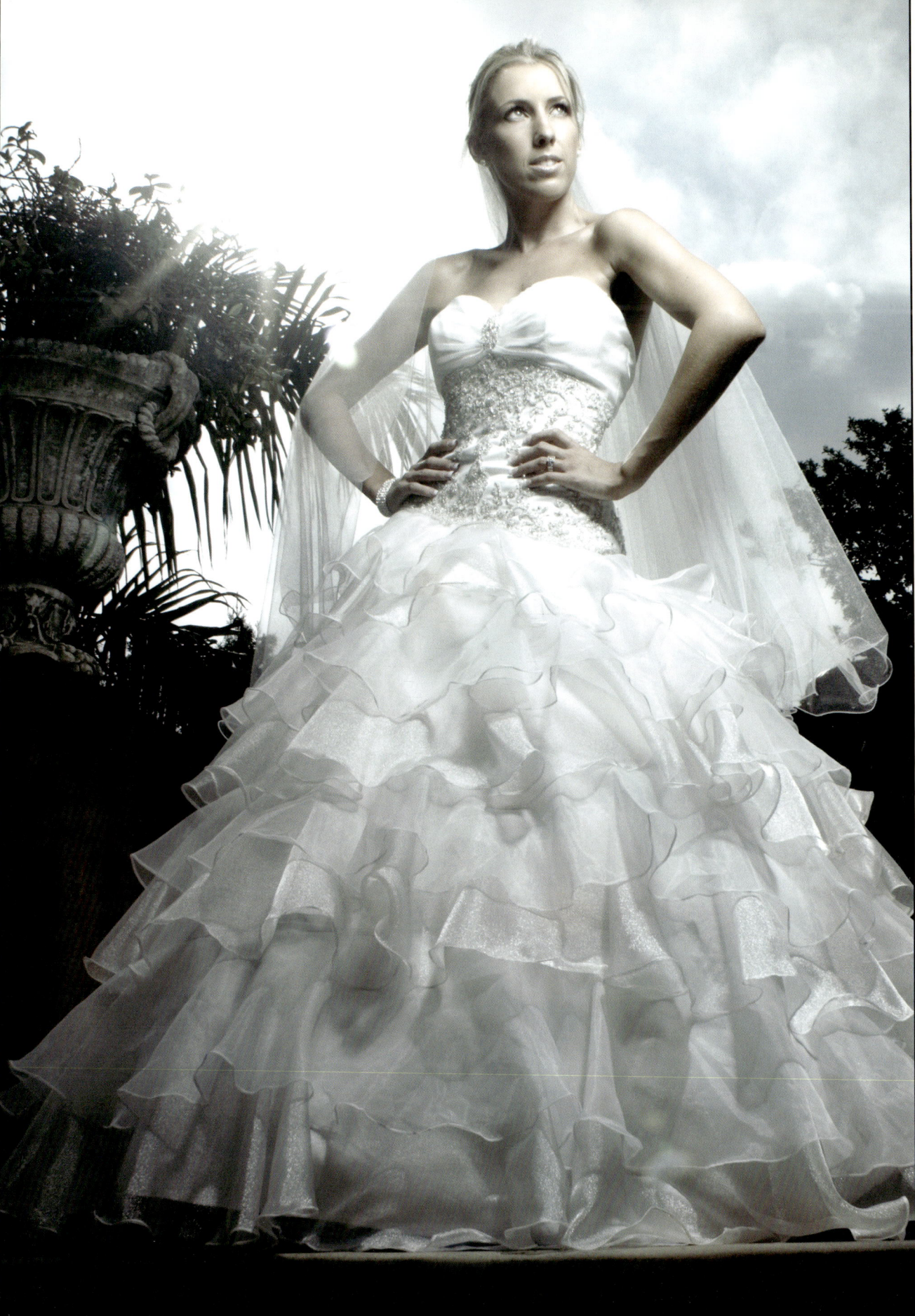

20. SIMULATED SUNLIGHT

This image was created on a cold, drizzling day, so I opted for a simulated sunlight effect (which put a bit of sunshine into the bride's heart too!).

To do this, I positioned my Elinchrom Ranger RX as a rim light behind her, so it looked like sunlight spilling around her sides and through her hair. The moisture in the air exaggerated the look, producing a bit of a halo effect around her torso.

To accentuate the angelic look, I asked the bride to stand in a very classic, simple pose—hands hung loosely by her side and her head tilted to the side with her chin slightly raised. The look is innocent, fresh, and peaceful.

I shot on shutter priority mode because I didn't want the shutter speed to go above my camera's flash sync speed; otherwise, I would have obtained a darker area on the image caused

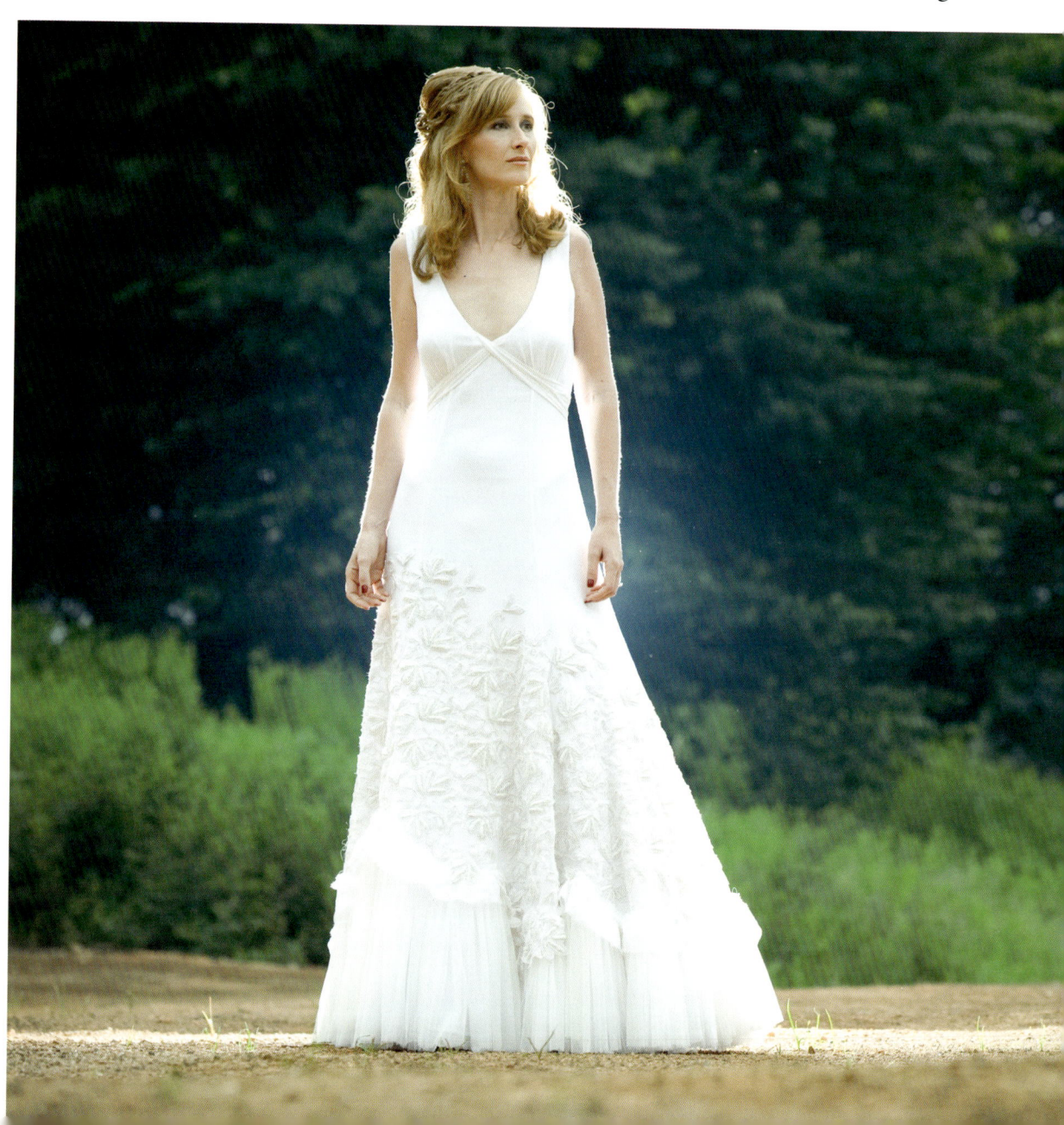

by the curtain closing. To avoid this happening, I set my shutter speed to $^1/_{160}$, and the camera selected an aperture of f/5.6.

Right: An alternate portrait from the shoot. **Bottom right:** The position of the flash.

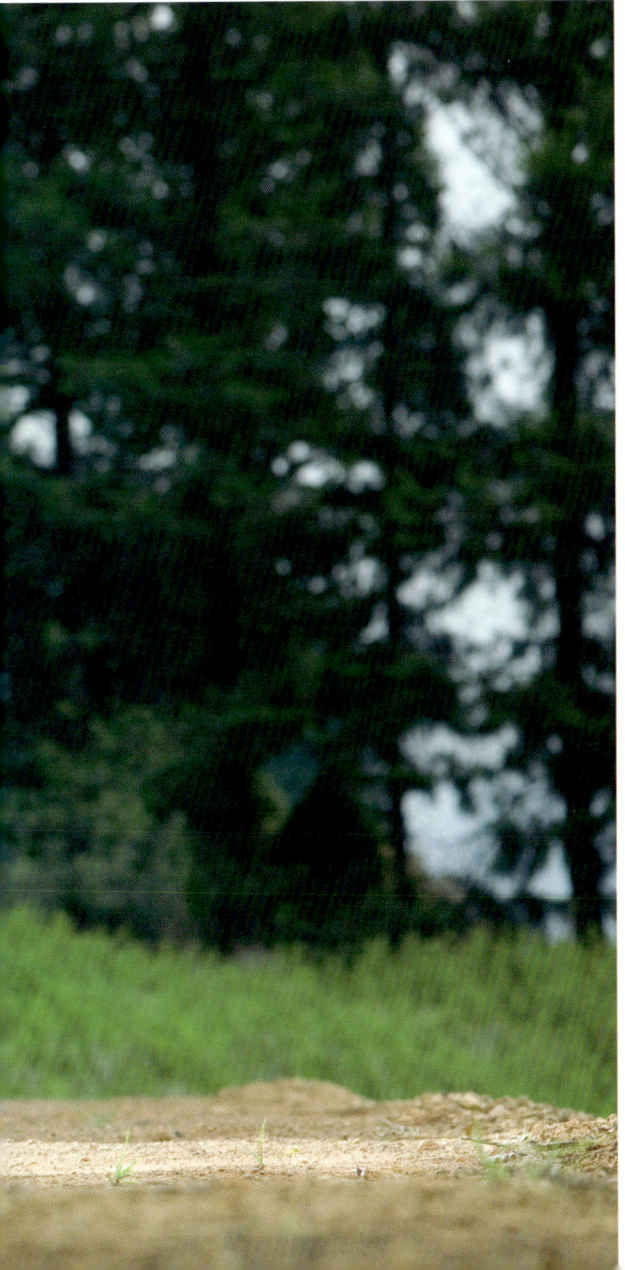

I had perfect control over the amount of back-lighting by either increasing or decreasing the power on the Elinchrom Ranger RX. This can be done from the Elinchrom Skyport, without the hassle of having to change it on the flash itself.

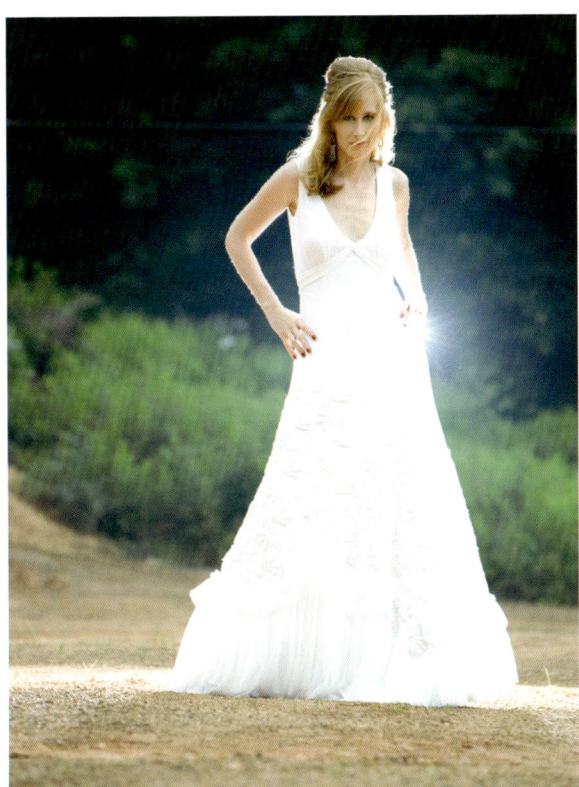

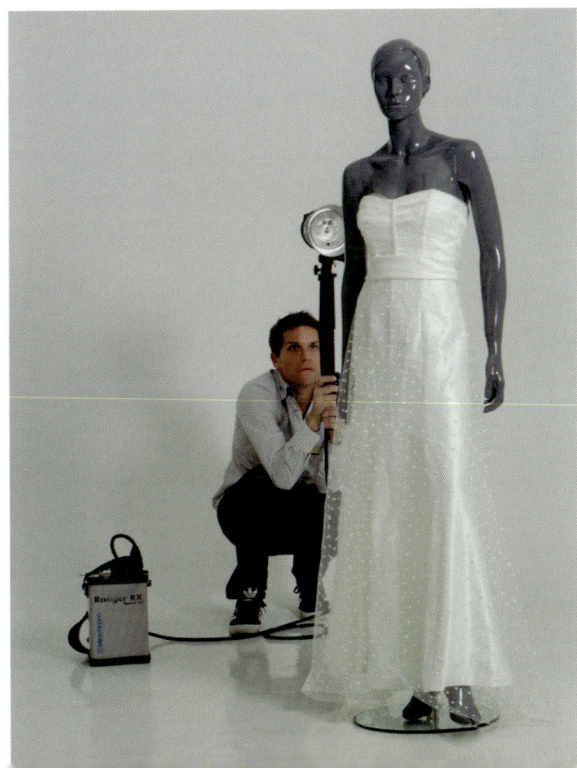

21. SHEER CURTAINS AS A SOFTBOX

A Studio Look on Location

White net curtaining has afforded me the opportunity to create a mini studio in the hotel or at the bride's home where she is getting dressed. Finding a large window—or preferably a glass door leading outside—that has net curtains, I pull this across and create a sort of giant softbox, with the ambient light from the window serving as my primary light source. If I don't have access to sheer curtains, I use a medium Lastolite Skylite. The Skylite has a collapsible but rigid aluminium frame, and it gives a great soft light.

This shot was made using curtains as a diffuser. I asked the bride to step far back into the fabric. The light almost enveloped her. This light behind her was the only source (I'd made sure that all other lights in the room were turned off).

The Exposure

I exposed for the skin, so I had to override the camera's light metering system. I shot this image at ⅔ stop over, resulting in blown-out curtains. It's no longer evident that the shot was made in a hotel room—it has a studio look.

Tip: Make sure you check your white balance for the light that is landing on the bride.

QUICK LOOK
CAMERA	Nikon D3s
LENS	Nikkor 70–200mm f/2.8G ED VR II
MODE	P
ISO	800
SHUTTER	$^1/_{250}$ +$^2/_3$ EV
APERTURE	f/5.6
LIGHTING	Window light diffused by a sheer white curtain.

Left: An alternate image from the session. **Right:** An alternate approach: the Lastolite Skylite.

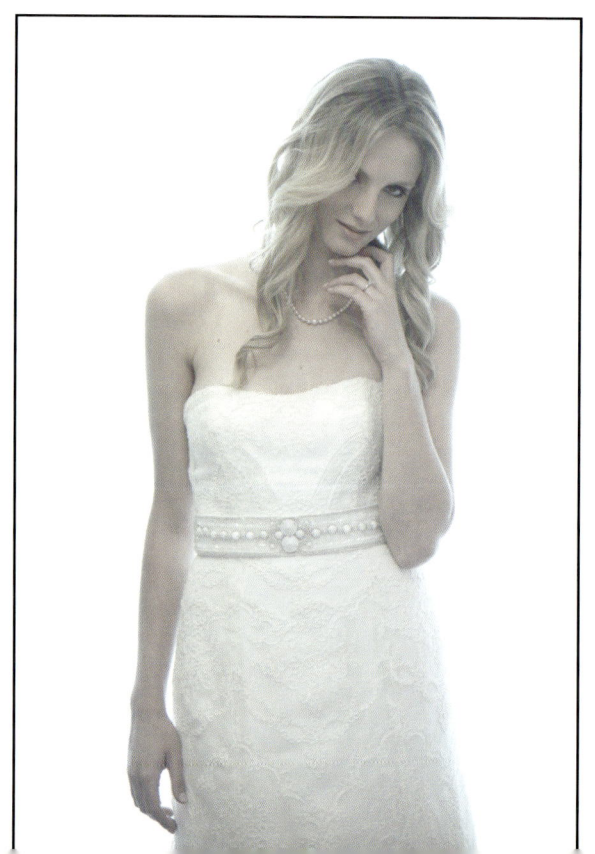

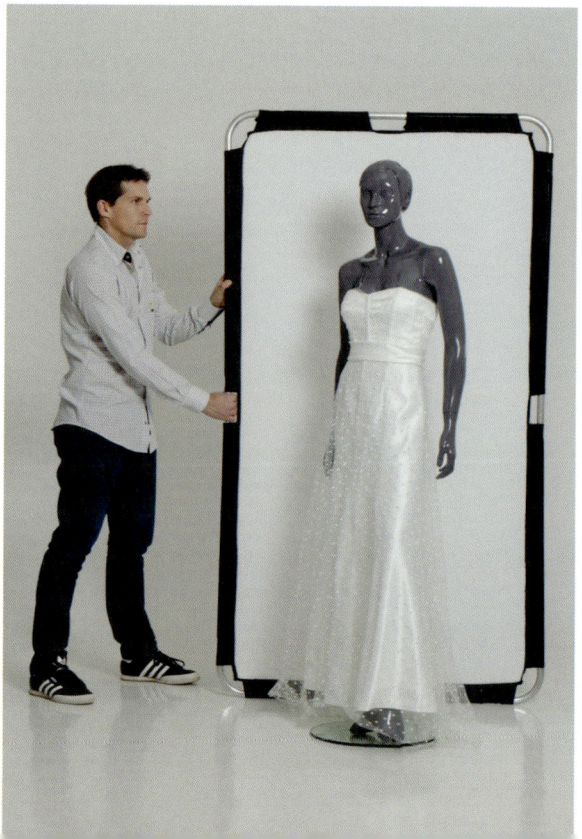

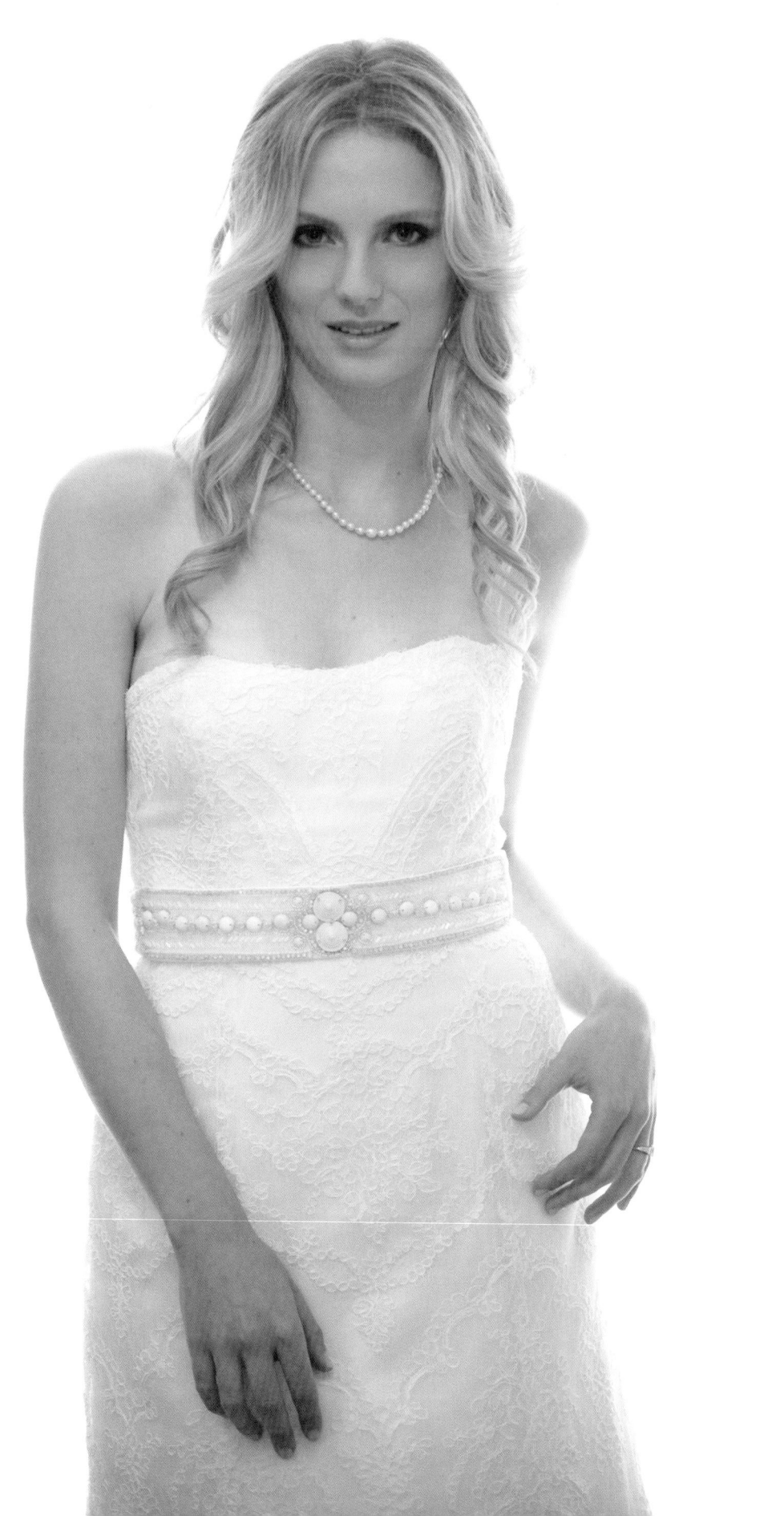

22. NEGATIVE SPACE

A Joyous Bride

Using my theories of utilizing dominant space, along with the rule of thirds, I placed my bride in the unexpected top right-hand corner of the frame and allowed for the shiny white floor of the location to play a significant role in the image as the predominant negative space, creating an image that I believe is highly impactful and contemporary.

QUICK LOOK

CAMERA	Nikon D4
LENS	Nikkor 70–200mm f/2.8G ED VR II
MODE	A
ISO	2000
SHUTTER	$^1/_{125}$ +2EV
APERTURE	f/2.8
LIGHTING	No additional lighting or manipulation

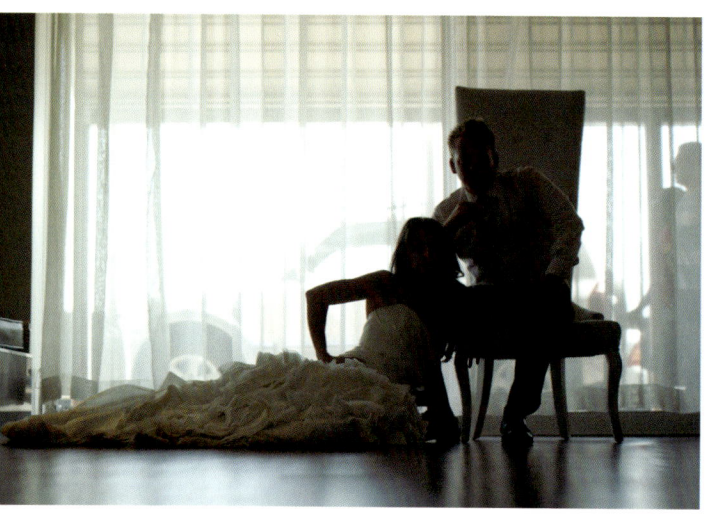

The location was actually a restaurant, and I had to move tables and chairs away from the window area to create the space that I desired. As the restaurant was on a busy street, there was lots of traffic and many people walking past the window.

The Pose

The bride's pose is a little cheeky, but also fun and spontaneous, with her dress tumbling down around her and head thrown back in laughter. Although it does have a spontaneous feel, I specifically structured and styled the pose in this way. Being able to articulate what you want from your subject in order to portray a certain mood is very valuable to you as a photographer.

An Alternate Image

The supporting image at the top left was actually my lighting test shot to see to what degree I needed to overexpose the image. I chose to overexpose it by 2 stops, which resulted in the bright white, high key image shown at the bottom left of this page.

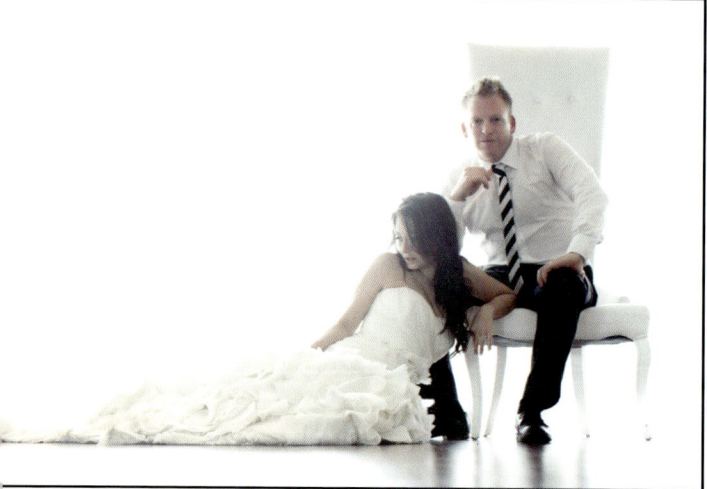

Top and bottom: Using the same lighting and setup, I was able to create a pose of the couple. The test shot (top) and final image (bottom).

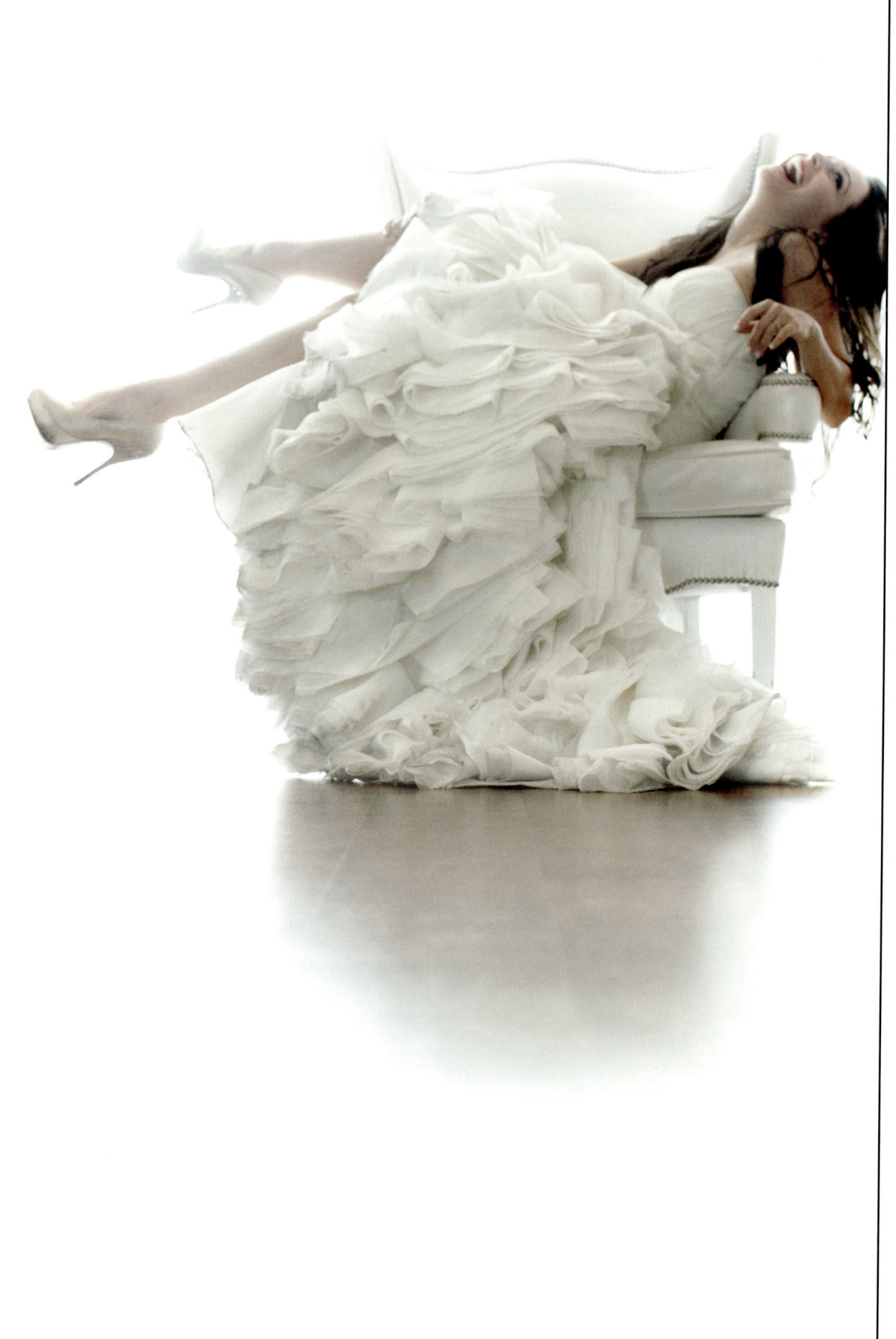

23. IN THE SPOTLIGHT

A Dramatic Look

Spotlights are synonymous with stage productions, and there certainly is something theatrical and dramatic about them. They highlight one subject, while all activity around them is negated and lost in the dark. The play on the spotlight lighting technique is very exciting for me, as I'm always looking for new ways to illuminate my brides, especially after dark, which is often the case when it comes to Jewish weddings.

The Setup

This image was shot on a verdant lawn outside the reception venue. I used my Elinchrom Ranger RX as my only light source—hence the spotlight effect. I used an asymmetrical system where the A flash head fires at 66.6 percent, and then the B flash head fires at 33.3 percent. I placed the B flash head behind the bride for beautiful rim lighting. The A flash head with a silver reflective umbrella was placed in front of the bride. This created the dimension I was looking for. Due to the very dark conditions, I chose a high shutter speed ($^1/_{200}$ second). The ambient light from the venue, which was a few meters off, did not affect the image. The resultant pitch-black background, in contrast to the circle of light around the bride, is just the look I was going for.

QUICK LOOK

CAMERA	Nikon D3s
LENS	Nikkor 70–200mm f/2.8G ED VR II
MODE	M
ISO	100
SHUTTER	$^1/_{200}$
APERTURE	f/11
LIGHTING	Elinchrom Ranger RX with a silver umbrella

Left: The groom is added in the same setup.
Right: The lighting setup for the main portrait.

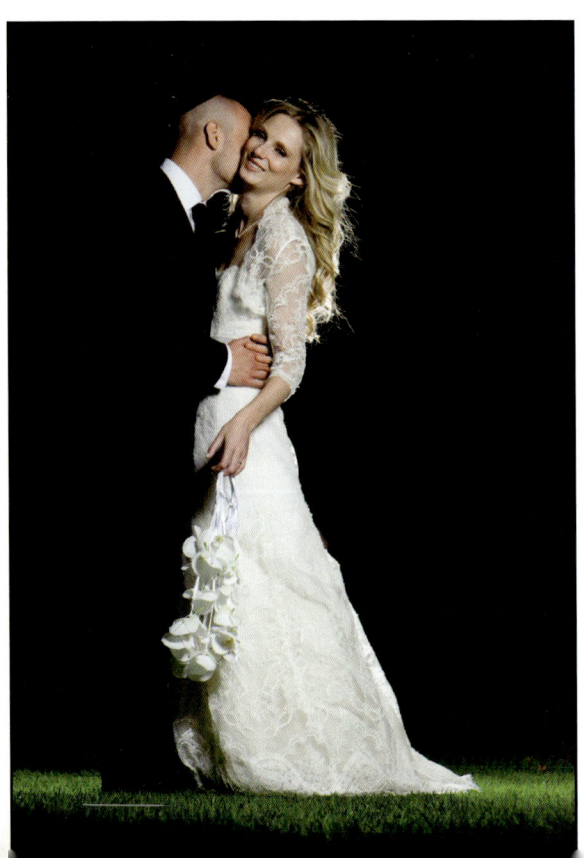

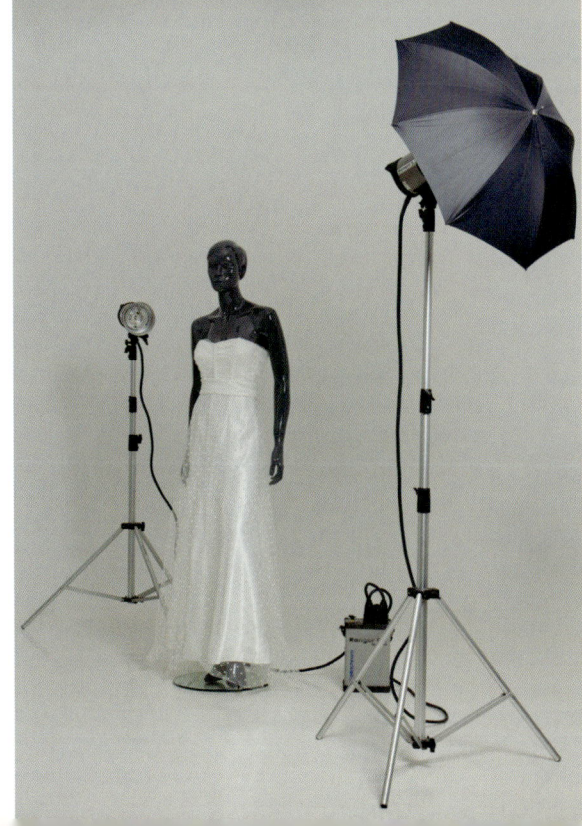

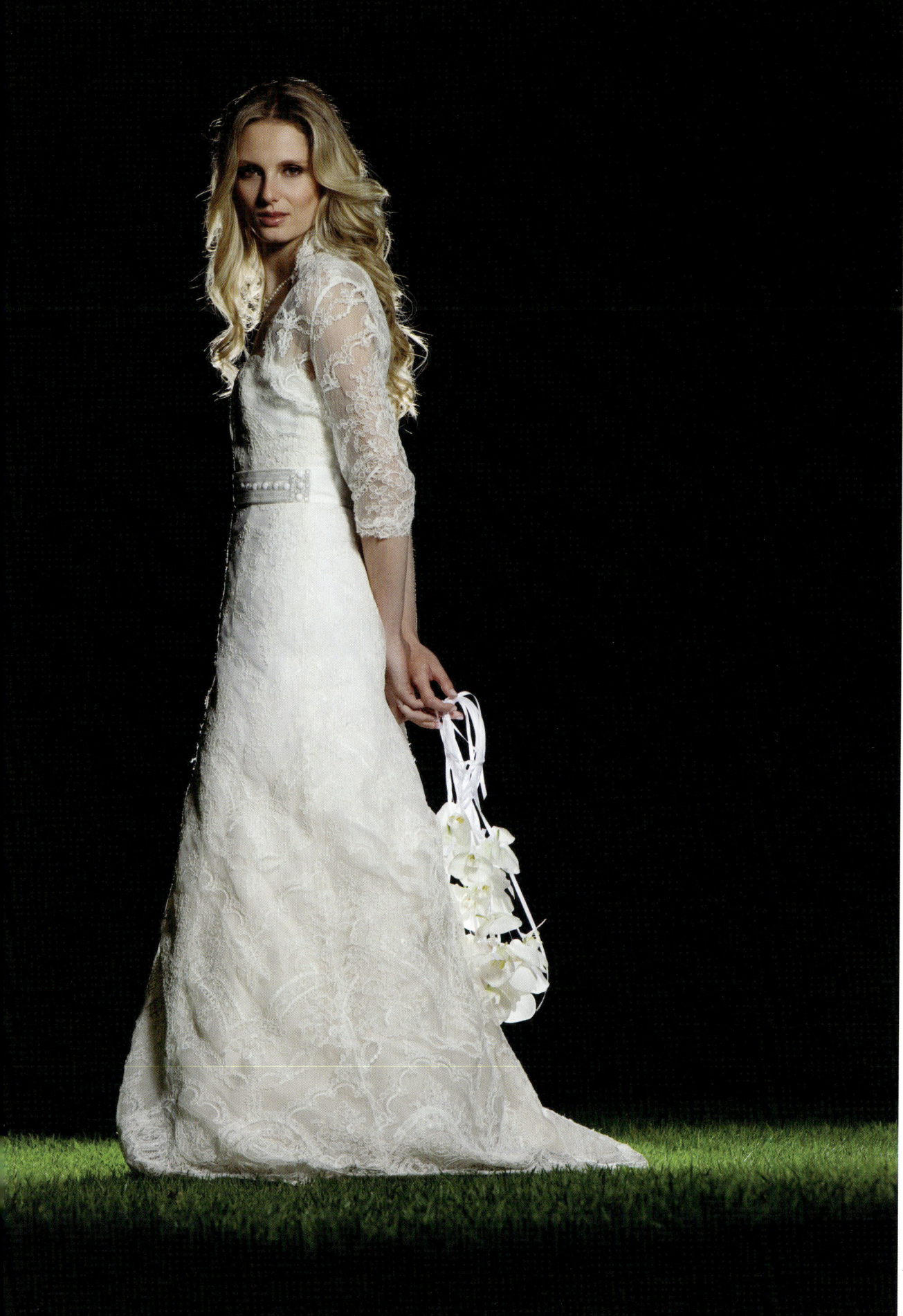

24. A BYGONE ERA

Grace and Poise

Evoking an era of traditional wedding photography, this image has a very strong, silent quality that I find particularly powerful.

The position of the bride's hands in this image also brings to mind a bygone time. The effect is enhanced by an arm positioned across her waist, and the other lifted to her shoulder where the hand touches ever so lightly.

Contrasty Lighting

I positioned the bride close to the window light, and using my 5-in-1 collapsible reflector with the black surface opposite the window, I blocked any ambient light that was coming from the room. This created a very contrasty, moody image, with a lovely dark shadow falling across her back, her hair at the back, and the back of her right arm. The front of her body was well lit, but the window light was not too harsh.

Contrasty images can highlight features that are not terribly attractive, such as a large nose or a pointed chin; they also enhance skin blemishes. As a photographer, you must be mindful of this. This bride had perfect facial features and skin, which allowed me to take this commanding image. The bygone era mood was further enhanced by the vintage curtains in the window, which my assistant pulled around the back of the bride to create a backdrop.

QUICK LOOK	
CAMERA	Nikon D3s
LENS	Nikkor 70–200mm f/2.8G ED VR II
MODE	A
ISO	400
SHUTTER	$^1/_{250}$
APERTURE	f/2.8
LIGHTING	Lastolite 5-in-1 collapsible reflector, black side to block light

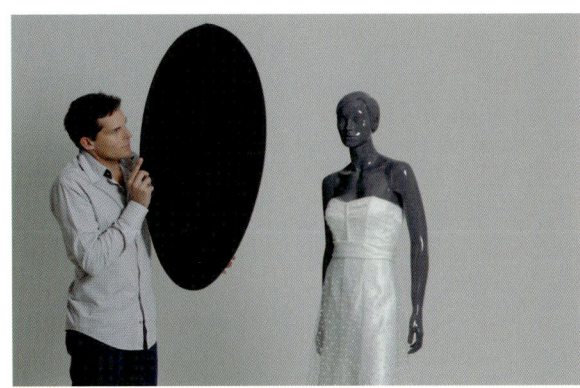

Left: An alternate portrait from the session.
Right: The position of the reflector.

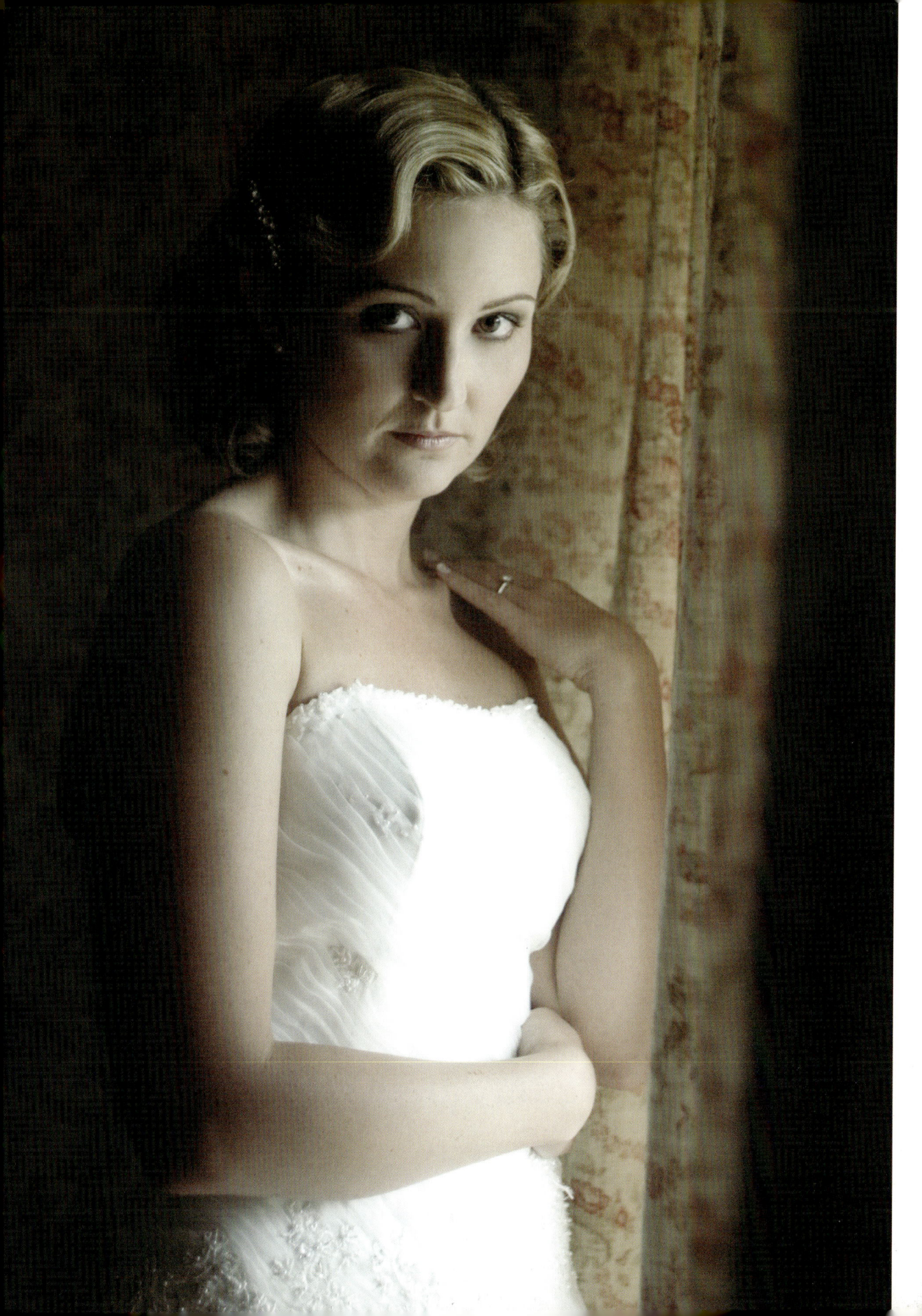

25. A COUNTRY SETTING

A Great Opportunity

Countryside locations always present a wealth of photographic opportunities. There's something magical around practically every corner. This particular wedding was held at a guesthouse where they kept horses. The horses were all quite used to people milling about, and this one was

Top: An alternate image from the session, before postproduction. **Bottom:** The edited final image.

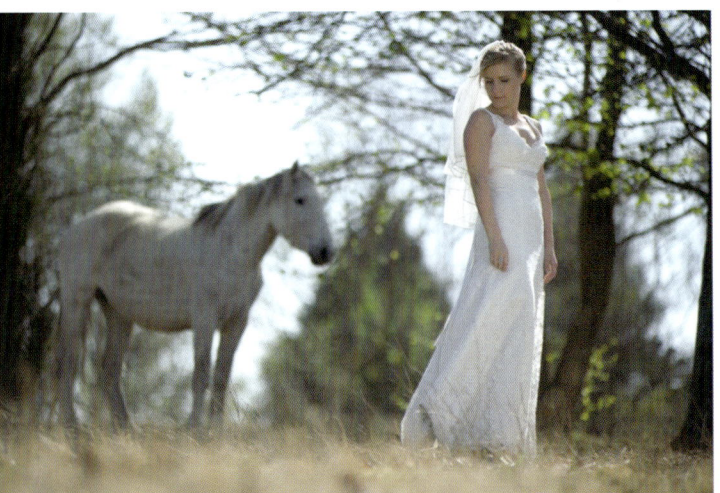

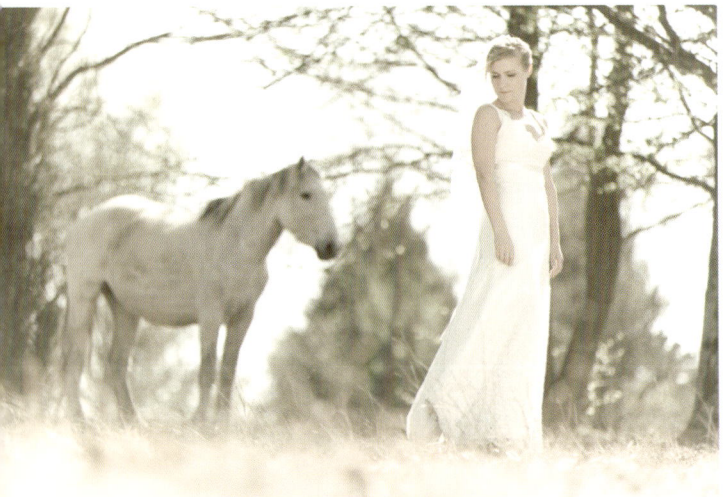

particularly tame, so we managed to get him into the right position where there was a glorious amount of backlight, as you can see here. Not knowing whether the horse would object to a bright modifier or flash, I cautiously chose not to use any artificial lighting, or even a reflector from the front. Luckily, there was a white outbuilding near the bride, and the light from the sun bounced off of this, so it acted as my reflector. When using backlighting, I'm always very careful not to allow any harsh light to fall onto my subjects' faces. Only their backs, shoulders, and necks have the full harsh light shining onto them—the light on the faces is always kept soft.

Artistic Considerations

Shooting this on f/2.8, one can see how blurred the background is, separating the subject from the background, which adds to the ethereal quality of the image. This was done by overexposing by 1 stop as there was a predominance of white in the frame. I then desaturated the image in postproduction using Nik Software's Color Efex Pro 4, adding a touch of warm orange color so as to make it look a bit old fashioned, like an old, faded photograph.

QUICK LOOK	
CAMERA	Nikon D3s
LENS	Nikkor 70–200mm f/2.8G ED VR II
MODE	A
ISO	200
SHUTTER	$^1/_{500}$ +1EV
APERTURE	f/2.8
LIGHTING	No additional lighting or manipulation

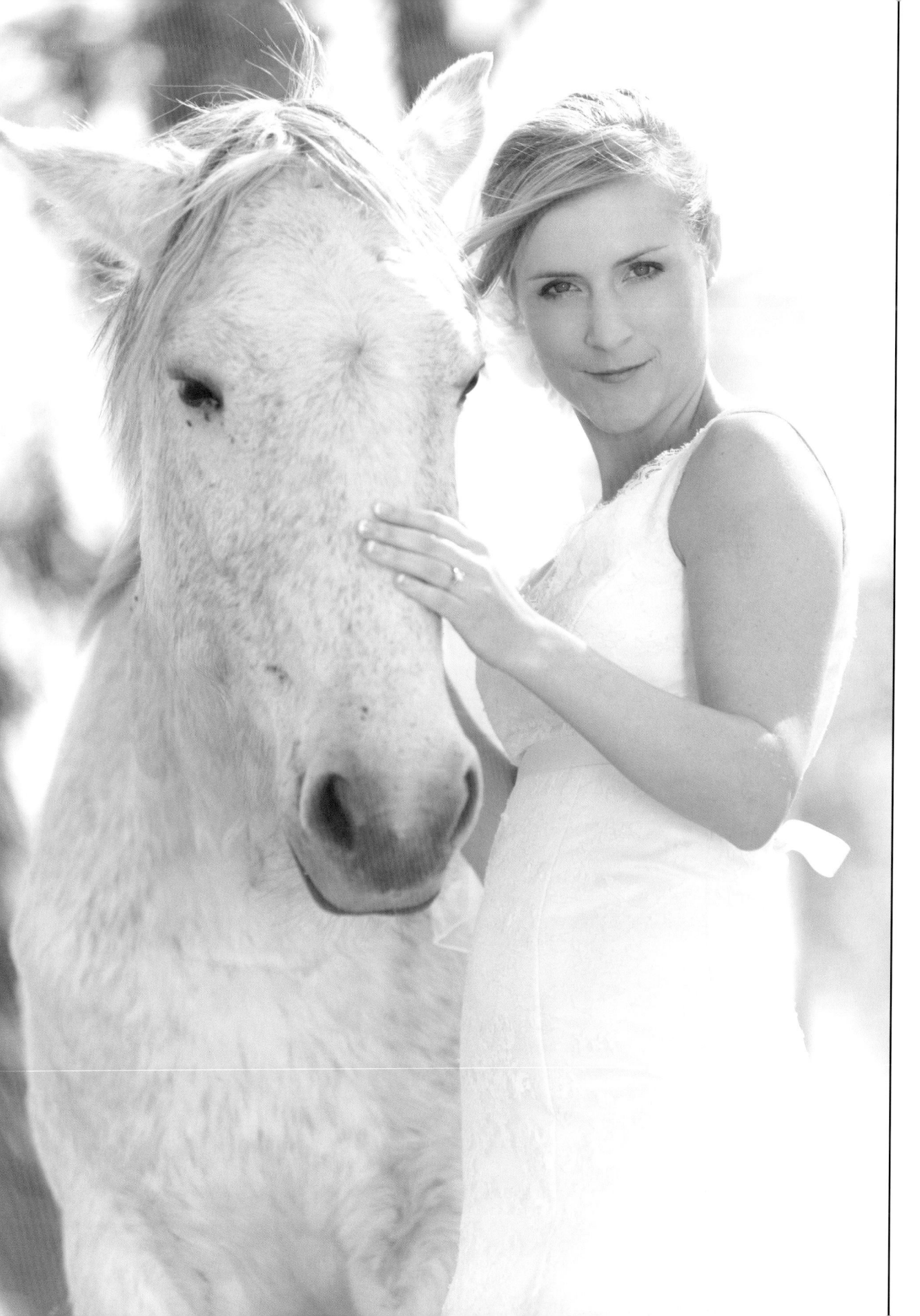

26. RAINY DAYS

A Beautiful Illusion

When it comes to weddings, you are at the mercy of nature. If it is raining, you really have to make the best of it because the couple is expecting you to produce the kind of images that they have seen in your portfolio. If the weather is dismal, the available light will seldom suffice, so it's imperative that you carry at least one off-camera flash (speedlight, studio strobe, or battery-powered strobe) so you can take fantastic photographs even when the weather falls short of fabulous.

This image was shot on a rainy, extremely overcast day, but you wouldn't know it by looking at the portrait. With my trusty Elinchrom Ranger RX, I created the illusion of sunlight pouring through a gap in the stone wall and onto the bride. I didn't use a light modifier, as

I wanted to emulate sunlight. My assistant was in front of the bride just out of the frame, and he bounced the flash back onto the bride with the gold side of the Lastolite collapsible 5-in-1 reflector, enhancing the golden "sunlight" glow.

Secret Garden

The bride positioned her head to protect her eyes from the bright light of the strobe, but the pose has an elegant, curious quality to it that also speaks of an exploration into a secret garden. The bridesmaids were standing by with a big umbrella so that the bride did not get wet!

Left: An alternate pose from the session. **Right:** The position of the flash.

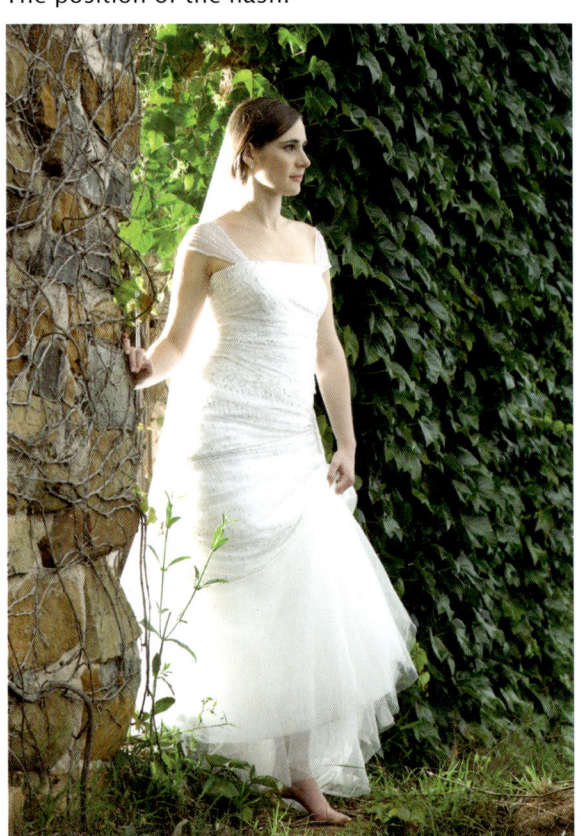

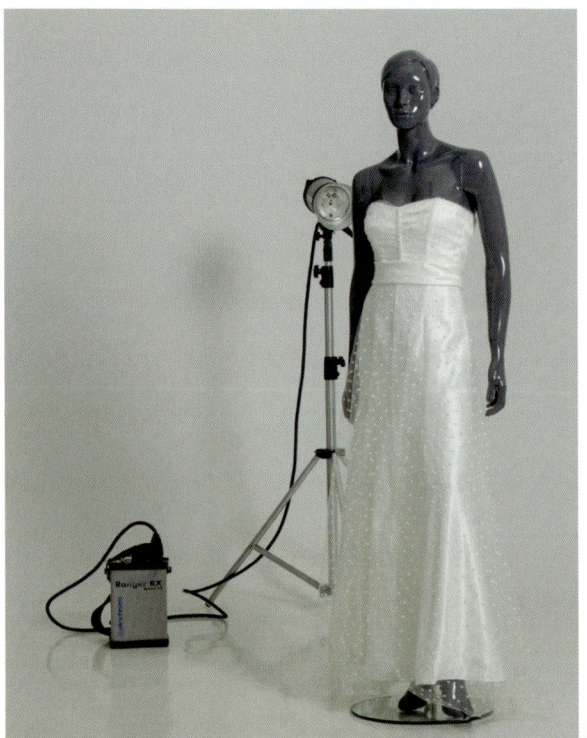

QUICK LOOK

CAMERA	Nikon D3s
LENS	Nikkor 70–200mm f/2.8G ED VR II
MODE	M
ISO	400
SHUTTER	$^1/_{125}$
APERTURE	f/5.6
LIGHTING	Elinchrom Ranger RX with a Lastolite 5-in-1 collapsible reflector

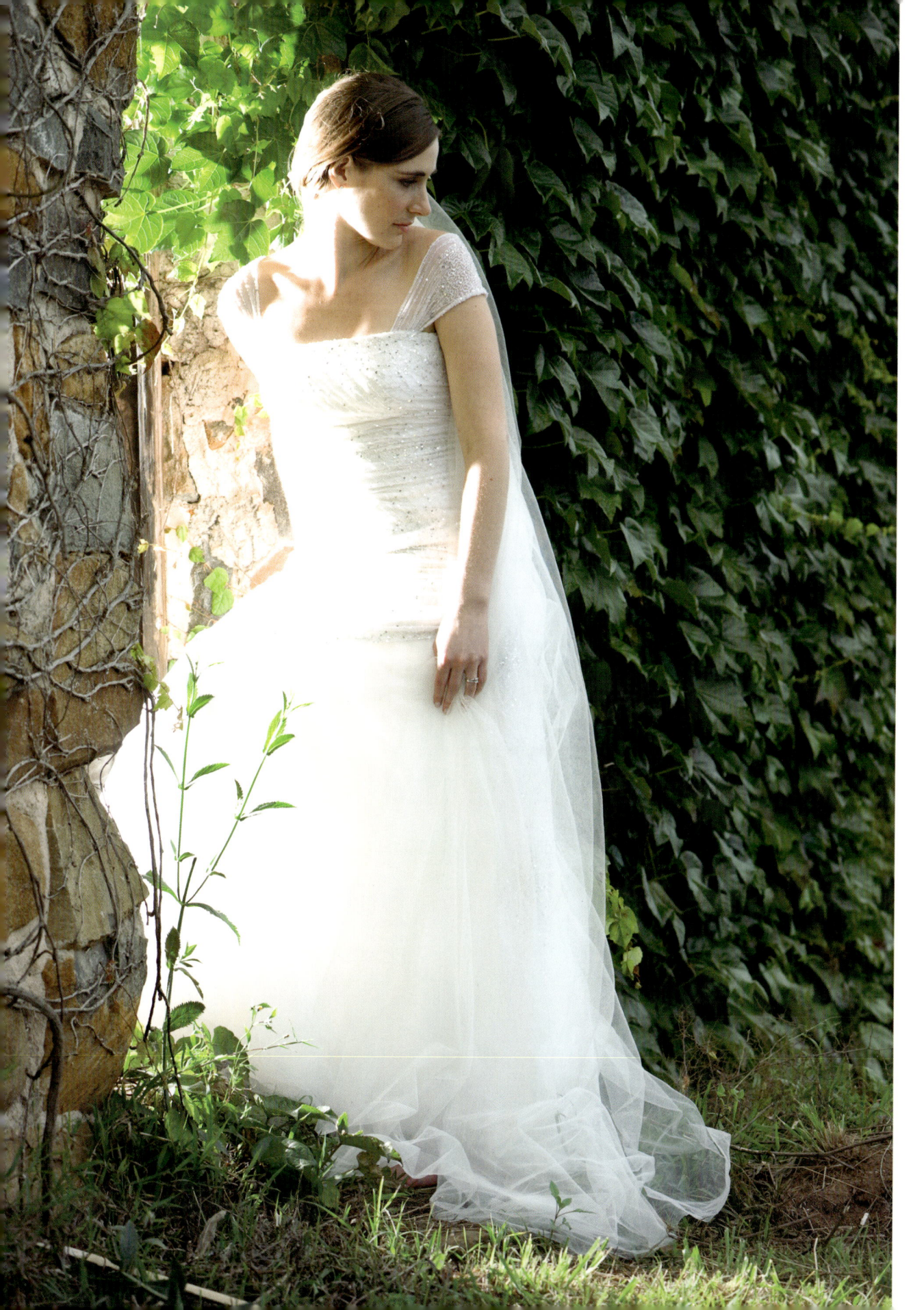

27. HEAD AND SHOULDERS

A Sultry Look

Head-and-shoulders portraiture is an essential element in the wedding album. Here, the gentle slant of the bride's shoulders and a corresponding tilt of her head creates a very feminine, flattering pose. Her eyes are peering down over her shoulder, but we can still see the dark iris beneath her eyelashes, and her mouth is gently open, with the faintest hint of a smile. Both of these facial features lend themselves to a look that is ever-so-sultry.

Window Light

I had positioned the bride very close to the window light, but unlike the side lighting I often favor when using window light, I posed her with her front facing the window at a 45 degree angle, while I shot from behind her. My assistant bounced just a touch of light back onto the

QUICK LOOK

CAMERA	Nikon D3s
LENS	Nikkor 85mm f/1.4
MODE	A
ISO	400
SHUTTER	$^1/_{500}$
APERTURE	f/1.4
LIGHTING	Lastolite 5-in-1 collapsible reflector

bride, but I tried to keep a lot of the contrast in the image, as you can see from the shadows across her bare back and three-quarters of her face.

The focus was very much on the "old world" fishnet veil, as it is the only material that we can see on an otherwise naked torso. I shot wide open so that the veil was very sharp. As you can see, the focus just falls off, even on the side of her cheek. In postproduction, I desaturated the image and added a slight sepia tone. I generally believe that images of the bridal preparation and portraits of her before she is fully dressed look best in black & white. When I am creating the storybook, the soft, serene images contrast nicely with the frenetic, fun images of the girls' preparation.

Left: An alternate presentation of the subject.
Below: The position of the reflector.

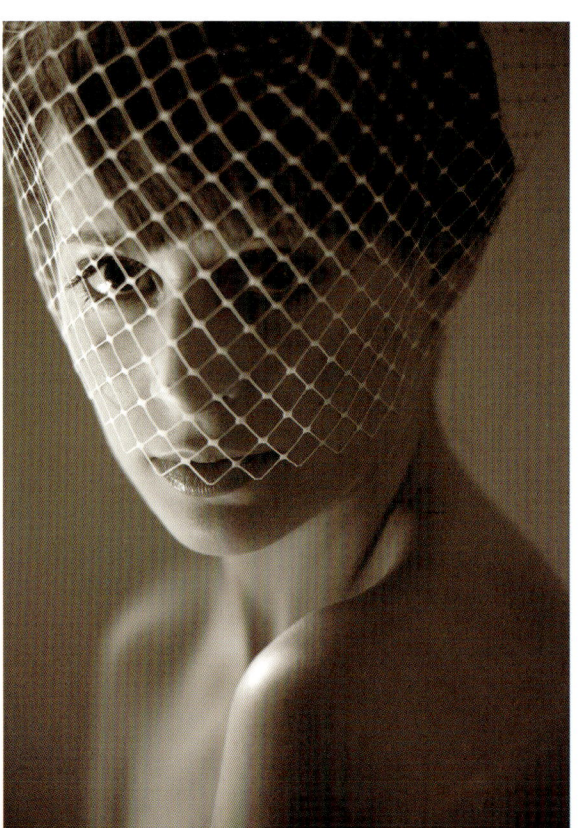

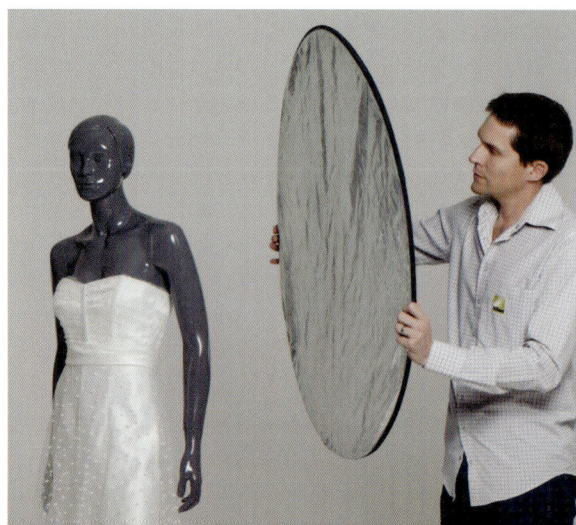

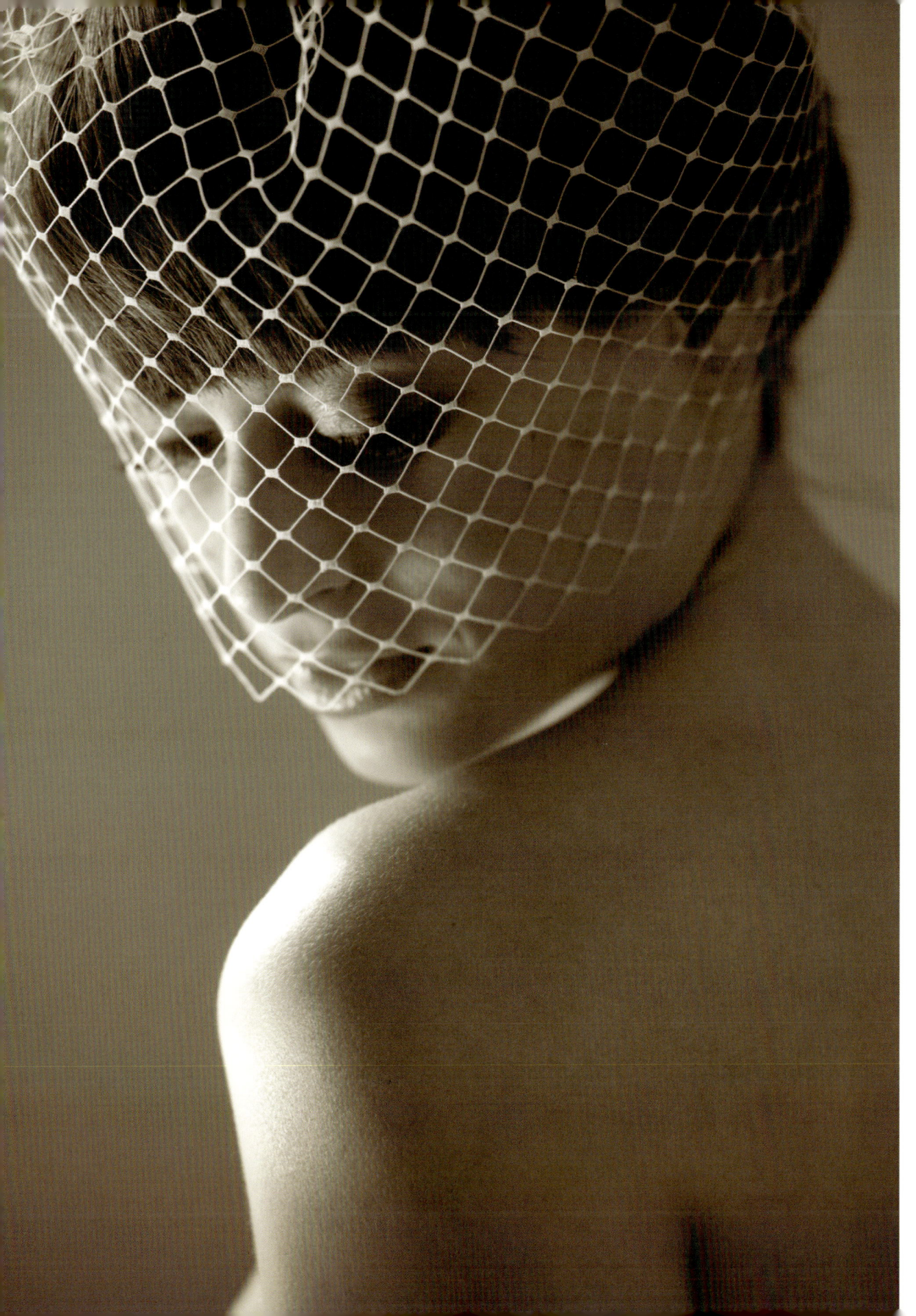

28. COMPOSITION

In wedding photography, one seldom has the opportunity to use lines as a compositional element. Lines—horizontal, vertical, or diagonal—can have a powerful impact on a photo. When I do find a pattern of lines, I'm happy to incorporate them into my wedding album.

This image was shot at the reception venue in a large, empty room. The white dado rail separating the two gorgeous pastel tones on the wall and the parallel skirting board between the wall and floor created five strong horizontal lines. The bride's dress featured horizontal paneling, which reinforced the horizontal theme. Horizontal lines convey a message of peace and stability. I believe that mood is evident in this image.

The Pose

The bride's pose is contemporary; she's leaning against the wall with one shoulder and her body is slanted away from it. One shoulder is higher than the other, creating another angle, with her head following the line. There is an implied line from the light to the camera-right side of her.

QUICK LOOK

CAMERA	Nikon D3s
LENS	Nikkor 85mm f/1.4
MODE	A
ISO	400
SHUTTER	$^1/_{250}$
APERTURE	f/1.4
LIGHTING	No artificial lighting or modification

Left and right Two alternate poses.

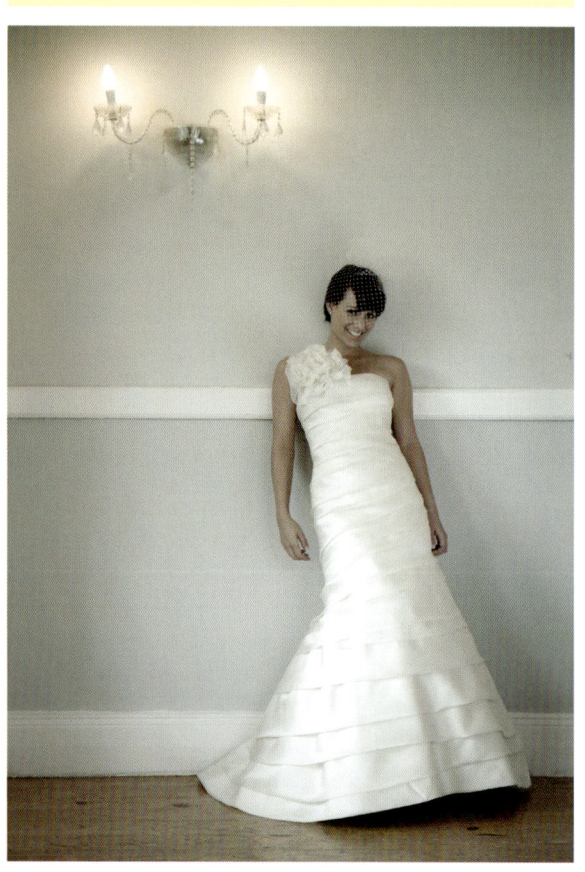
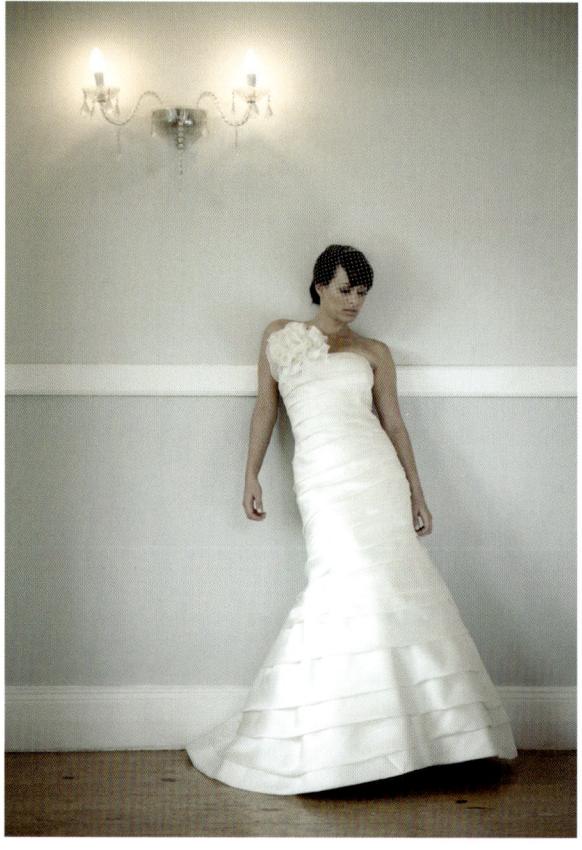

The Lighting

I dimmed that candelabra to create a slight orange cast on the bride. For the most part, she was illuminated by the window light, pouring in from three windows opposite her, as you can see from the shadows on the wall. In postproduction, I desaturated the image to enhance the pastel shades on the wall.

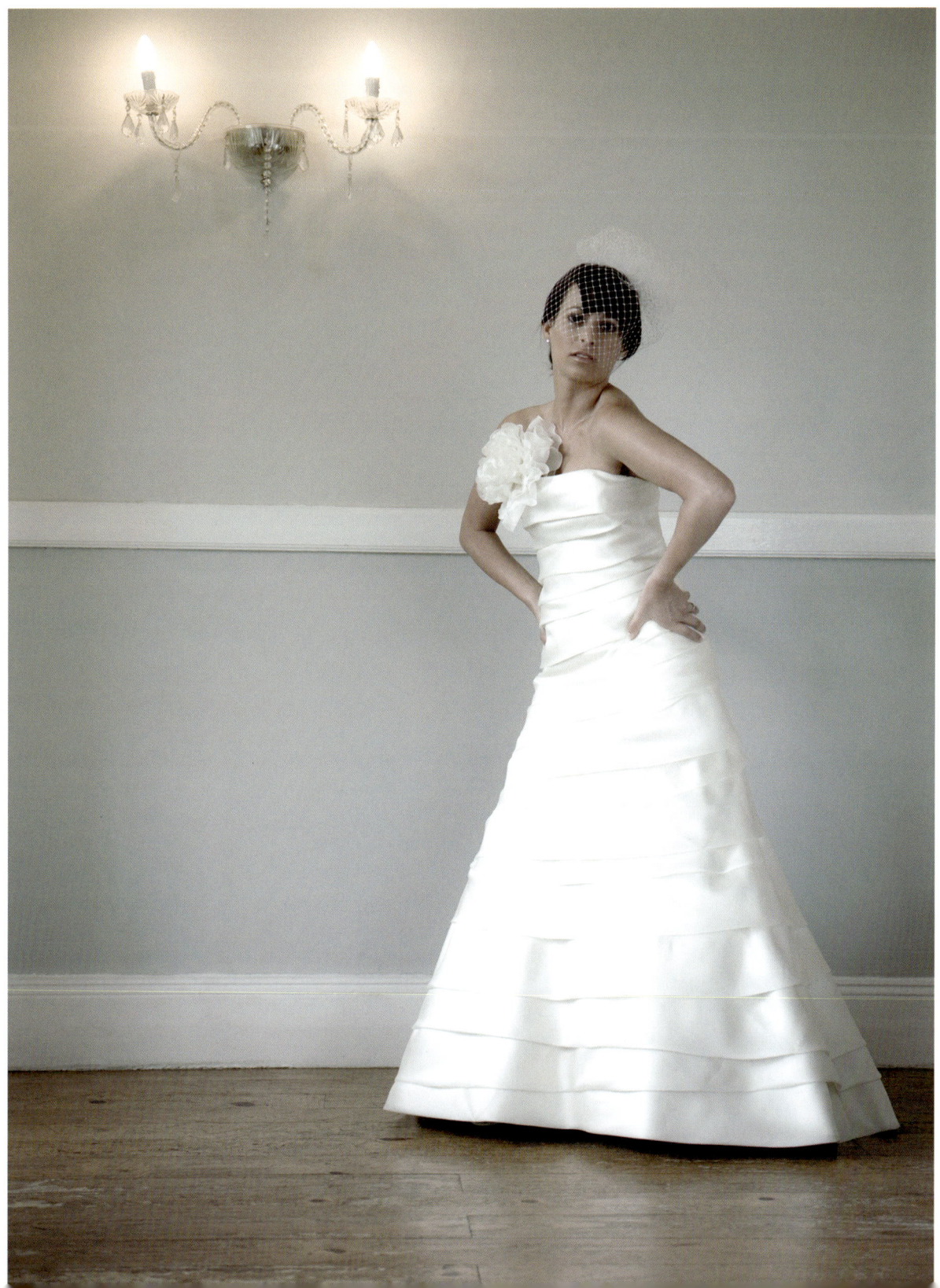

29. ANOTHER TAKE

Available Light

This image was shot in the same sequence as the previous photograph, with the purpose of positioning the photos opposite each other in the wedding album. I adjusted the lighting slightly by placing the bride in front of the candelabra, far enough from the light so that it was hidden behind her head. I turned up the dimmer and controlled the amount of orange tungsten light that this light emitted, giving the bride a lovely orange halo of light behind her veil and head.

The Rule of Thirds

This positioning highlights the bow on her '30s style veil beautifully. Note that her head is positioned according to the rule of thirds—this is one of photography's most basic rules of composition. The photographer mentally divides the image into thirds vertically and horizontally (think of a tic-tac-toe board), then composes the image so that the point of interest sits on two of the dissecting lines. This is a foolproof way to achieve a composition that is balanced and interesting. Of course, this rule can be broken, and it is possible to achieve wonderful images that defy the principle, but for the most part, I tend to adhere to the code, because it gives me an innate sense of harmony—it just feels right!

QUICK LOOK	
CAMERA	Nikon D3s
LENS	Nikkor 85mm f/1.4
MODE	A
ISO	400
SHUTTER	$^1/_{250}$
APERTURE	f/1.4
LIGHTING	Unmodified ambient light only

Left: An alternate pose. **Right:** The rule of thirds grid.

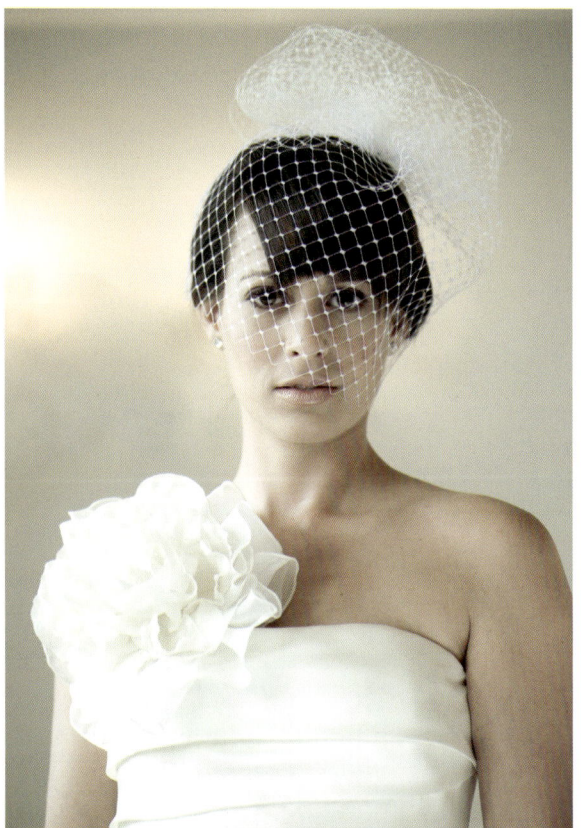
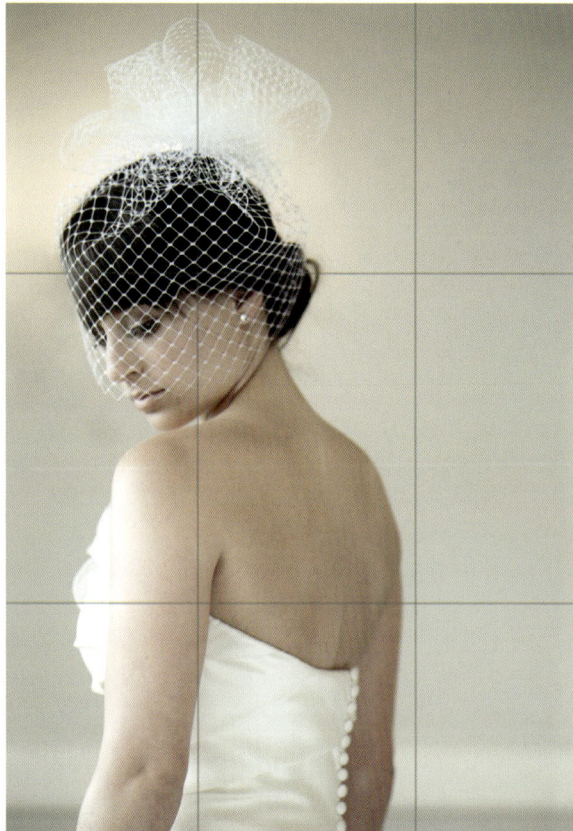

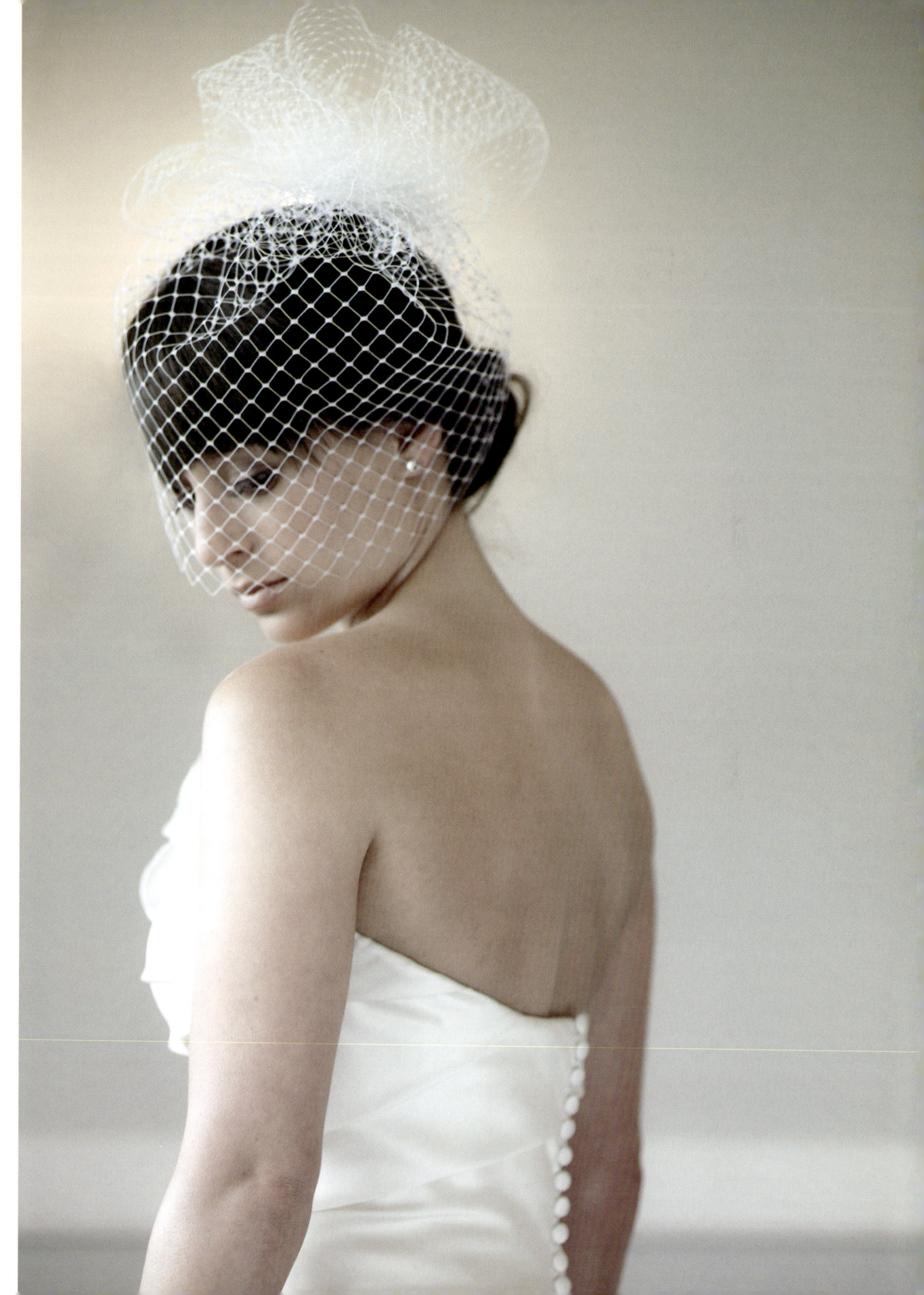

30. BEHIND THE VEIL

Pure Romance

The use of the veil in the bridal portraits always has such a wonderfully romantic, pure, and feminine effect. Nothing can be more symbolic of a bride in all her innocence before she walks down to the altar than the veil.

An Unlikely Shooting Space

I shot this in the bathroom where the bride was getting ready; the lighting happened to be really good. I'm never shy to use what some deem "private territory" if it works for me and, ultimately, the client. In this bathroom, the tiles were pale and acted like a large reflector. There was beautiful window lighting pouring in from the bride's right-hand side, as you can see from the catchlights. Draping the veil over her face

Left and right: Additional shots from the session.

and shoulders gave a soft, feminine feel to the pose. Not yet fully clothed, her bare torso added to the sense of purity. I posed her to look up at me, which tends to give a strong jawline and highlights the separation between her chin and her chest—the chest being that much darker. Her arms were strategically placed to cover her breasts, and I asked her to lift her left hand to rest gently on her shoulder, just to add a bit more depth and interest to the composition. The hint of a smile is very alluring, as is the intensity of her stare.

QUICK LOOK

CAMERA	Nikon D3s
LENS	Nikkor 70–200mm f/2.8G ED VR II
MODE	A
ISO	400
SHUTTER	$1/200$
APERTURE	f/2.8
LIGHTING	Available light only

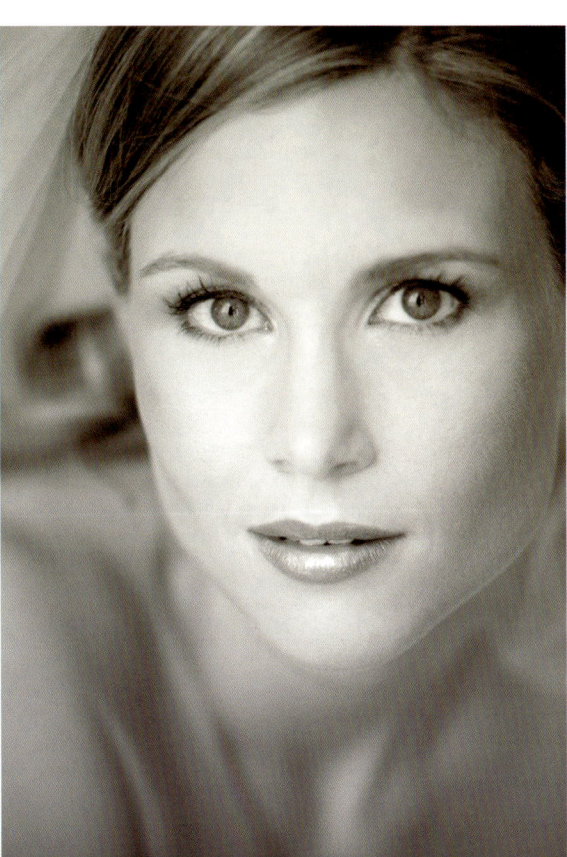

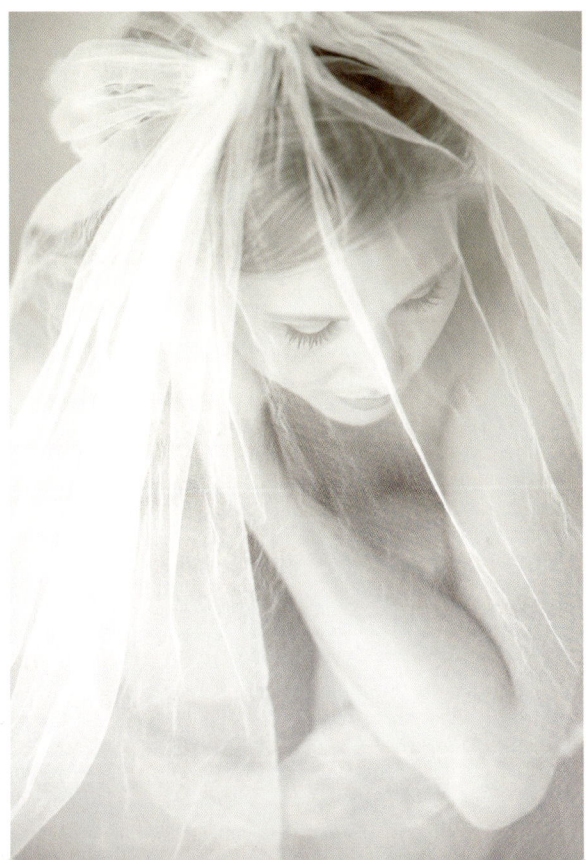

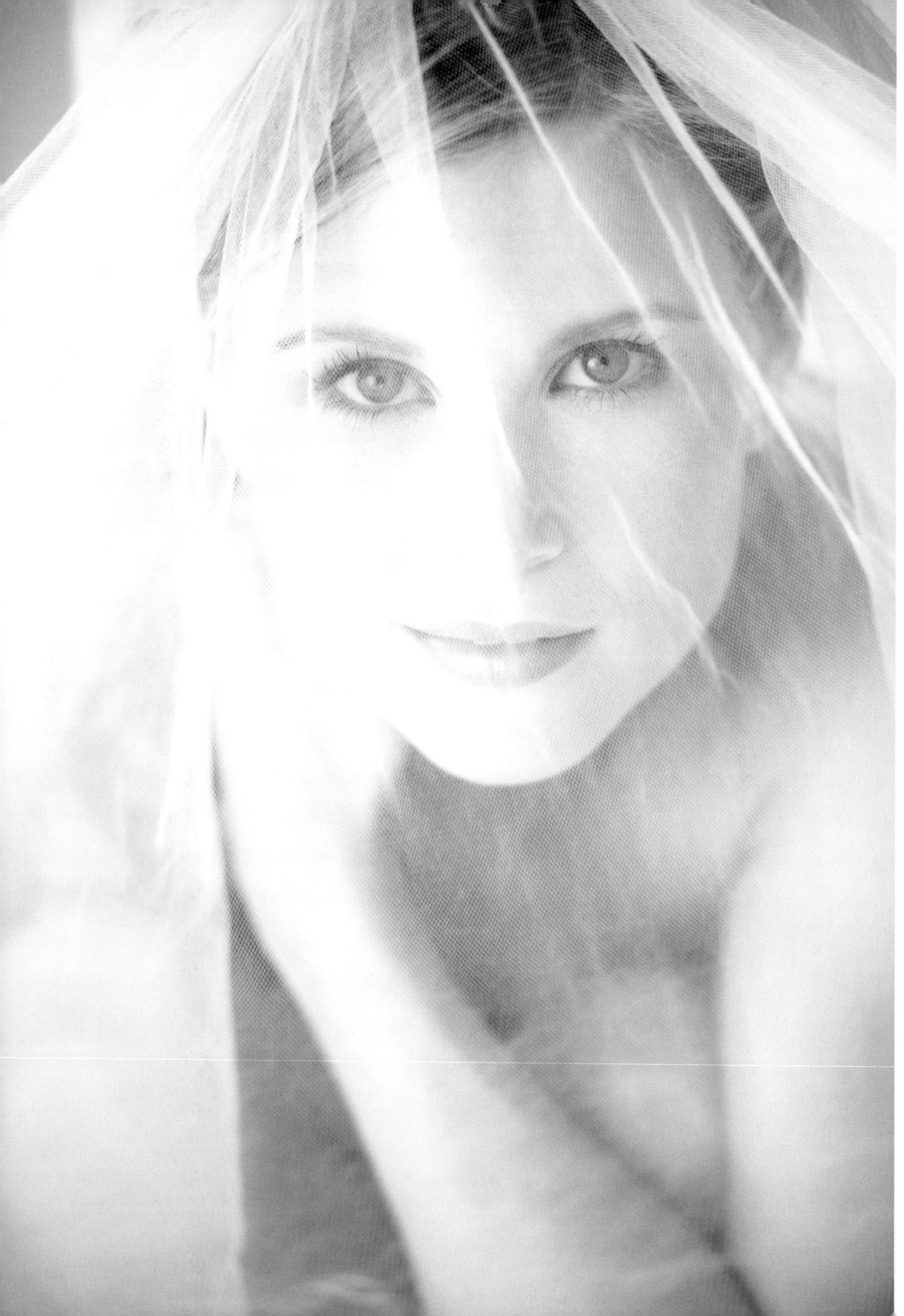

31. AN ANGELIC EFFECT

Net Curtains

Here, I once again used net curtaining to create a beautiful softbox lighting effect and a feeling that the light is enveloping the bride. There is an angelic quality to the image, and this is due to the predominance of the white, glowing light that creates a halo not only around her head, but also around her whole body.

Tone on Tone

I desaturated the image and added a magenta cast to it in postproduction. The magenta is within the color spectrum of white, and as you can see, there are several near-white shades that fade in and out, almost like a vignette: from light gray to a very soft pink and then a very bright white. This has created a prominent vertical pattern to the photograph, with the vignetted stripes of the curtaining and the very vertical pose of the bride's body juxtaposed only by the triangles of her elbows. Vertical patterns in photography have a very commanding and strong effect, so while the image is very soft and angelic with floral colors, there is an innate sense of power to the photograph as well. The bride's pose reiterates this; she looks beautiful and angelic, but she is strong and confident too. The hands on her hips and the strong triangles her arms have created emphasise this confidence.

QUICK LOOK
CAMERA	Nikon D3
LENS	Nikkor 24–70mm f/2.8G ED
MODE	A
ISO	400
SHUTTER	$^1/_{250}$
APERTURE	f/4 (+3EV)
LIGHTING	Available light only

Left: An alternate pose. **Right:** The setting.

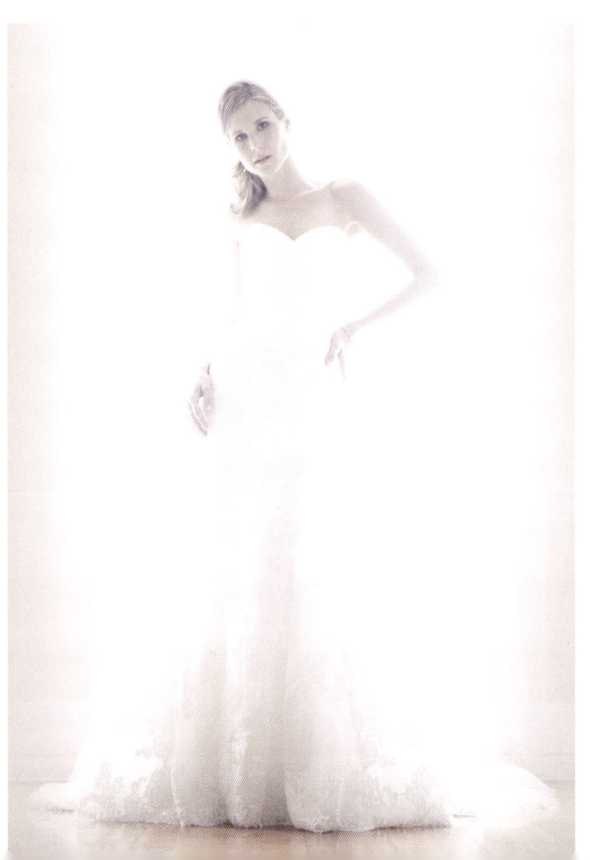

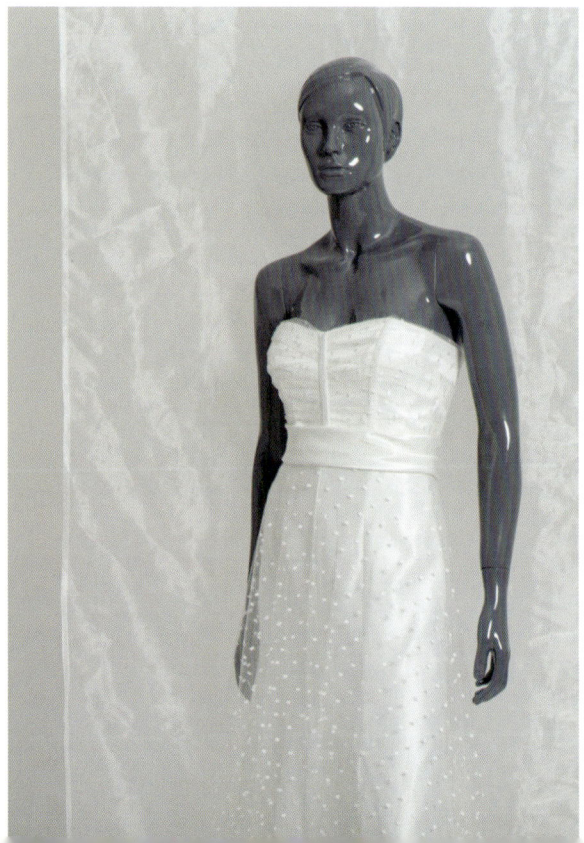

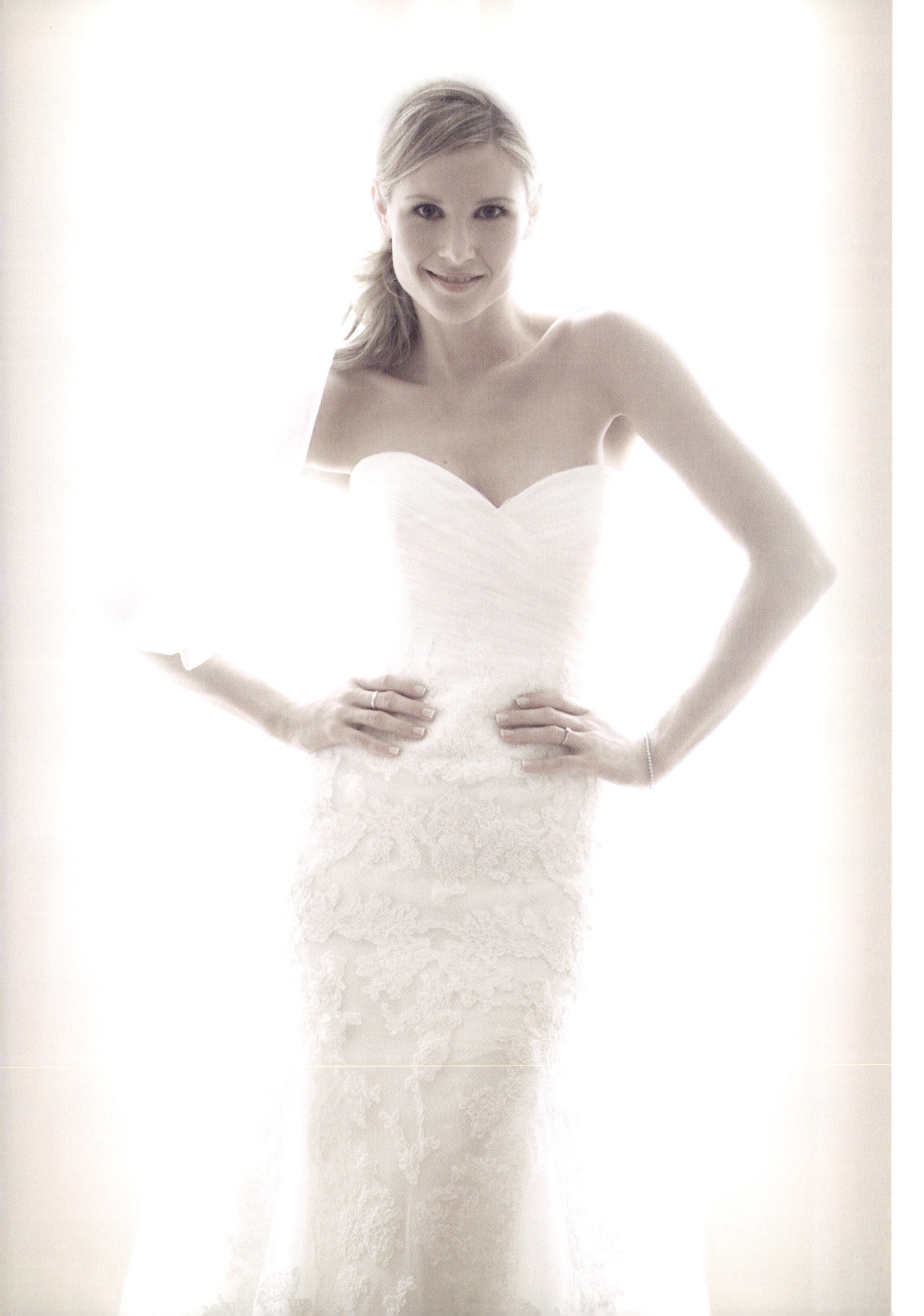

32. FEMININITY AND GRACE

Traditional Appeal

A three-quarter pose against a very clean backdrop, with the bouquet cradled in her arms—this is the ultimate in classical bridal poses and one that, in my opinion, should never be missed. As I've mentioned, there are a number of "must have" shots, or perhaps one could even call them the "money shots" because these are the images that most of the close family members will want to have reprinted so that they can frame them and put them in a prominent place in the home for all to see. Classical images have a cross-generational appeal, and it would be foolish to ignore them merely because they seem "old fashioned." In fact, it could be noted that there is a resurgence of traditional portraiture and traditional wedding photography, with good trustworthy posing and masterful lighting techniques.

The Lighting

Here, the bride was posed near a window with her body positioned to face the light. I asked her to then turn her head toward the camera, also making sure that her chin is angled down. This technique means that one is shooting from the darker, narrow side of the face, which is a lot more flattering, and although this particular bride was not at all overweight, it does have the effect of thinning your subject down a bit.

My assistant held a collapsible 5-in-1 reflector, bouncing the window light onto her to fill the darker areas on her right-hand side. The arms support the bouquet gently right close to her body, and she has a faint smile on her lips. The overall look and feel is one of femininity and grace.

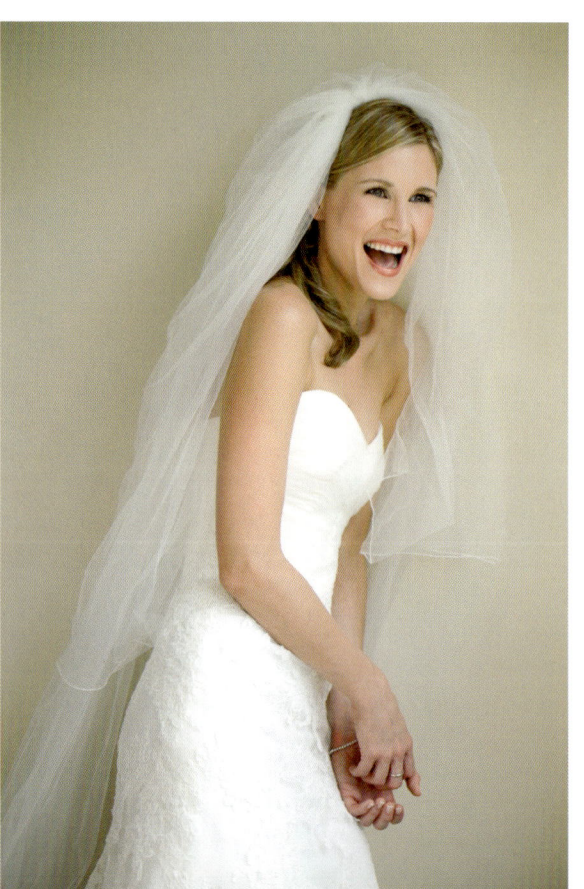

QUICK LOOK

CAMERA	Nikon D3s
LENS	Nikkor 85mm f/1.4
MODE	A
ISO	400
SHUTTER	$^1/_{250}$
APERTURE	f/5.6
LIGHTING	Lastolite 5-in-1 collapsible reflector

Left: An alternate portrait from the session.
Below: The position of the reflector.

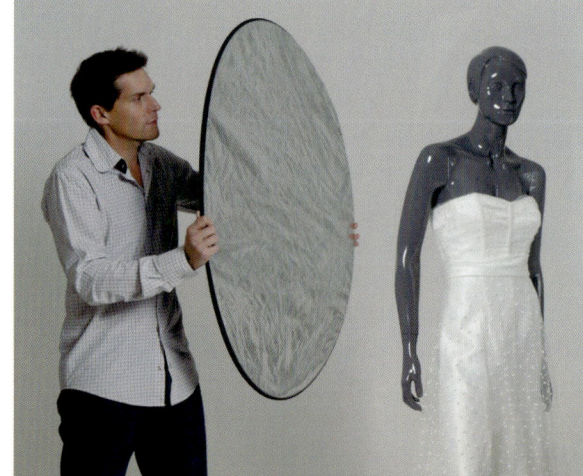

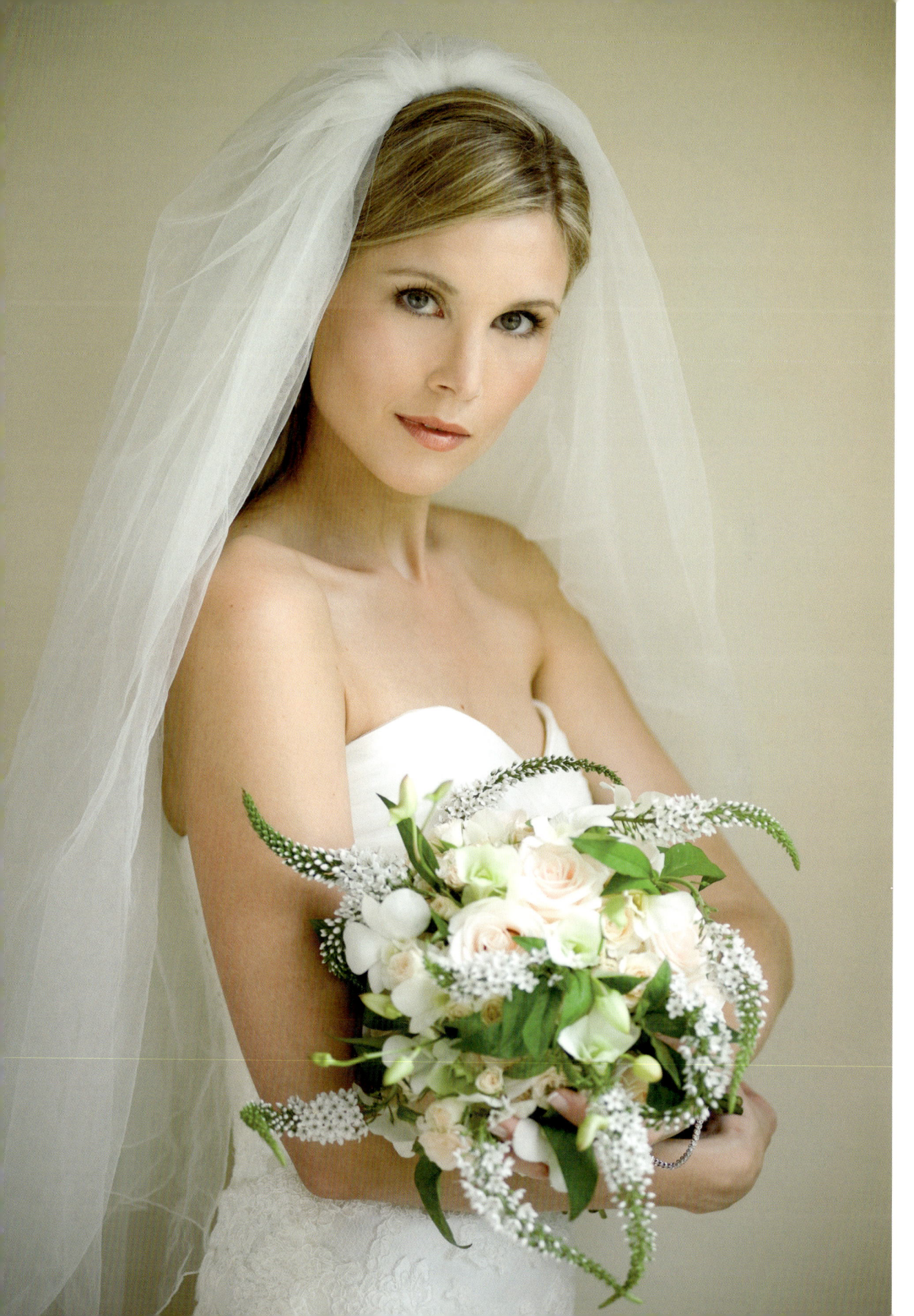

33. BACKLIGHTING

The Lighting

Study any romantic movie, and you'll probably notice that the starry-eyed and adoring sequences are not only set to moving melodies, but they are also generally beautifully backlit. Backlighting is a technique that I really favor for my bridal portraits, and this is because backlighting exudes the feeling of romance and love. Here, I was exposing for the bride's skin tone, to keep it perfectly true to life, so the very delicate detail in the stained glass windows is almost lost; however, I don't think that it is really important

because I feel that the focus shifts back to the bride, her skin, and the dress. My assistant was standing with a 5-in-1 reflector to the bride's left in a doorway that was near her, just out of the frame, bouncing some of the window light back onto her front. The backlighting has starkly brightened the bride's veil and the train of her dress, the intensity of the light mirroring that of the bright light illuminating the windows.

The Pose and Composition

The curvaceous silhouette of the bride can be seen beneath her garment, and along with the slight arch in her back and the position of her arms, the pose is very sensual and alluring. The composition is very true to the rule of thirds, and I love the contrast of the very rectangular and square shapes of the windows and wall to the shapely bride. I desaturated this image in post-production giving it even more of a romantic quality. Because of the very intense light coming through the window, I shot this on f/4 on aperture priority overexposing by three stops, at $^1/_{125}$ and 400 ISO.

Left: An alternate pose. **Right:** The reflector position.

QUICK LOOK
CAMERA Nikon D3
LENS Nikkor 70–200mm f/2.8G ED VR II
MODE A
ISO 400
SHUTTER $^1/_{125}$ (+3EV)
APERTURE f/4
LIGHTING Lastolite 5-in-1 collapsible reflector

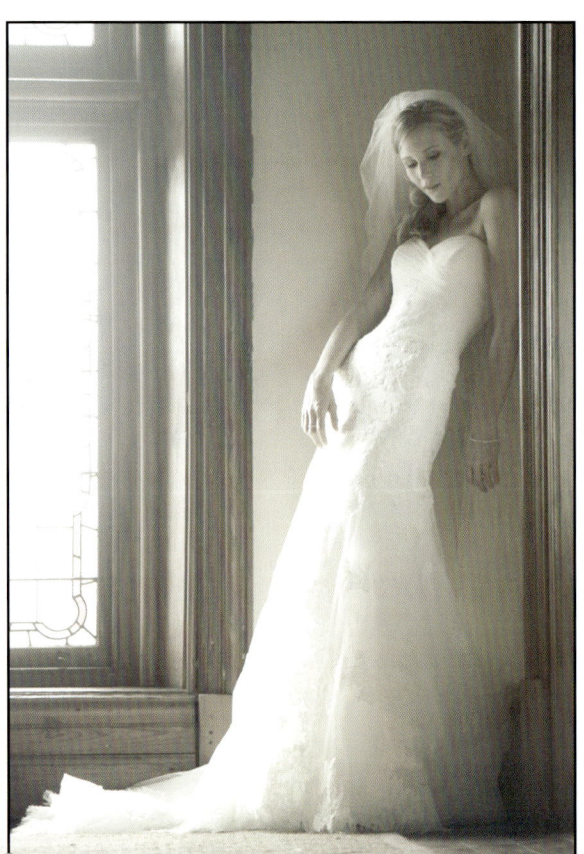

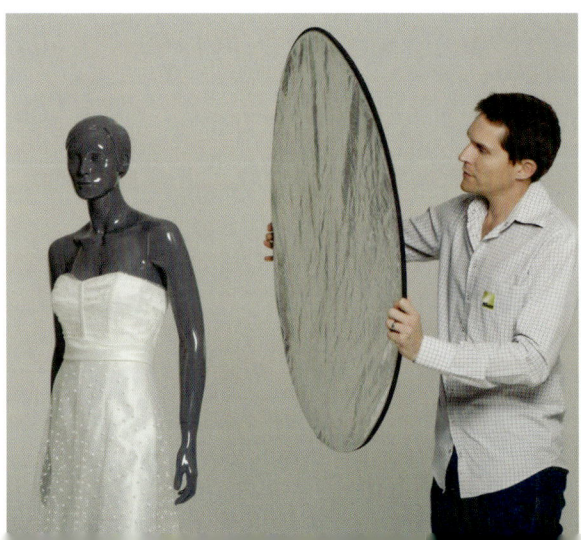

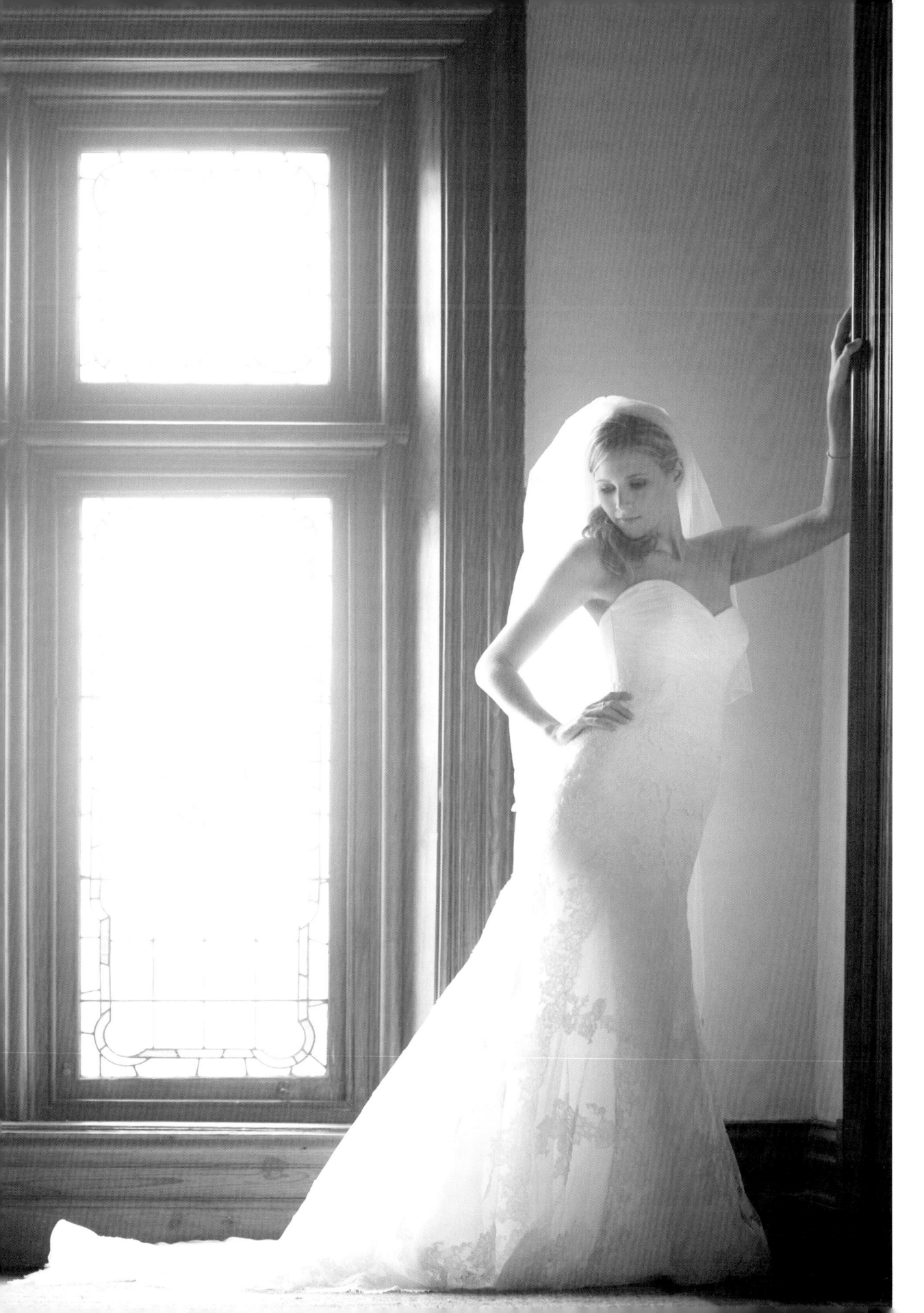

34. THE MODERN BRIDE

An Assistant

Whenever possible, I'm in favor of using available light. A collapsible reflector will enhance and modify this natural light if held correctly—this is where an assistant is, in my opinion, a non-optional part of your camera kit! Seriously though, an assistant who learns quickly how to modify the light for you with a reflector to reduce contrast and produce soft, flattering light is worth his weight in gold.

Beautiful Ambient Light

Having scouted the bride's home, I found an area near the kitchen door where there was an abundance of beautiful ambient light. I had to remove a painting from the wall so that the bride was positioned with a perfectly clean background, the available light coming in from the bride's left-hand side. My assistant bounced the light back onto the bride with my 5-in-1 collapsible reflector using the very reflective silver side.

The Pose

This three-quarter body pose differs somewhat from the typical classic portrait shot in that I had this bride face me square on. Being a model in her everyday life, she was obviously confident in front of the camera. We wrapped the veil around her body like a shawl, creating lovely volume to the arms.

The pose is linear in feel, with her straight shoulders, and one arm folded across her waist, while the other is lifted at a right angle to her side, holding the veil. This linear quality, along with her direct stare into the camera, gives us an image that exudes confidence and purpose. We understand that she is a modern, beautiful woman who knows what she wants and how to get it.

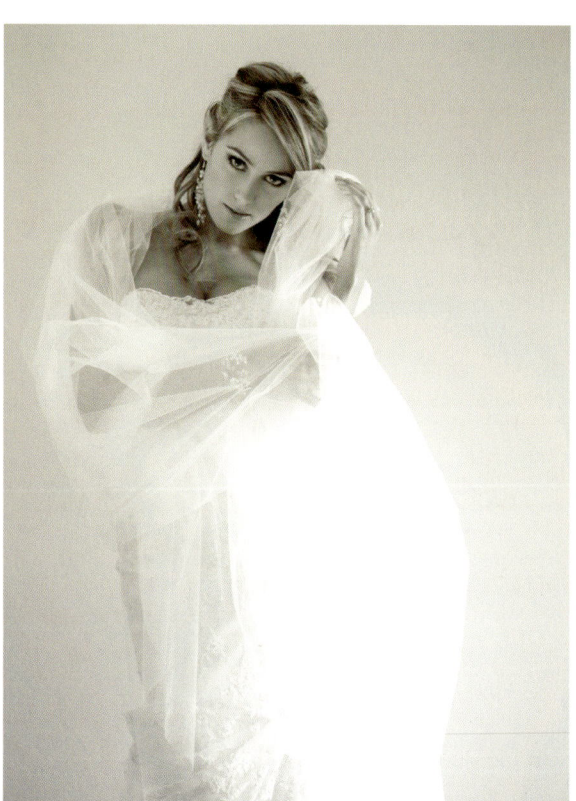

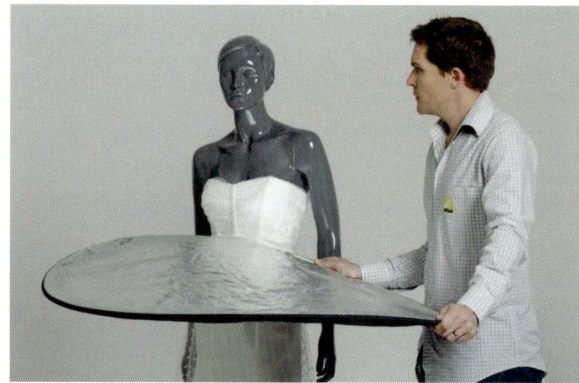

Left: An alternate pose from the session. **Above:** The position of the reflector.

> ### QUICK LOOK
> **CAMERA** Nikon D3s
> **LENS** Nikkor 70–200mm f/2.8G ED VR II
> **MODE** A
> **ISO** 400
> **SHUTTER** $^1/_{400}$
> **APERTURE** f/2.8
> **LIGHTING** Lastolite 5-in-1 collapsible reflector

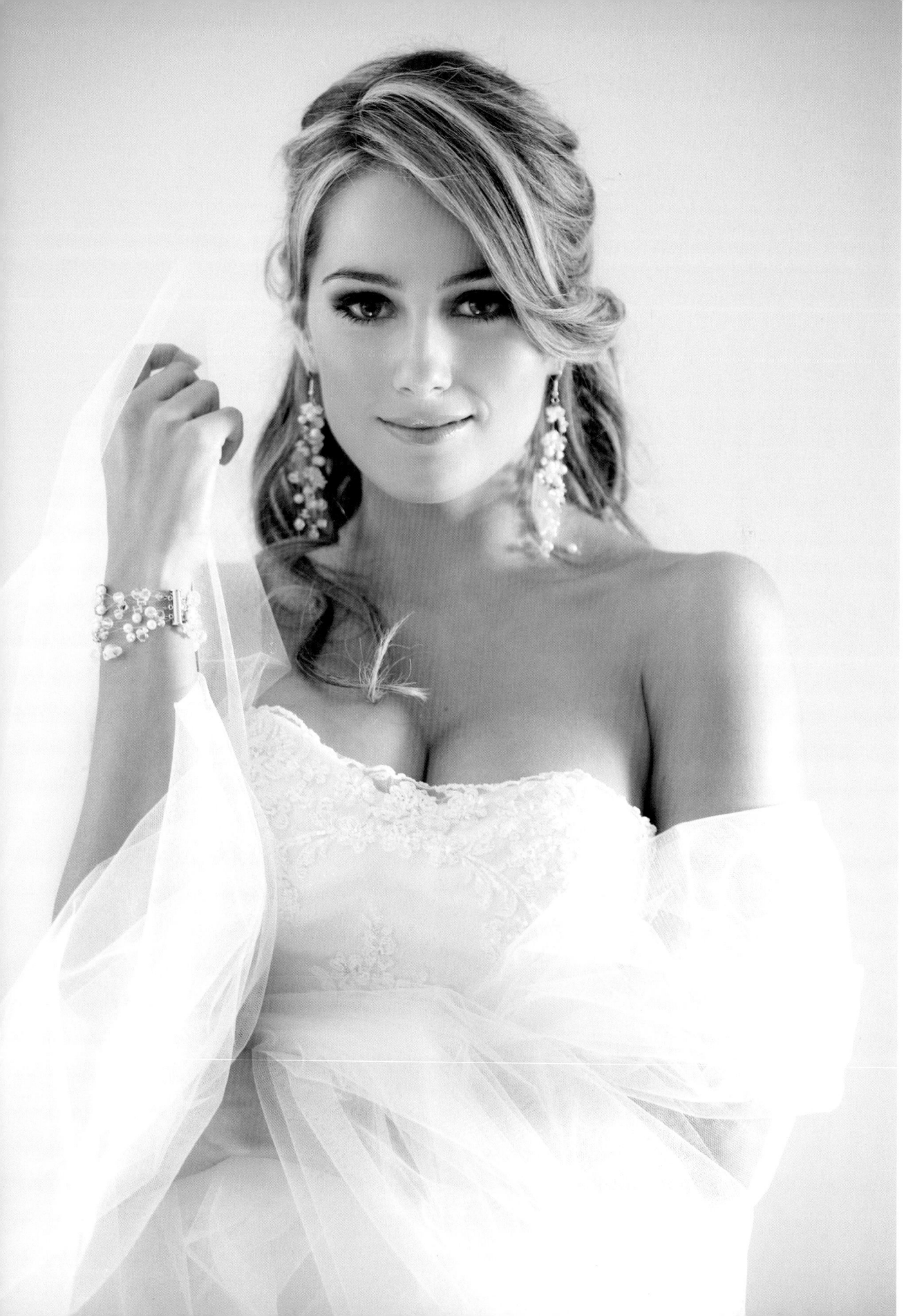

35. BOUGAINVILLEA BRIDE

What can be more gorgeous than a blossoming tree or bush, abundant in blooms and bursting with color? As luck would have it, there were a number of blossoming bougainvillea bushes near the bride's home, and she was enthusiastic about having these vibrant flowers as a backdrop for a few of her bridal portraits.

Lighting

I used the Ranger RX portable strobe and shot this image using the 5-in-1 scrim. By removing the reflective material, one is left with the scrim fabric, which diffuses light into a circular type motion. This is similar to a round softbox, emitting a gentle light that wraps around the bride to the right.

Left: The image before postproduction. **Right:** The lighting setup.

Postproduction

Although the bush appears to be in full bloom, I did have to resort to postproduction manipulation to fill in the gaps in the bougainvillea bush. In order to do this, I made sure that I had shot some of the blossoms on their own. We then used these in Photoshop and created a bush that fully surrounded the bride, producing a patterned backdrop that is incredibly striking.

<table>
<tr><td colspan="2">QUICK LOOK</td></tr>
<tr><td>CAMERA</td><td>Nikon D3s</td></tr>
<tr><td>LENS</td><td>Nikkor 70–200mm f/2.8G ED VR II</td></tr>
<tr><td>MODE</td><td>M</td></tr>
<tr><td>ISO</td><td>100</td></tr>
<tr><td>SHUTTER</td><td>$^1/_{200}$</td></tr>
<tr><td>APERTURE</td><td>f/5.6</td></tr>
<tr><td>LIGHTING</td><td>Elinchrom Ranger RX and scrim from Lastolite 5-in-1 collapsible reflector</td></tr>
</table>

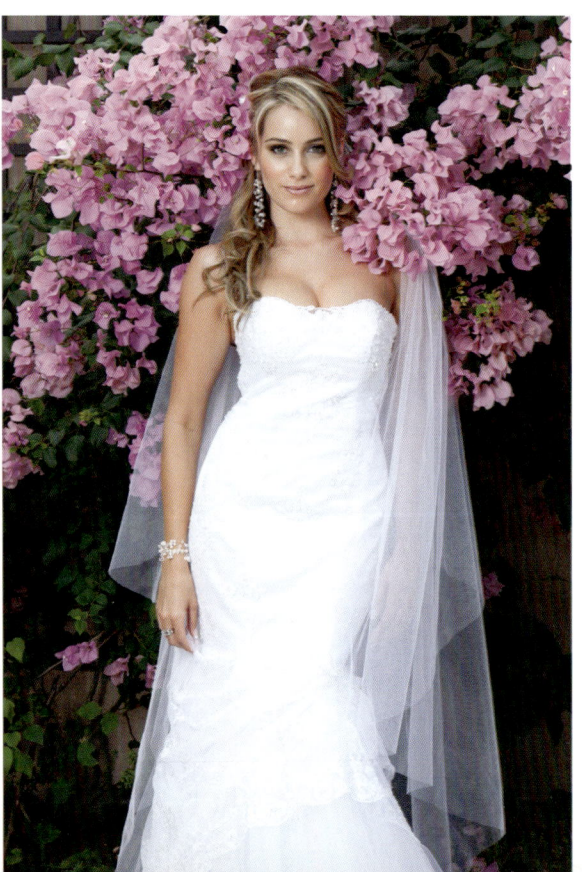

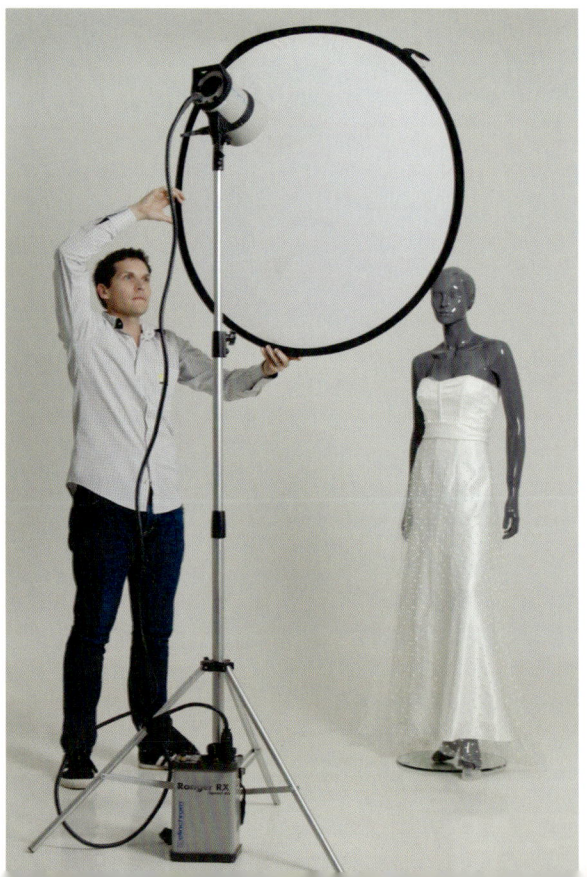

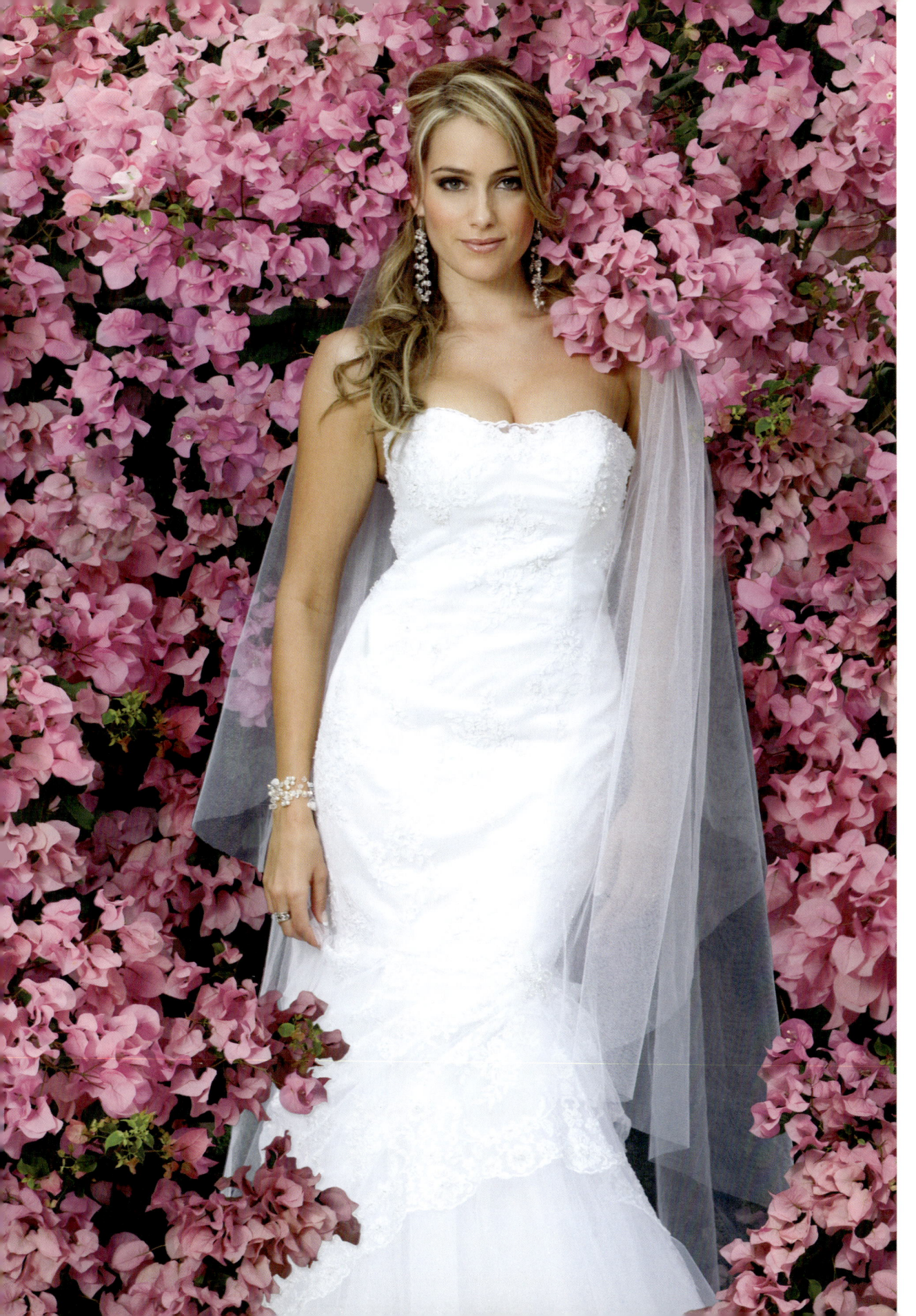

36. THE LUSH TROPICS

Lush, tropical vegetation is not hard to find in the area that I live, which is Durban, South Africa. Enormous leaves called "elephant ears," palms, ferns, and vines grow prolifically in this very humid climate—and the climate and vegetation, I believe, is very similar to that of Hawaii. So, creating a scene that is reminiscent of *A Midsummer Night's Dream* or *Blue Lagoon* is relatively easy!

Location

This location was literally found on the side of the road. I was standing on the verge of the road, and I seated the bride on a picnic blanket in a

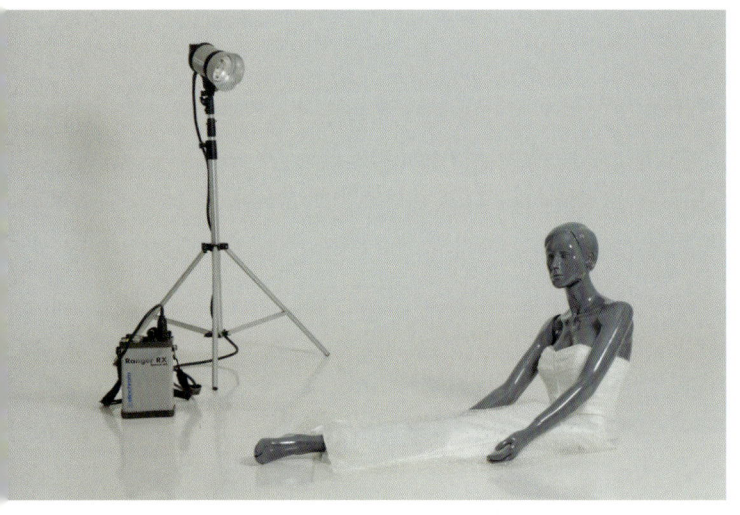

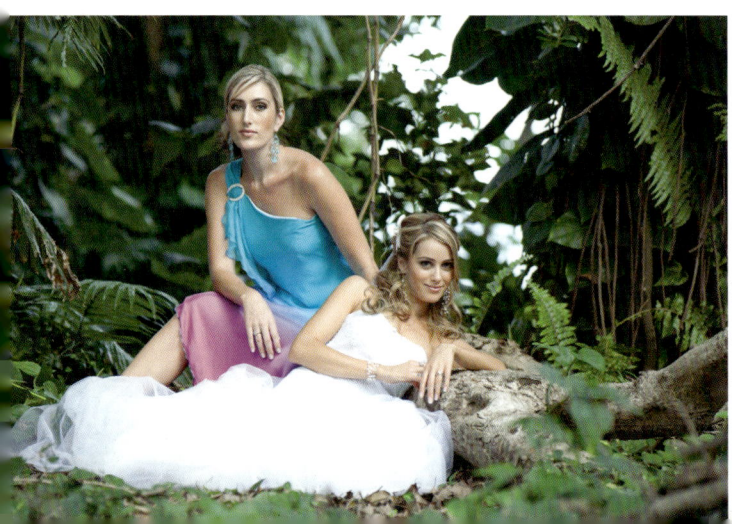

spot next to a fallen tree. I posed her casually leaning into the log, and my assistant made sure that her dress was beautifully puffed up and covered the blanket. I had her stretch her left arm along the log, which made her recline even more. Her right hand was gently posed onto her right shoulder in a very elegant fashion. The bride's turned head and expression create a lovely wistful, peaceful ambience to the image.

The Lighting

I placed my external strobe, the Ranger RX, behind the bride and to the right, creating the effect of sunlight pouring through the tropical foliage. There was no light modifier on the Ranger, it was simply a bare bulb, which created a very strong light, the intensity of which you can see at the bottom-left edge of the frame.

My assistant held the 5-in-1 reflector just out of the frame to the bride's left side, bouncing some of the external strobe light back onto the subject. The lighting gave the image a great deal of depth and helped create atmosphere, which (as you can see from the supporting image, shot without the external strobe) was lacking.

QUICK LOOK

CAMERA	Nikon D3s
LENS	Nikkor 70–200mm f/2.8G ED VR II
MODE	S
ISO	500
SHUTTER	$^1/_{100}$
APERTURE	f/5.6
LIGHTING	Elinchrom Ranger RX and Lastolite 5-in-1 collapsible reflector

Top: The lighting setup for the final image. **Bottom:** An image of the bride and bridesmaid, shot without flash.

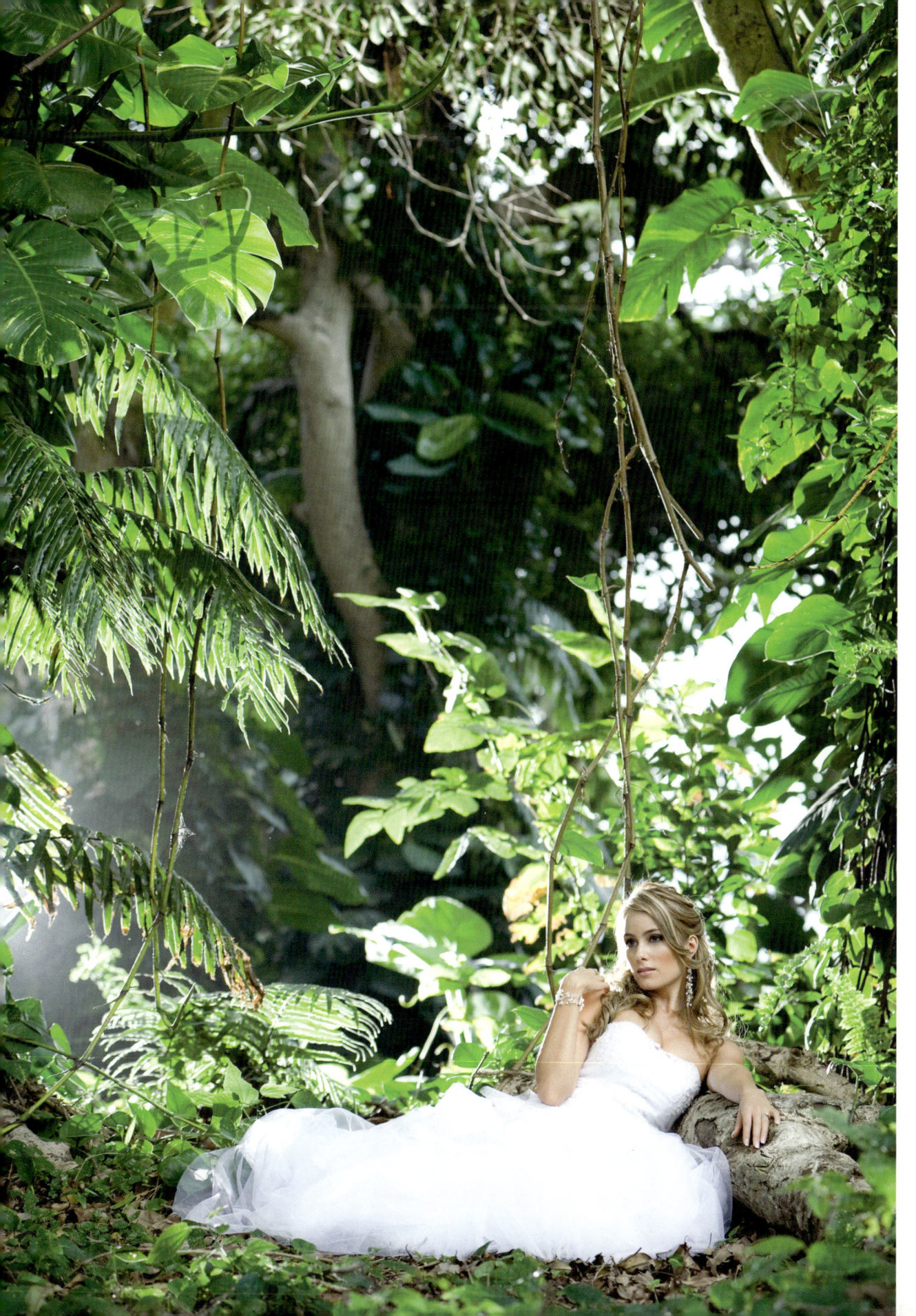

37. HIGHLIGHT AND SHADOW

Conceptualizing the Shot

This image was created in the same overgrown area shown in the last image. It was found just off the side of the road in the quiet suburb where the bride was getting ready. Realizing the potential of the gorgeous vegetation and wanting to create almost a fairy-tale look that represented something like a secret tunnel to a mysterious faraway land, I knew that I would be using quite a lot of special effects in postproduction.

With this in mind, I positioned the bride in a slight clearing and placed my Elinchrom Ranger RX behind a tree to the bride's right. Using only a bare bulb for the maximum luminosity, the light streams onto her as if it were strong sunlight filtering through the forest, beautifully backlighting her veil and hair and giving the bride a very ethereal, other-worldly quality. My assistant held the 5-in-1 collapsible reflector to her left just off-camera and bounced some of this artificial light back onto the bride's face using the highly reflective silver side. The light that falls back onto her is lovely and soft, providing the perfect balance of highlights and shadows in her dress, her cheekbones, and her body.

Postproduction

Enhancing the whole atmosphere in postproduction, I converted the image in Nik Software's Silver Efex Pro using a dark vignette in a circular pattern to draw the focus onto the bride and to create the "magical tunnel."

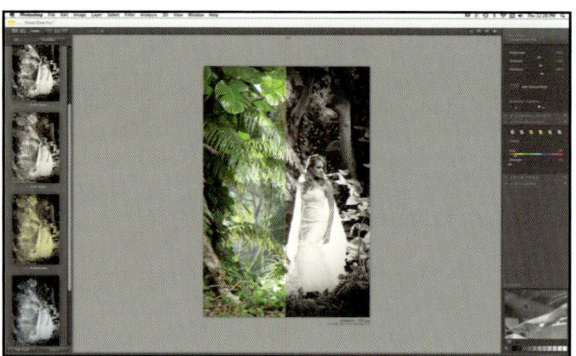

Left: The image in Nik Silver Efex Pro. **Right:** The strobe position.

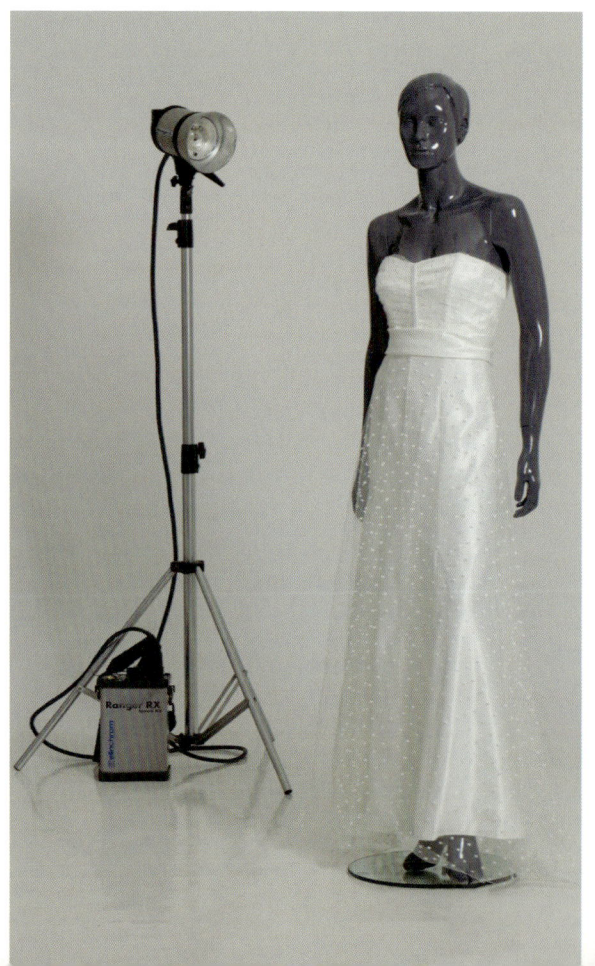

QUICK LOOK

CAMERA	Nikon D3s
LENS	Nikkor 70–200mm f/2.8G ED VR II
MODE	S
ISO	500
SHUTTER	$^1/_{100}$
APERTURE	f/5.6
LIGHTING	Elinchrom Ranger RX and Lastolite 5-in-1 collapsible reflector

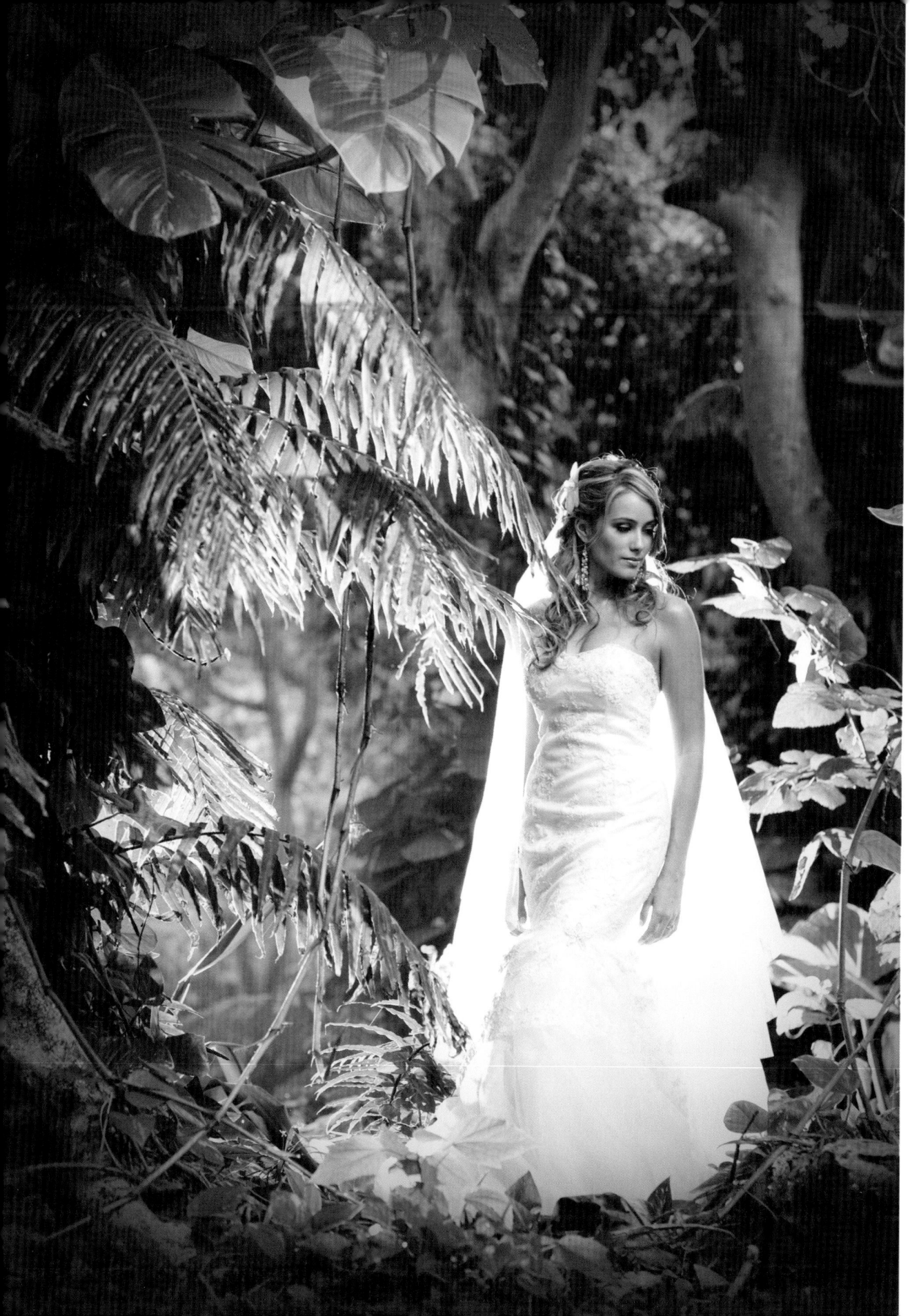

38. UNUSUAL LOCATIONS

Unique and Beautiful

Unusual locations can yield beautiful images. I get excited when I find an old building with peeling paint and broken walls, big empty warehouses with rusty windows and high ceilings, and dishevelled barns where wooden slats allow shafts of light to run through. The contrast to the impeccable bride and groom is always delightful.

This full-length image was photographed in an unused swimming pool with a marblelite surface that had cracked into some amazing patterns. The predominately light surface (in open shade) bounced the late-afternoon light in every direction, creating incredibly soft light on the bride. There was no need to add any lighting or even a reflector to manipulate the available light. The elements and the location just came together. Had it been much earlier, the sunlight would have been too bright to handle.

Pose and Perspective

The bride's pose is classic; she's at a slight angle to the camera, and her head is tilted toward her higher shoulder. This is a typically feminine pose with characteristics of grace, vulnerability, and mystery. The angle is not entirely typical, though; I shot from a slightly higher vantage point, standing on the edge of the pool, looking down at her. As a result, we see the top of her head and the train of the dress behind her.

> **QUICK LOOK**
> **CAMERA** Nikon D4
> **LENS** Nikkor 85 f/1.4G
> **MODE** A
> **ISO** 200
> **SHUTTER** $^1/_{500}$
> **APERTURE** f/1.4
> **LIGHTING** Available light only

Left: The same location was used here, but the groom was added and I changed my perspective. **Right:** An alternate pose.

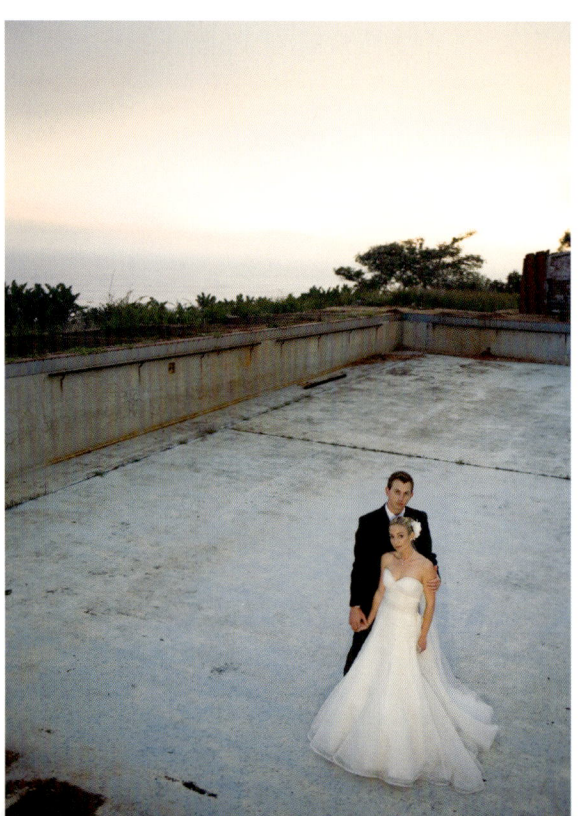

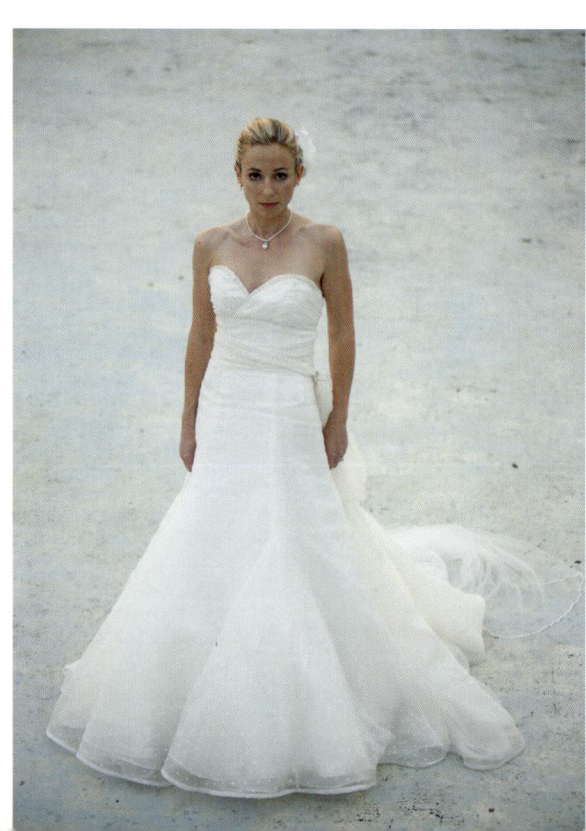

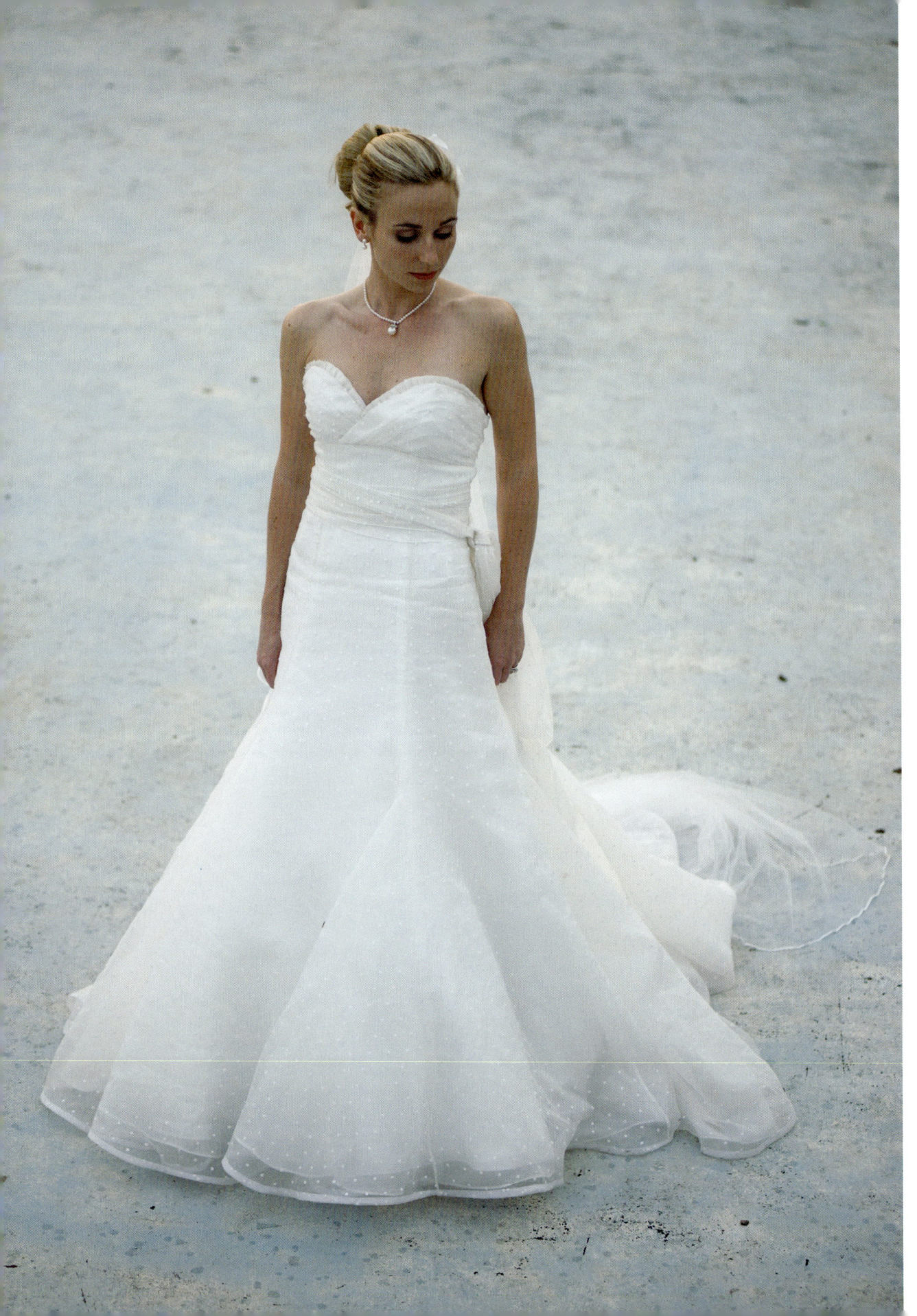

39. DISTINCTIVE SHADOWS

Midday Sun

This photograph is a great example of balancing ambient light with off-camera strobes—in this case, the Elinchrom Ranger RX. Here, I used a beauty dish, which produces sharper shadows than a softbox or umbrella (with these modifiers, the light is more diffused and wraps more evenly around the subject). Because this bride had beautiful aquiline features, I felt that she could carry off the more distinct shadows very well.

Looking at the sky, one can see that the exposure on the background is normal and realistic.

QUICK LOOK
CAMERA	Nikon D4
LENS	Nikkor 70–200mm f/2.8G ED VR II
MODE	M
ISO	100
SHUTTER	$^1/_{200}$
APERTURE	f/16
LIGHTING	Elinchrom Ranger with beauty dish

Had I not used the flash, the bride would have been quite dark.

Just Add Light

This was shot at about 2:00PM, so the sun was still very intense. If I had used my 5-in-1 reflector, the bright reflected light would have caused the bride to squint, which clearly is a no-no for any bridal portrait. Using my strobe, I could balance the light perfectly, causing no discomfort to the bride at all. The control that I have with the Elinchrom Ranger in terms of light direction and intensity is superb. It allows me to shoot out in the open during the brightest hours of the day and still produce images that are free of unflattering shadows and hot spots.

Left: An image of the bride and groom made under the same conditions. **Right:** The position of the beauty dish.

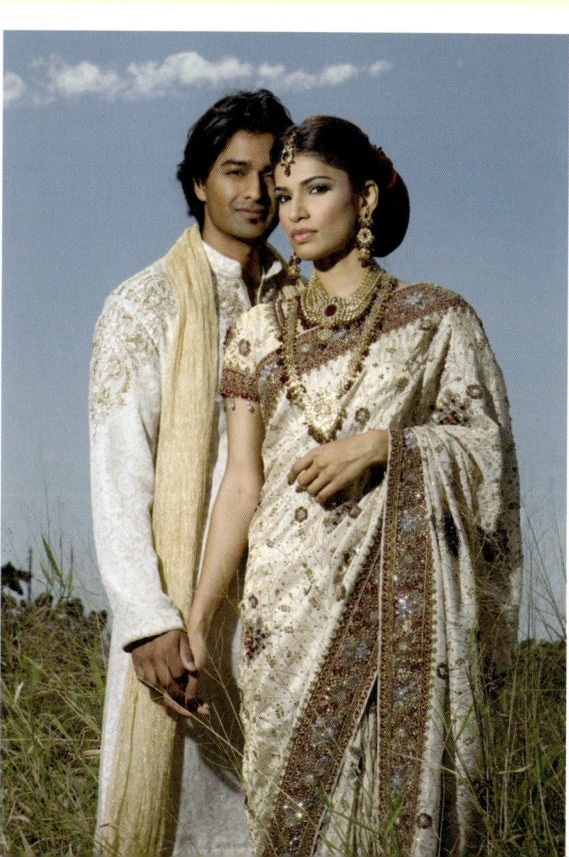

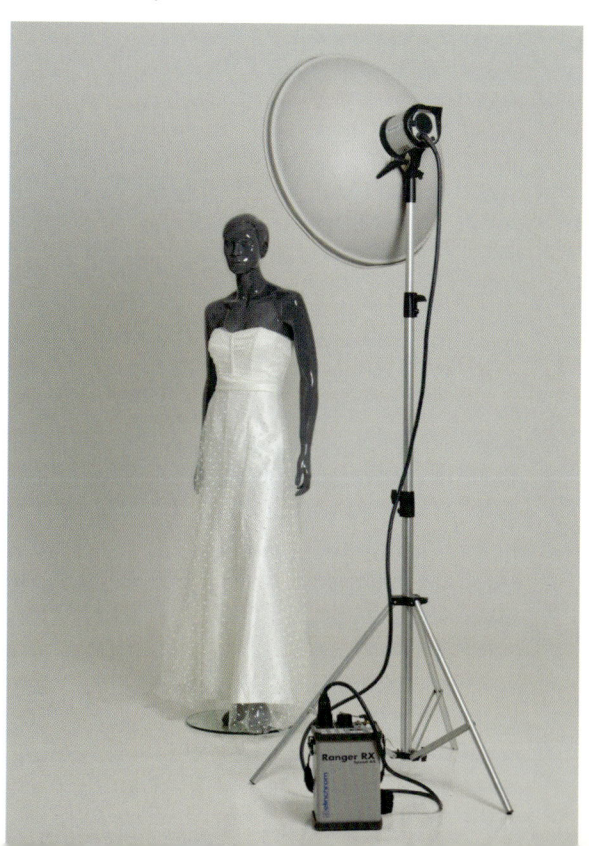

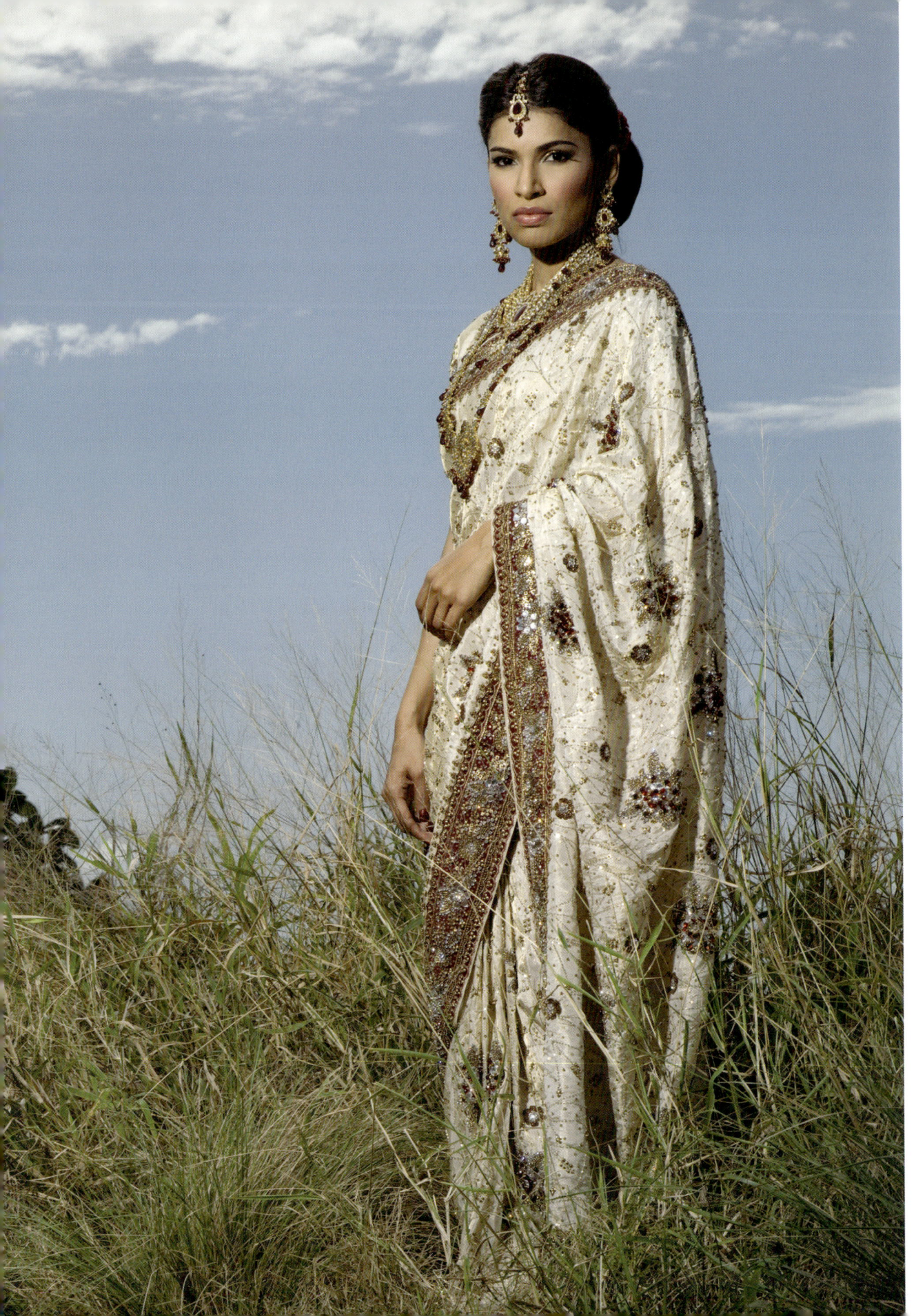

40. BREAKING THE RULES

The Composition

Sometimes rules are meant to be broken! I'm referring here to the rule of thirds, because in this very rare case, I positioned my bride almost exactly in the middle of the photo. In a way, her body is repeating the pattern of the vertical lines that we see in the bay window—she dissects the window into halves. Only the tilt of her head and twisted shoulders take her slightly off center. Without this obvious pattern being created, I'm sure I would not have found that this central stance worked, but I am confident that it does.

Her stance is one of confidence and strength. The position of her arms, especially the left, speaks of a woman who is very much in control of her destiny. The direct gaze into the camera also indicates that she is very self-assured.

Left: An alternate image from the session. **Right:** Image without exposure compensation.

Lighting and Exposure

The subject is clearly backlit, with the intense light wrapping around her and highlighting her head and curvaceous body.

I exposed for her skin, which resulted in the areas of the dress around her knees being completely blown out, obscuring detail. The highlights on her cheekbones are very flattering, and the light that enfolds her shoulders is also very sensual. The background is blown out, which I think adds to the geometric pattern of this image.

QUICK LOOK

CAMERA	Nikon D3s
LENS	Nikkor 70–200mm f/2.8G ED VR II
MODE	A
ISO	400
SHUTTER	$^1/_{200}$ +2EV
APERTURE	f/2.8
LIGHTING	Available light only

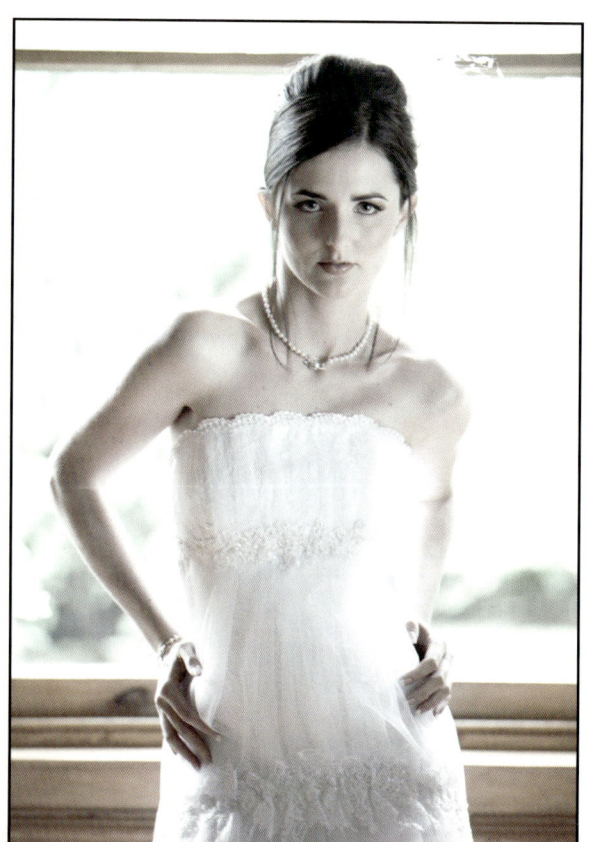

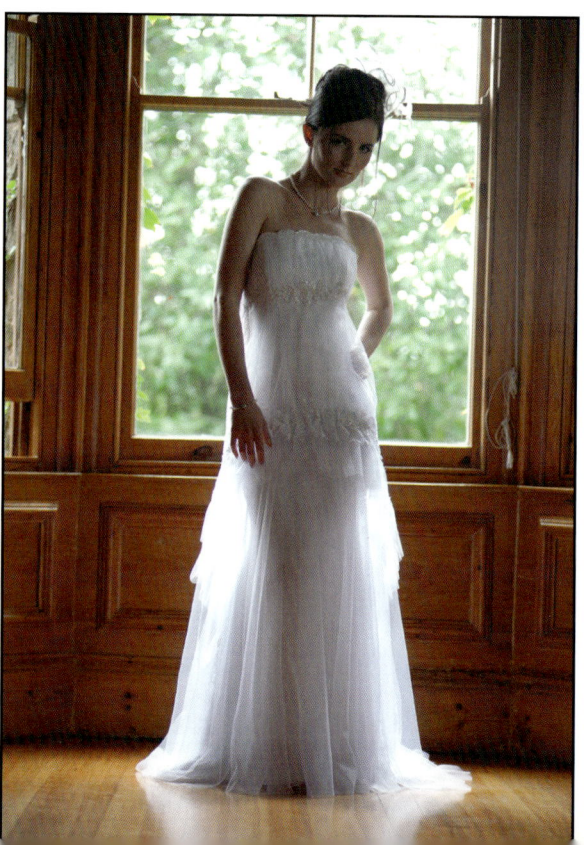

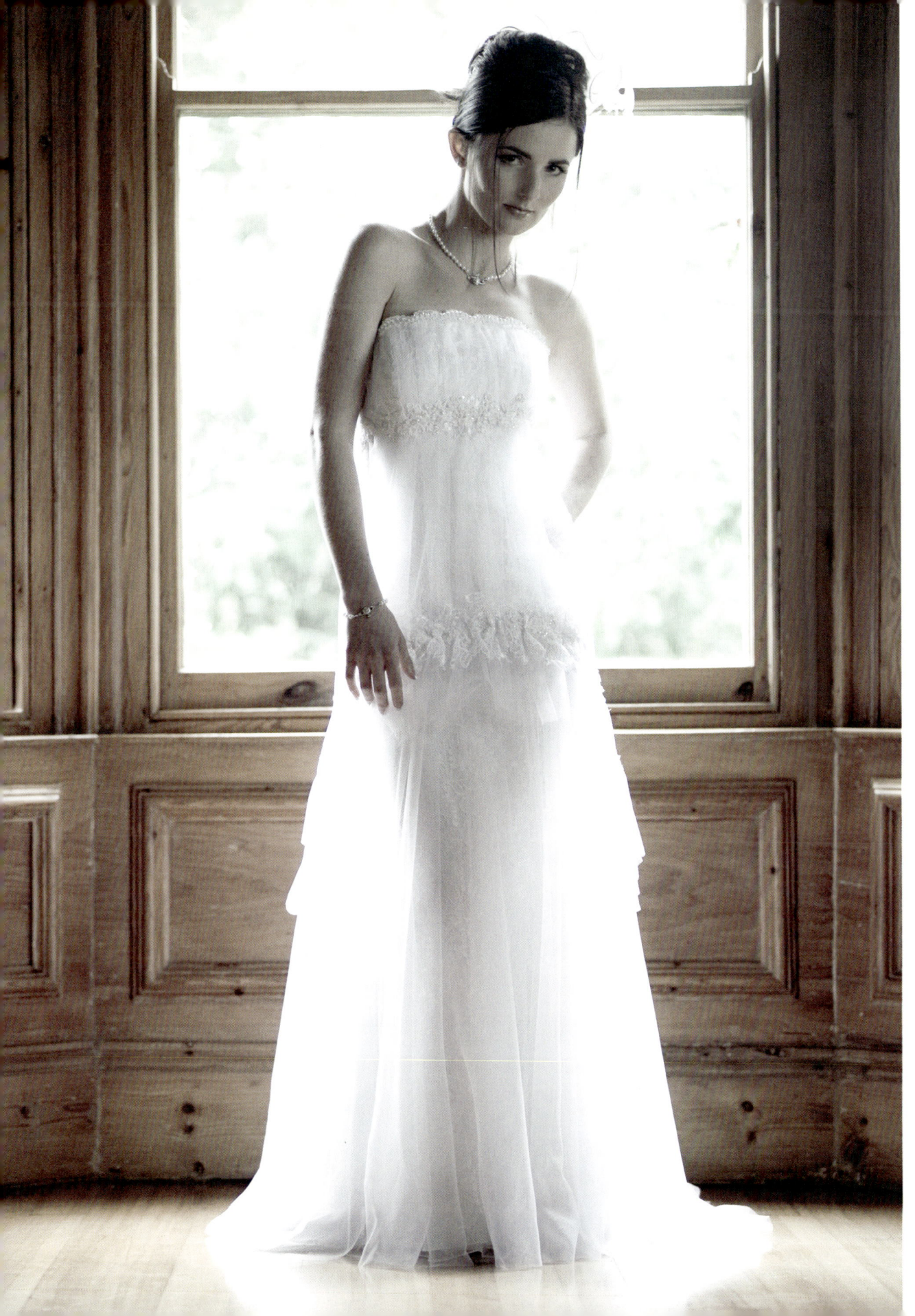

41. VARIETY

Timing

Timing is crucial during a wedding, and as a professional, you have to ensure that you are never the one to make the bride late for her walk down the aisle! I usually allow for 90 minutes before the ceremony to photograph the bride getting ready, the detail shots, her portraits, and the images of her bridesmaids and the mother of the bride. However, if the bride is running late, the time that you have allotted for the beautiful portraits may be whittled away to a mere 20 minutes.

A Change in the Lighting

Variation in the album is key, and a change of lighting can create a completely different look and feel to the image. Here, I shot with the Elinchrom Ranger RX as my primary light source, as opposed to the natural light in the previous shot. The background is a lot darker due to the fact that I chose a smaller aperture and lower ISO. The shape of the light is also very different, as this time I used a 50cm beauty dish, giving me a truly structured shot in terms of the lighting. It is also balanced with the background lighting.

Pose and Composition

Her pose is elegant and confident. In terms of composition, the chair is dead center, but the positioning of the bride's head is on a thirds line.

Left: Another pose from the session. **Right:** The placement of the lights.

> ### QUICK LOOK
> **CAMERA** Nikon D3s
> **LENS** Nikkor 70–200mm f/2.8G ED VR II
> **MODE** M
> **ISO** 100
> **SHUTTER** $^1/_{200}$
> **APERTURE** f/8
> **LIGHTING** Elinchrom Ranger RX

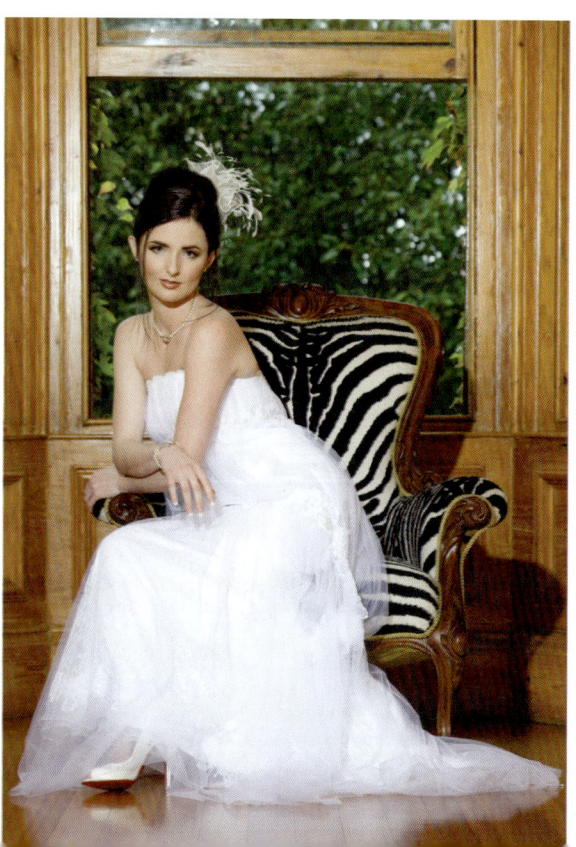

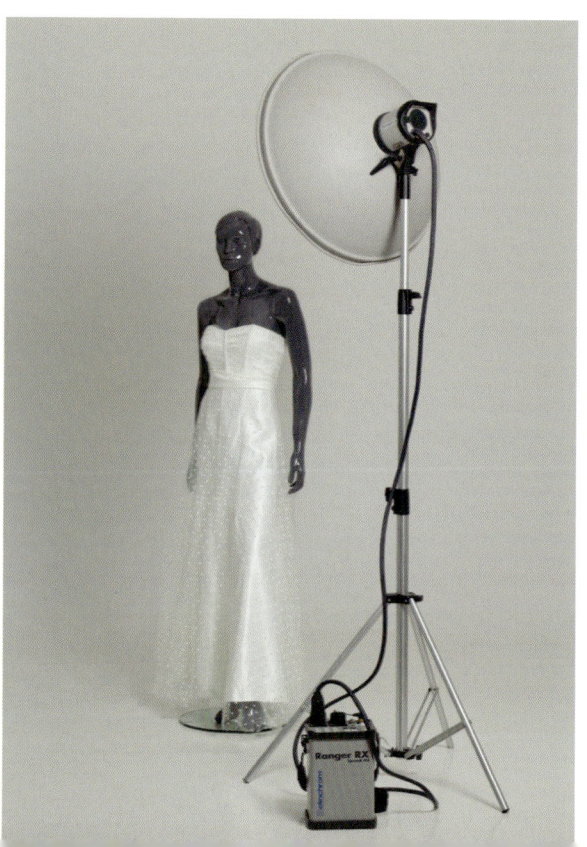

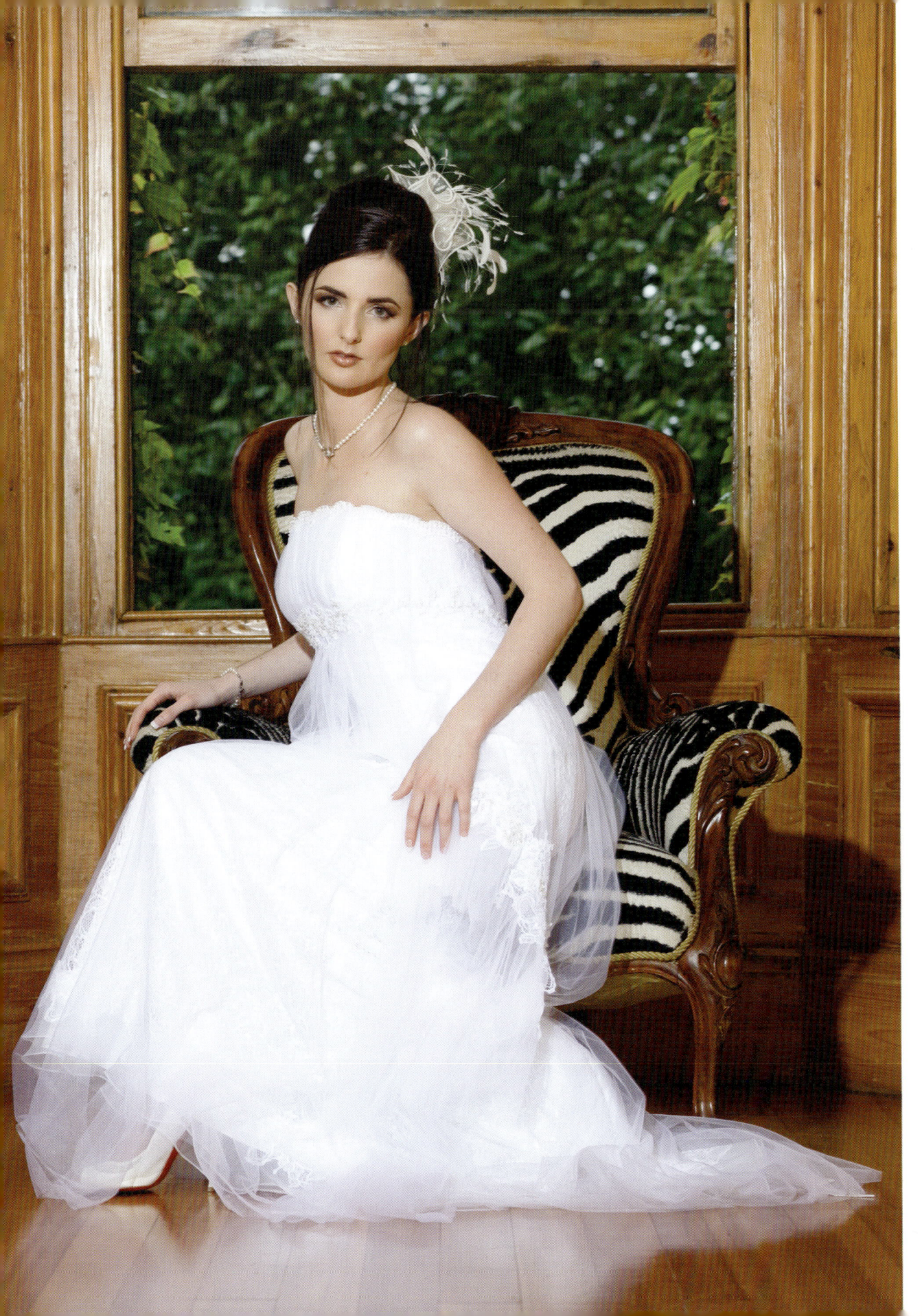

42. SPLENDOR

Building the Mood

Clouds have a big influence on the ambience and splendor of an image. Whether wispy and white or heavy and brooding, they have a mysterious energy that can make the difference between a nice photo and a spectacular one.

I had a friend who was a master at landscape photography. He was known to hike for days to find the perfect location, set up his camera, and wait for a cloud to cross the sky. As a wedding photographer, I can't wait for the perfect sky, so when atmospheric clouds are present, I'm happy to incorporate them into my images.

About the Image

This shot was made after a late-afternoon thunderstorm. The clouds were dissipating, and the sun was streaking through the thin clouds, creating an almost spotlight effect behind the bride, lighting her dress through the layers of tulle. An Elinchrom RX (with a beauty dish for added drama) was my main light. It was placed to the bride's front left, and I exposed for her skin. The background appeared a bit darker, as it was slightly underexposed. This enhanced the brooding clouds and had an almost HDR effect on the image. The pose is cheeky and confident, with the hitched-up dress exposing her legs. I like that it shows off the textures and layers of the dress.

Left: An alternate pose. **Right:** The stobe-with-beauty bowl placement.

QUICK LOOK

CAMERA	Nikon D3s
LENS	Nikkor 70–200mm f/2.8G ED VR II
MODE	M
ISO	100
SHUTTER	$^1/_{200}$
APERTURE	f/22
LIGHTING	Elinchrom Ranger RX with beauty dish

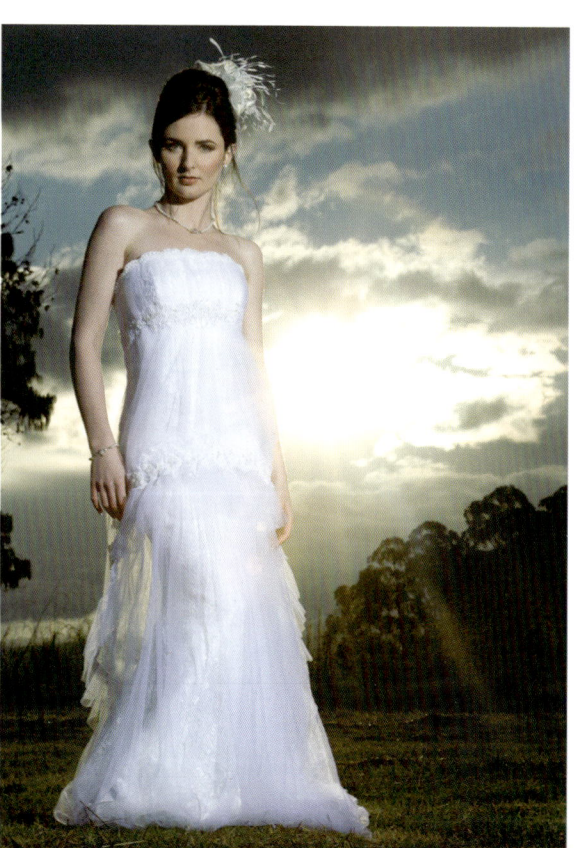

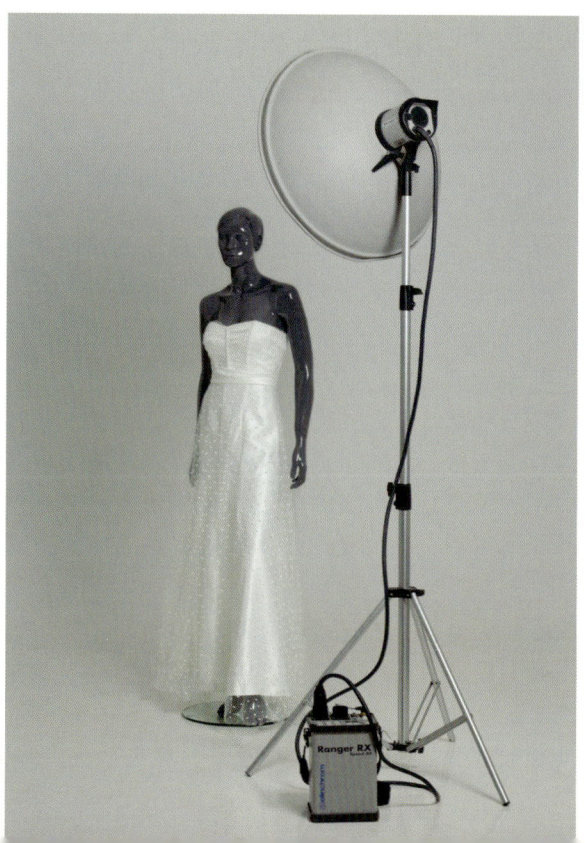

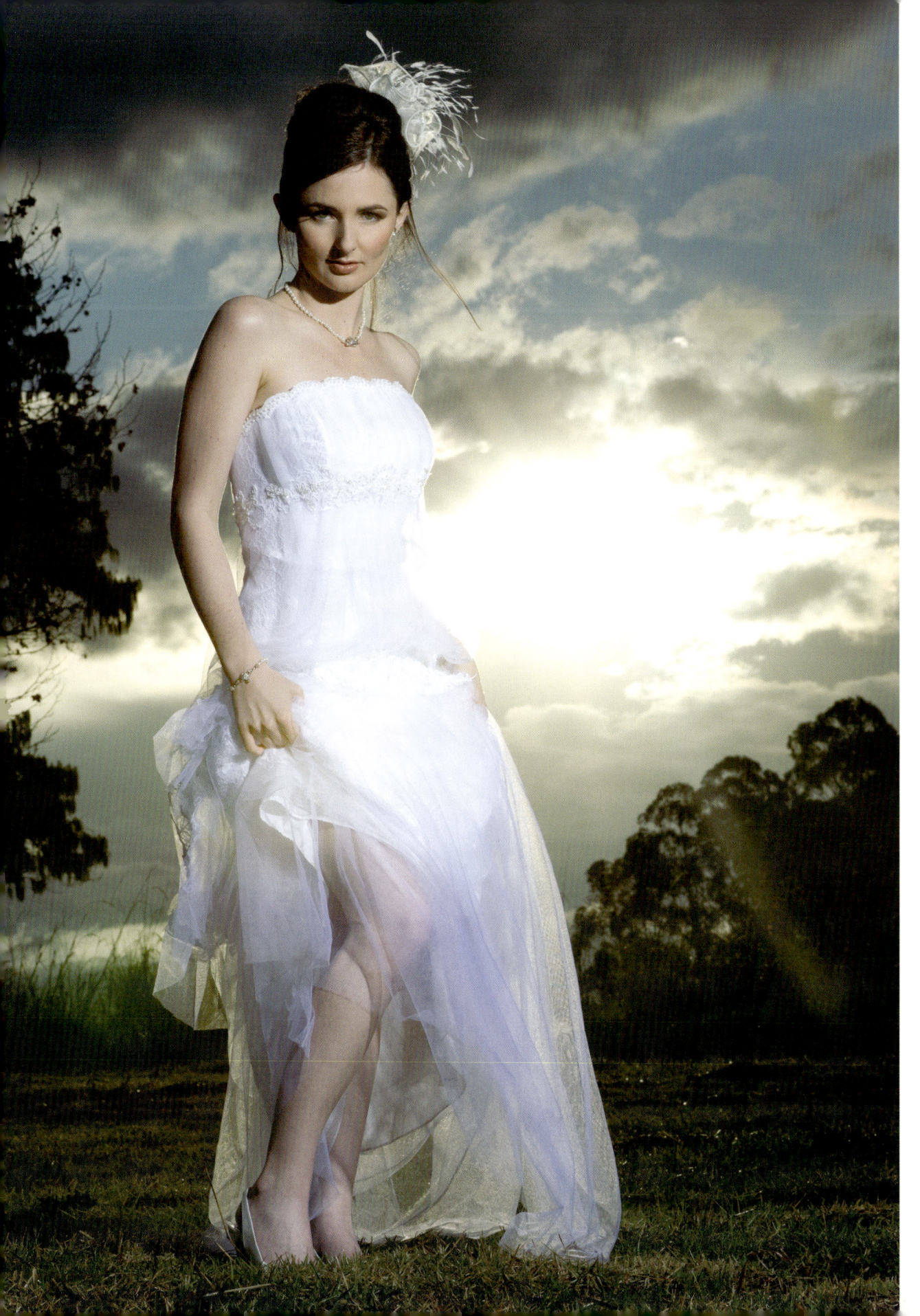

43. THE DAY AFTER

A New Freedom

I offer a "day after" shoot in one of my packages. It's popular with bridal couples for many reasons: time constraints are eliminated, we don't have to worry about the gown getting dirty, and we can choose a location that suits the clients' personalities without needing to remain near the venue.

QUICK LOOK

CAMERA	Nikon D3s
LENS	Nikkor 70–200mm f/2.8G ED VR II
MODE	M
ISO	100
SHUTTER	$^1/_{80}$
APERTURE	f/6.3
LIGHTING	Elinchrom Ranger Quadra RX

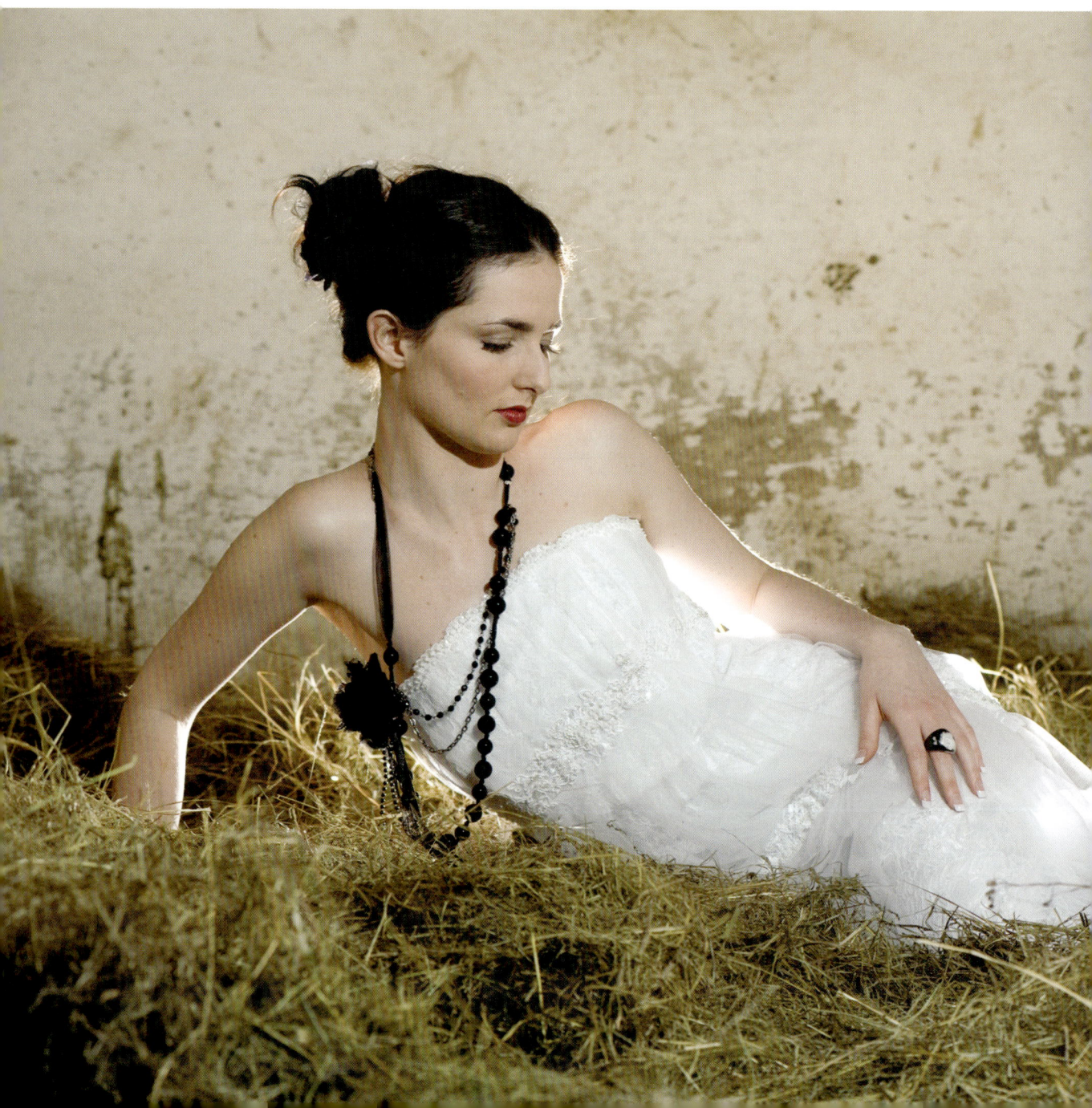

This shoot was held at the wedding venue, which happened to be on a stud farm in the countryside. The couple was very laid back and wanted portraits that were casual but beautiful.

I love shooting in locations that offer a visual contrast to the bride and groom in all their finery. The stables on this farm had thickly painted green barn doors and paint-worn interiors with mounds of fresh hay; this made it easy for me to hide the cord leading to my second flash head, which was placed behind the bride to give me the great rim light coming from behind her. The rim lighting gives a wonderful 3D effect, separating her from the background and adding dimension to the shot. I used the Elinchrom Quadra, as I did not need the power of the Ranger RX. The front flash head had an umbrella, and the flash head behind the bride was a bare bulb.

A Reclining Pose

The pose is reminiscent of Manet's *Olympia*, but my bride is fully clothed! Nevertheless, it is a beautifully sensual and feminine pose.

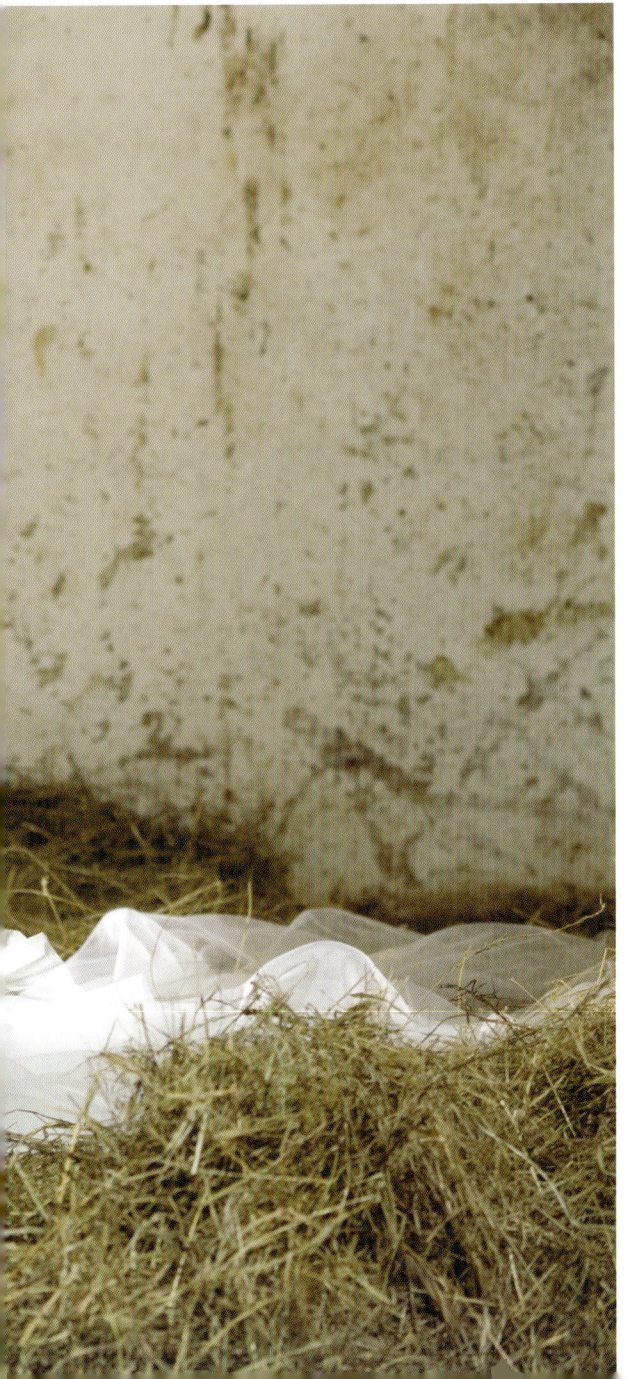

Top: Without a change to the setup, the groom was added to the scene for another portrait look. **Bottom:** The lighting setup.

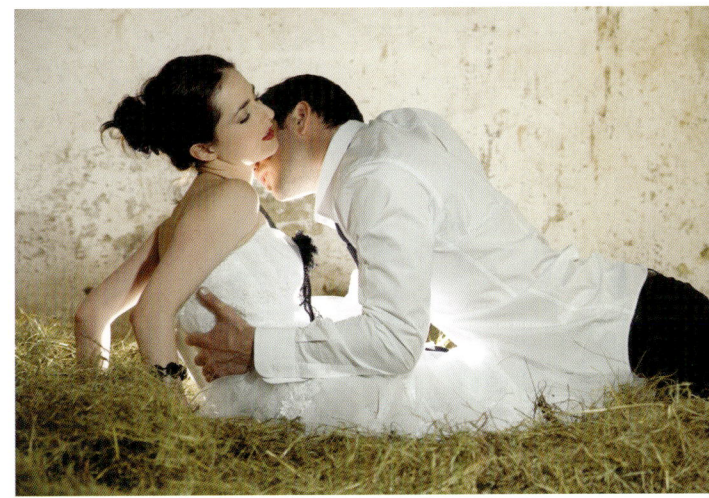

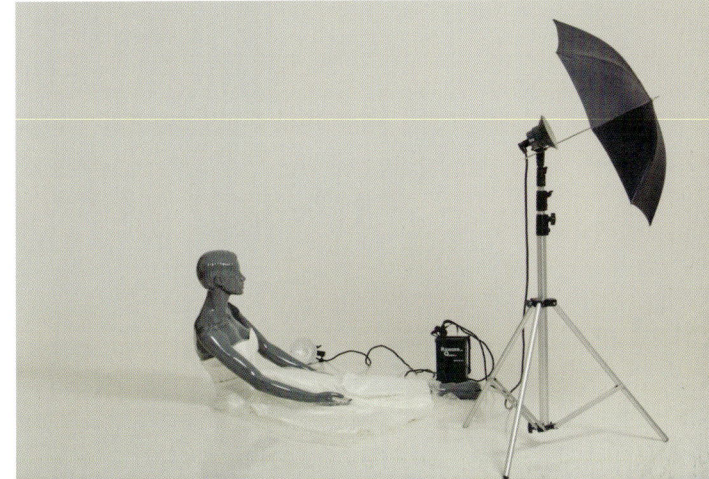

44. THE ROARING '20s

There are certain images that, due to the lighting and location, or possibly the clothing, seem to take the viewer to a bygone era. In this case, the photo could have come out of the roaring '20s, when life was opulent, the décor was dazzling, and the mood was very party-going and carefree.

This image was shot in a hotel bar. The bride's dress is reminiscent of the flapper-style fashion of the '20s, and her pose is appropriately self-assured. The decadent interior consisted of round white leather booths surrounded by glass beads that cascaded down like the glittery droplets of a waterfall, creating an opulent, vintage feel.

The Lighting

I placed the Elinchrom Ranger RX flash behind the bride, hoping that I would get some interesting lighting coming through the beads, but I was even more pleasantly surprised—the reflections and refractions that were created lit up the bride beautifully, in a soft and magical way. There was now no need to light the bride from the front—the incredible light bouncing off the beads was enough to wrap around the bride and give me exactly what I needed in terms of illumination.

Postproduction

I desaturated the image in postproduction, lifting the exposure to create a pastel, washed-out look, along with this very harsh backlighting.

Left: An alternate pose. **Right:** The lighting setup.

QUICK LOOK	
CAMERA	Nikon D4
LENS	Nikkor 70–200mm f/2.8 ED VR II
MODE	M
ISO	250
SHUTTER	$^1/_{80}$
APERTURE	f/2.8
LIGHTING	Elinchrom Ranger RX

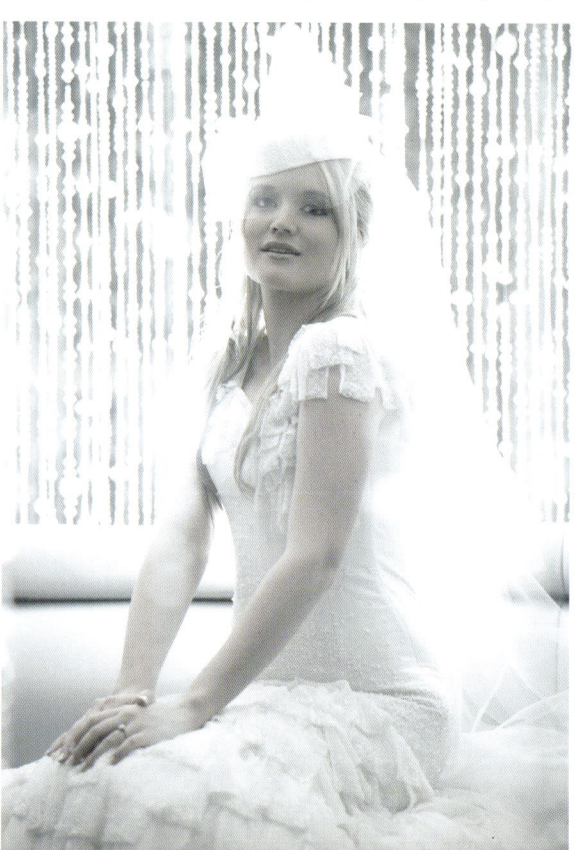

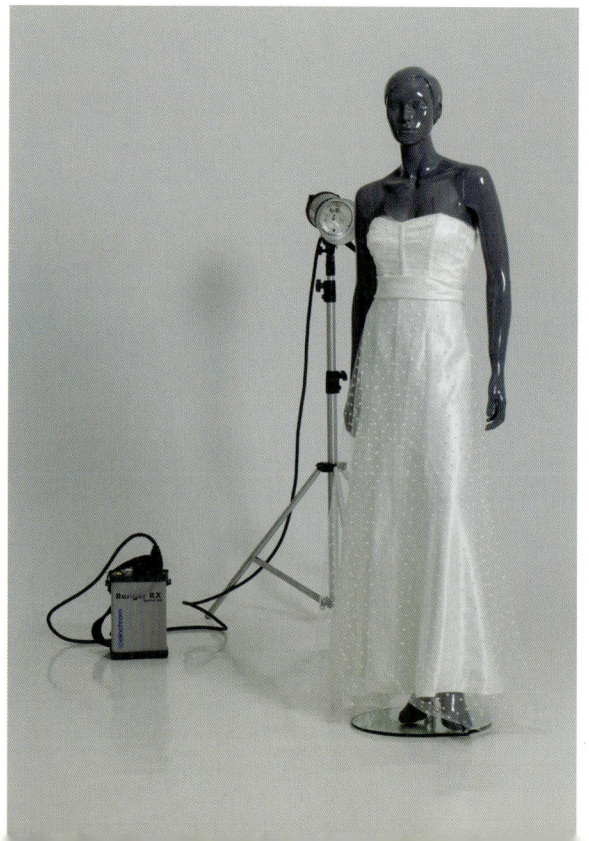

45. LARGER THAN LIFE

This image takes me back to a childhood story, where Alice falls down a rabbit hole and enters a mysterious world and, after drinking a small vial of potion, shrinks ten times smaller than her original size!

Serendipity

While I was photographing the bridesmaids, I noticed that the bride was waiting patiently for her turn, and the window light was falling on her, creating this beautiful, natural rim lighting. Near her feet, there was a door leading to the outside area of the bar, and being 2:00PM, gorgeous golden sunlight was pouring in onto the bride.

I shot this image at a low angle along the lounger, making "Alice" appear very small against the large, imposing furniture. I also felt

that in terms of the composition and the rule of thirds, it was very pleasing. The bride's pose seemed innocent and childlike, with her arm pushed straight next to her and her open fingers. Her gaze also has a youthful quality.

A Composite Image

I had to extend the leather cladding on the wall just beyond the bride's knee to perfectly finish off the image. To do this, I shot the leather upholstery separately and dropped it into the image in postproduction.

QUICK LOOK
CAMERA Nikon D4
LENS Nikkor 70–200mm f/2.8G ED VR II
MODE A
ISO 1000
SHUTTER $^1/_{160}$
APERTURE f/2.8
LIGHTING No artificial lighting or modification

The two images used for the composite shot.

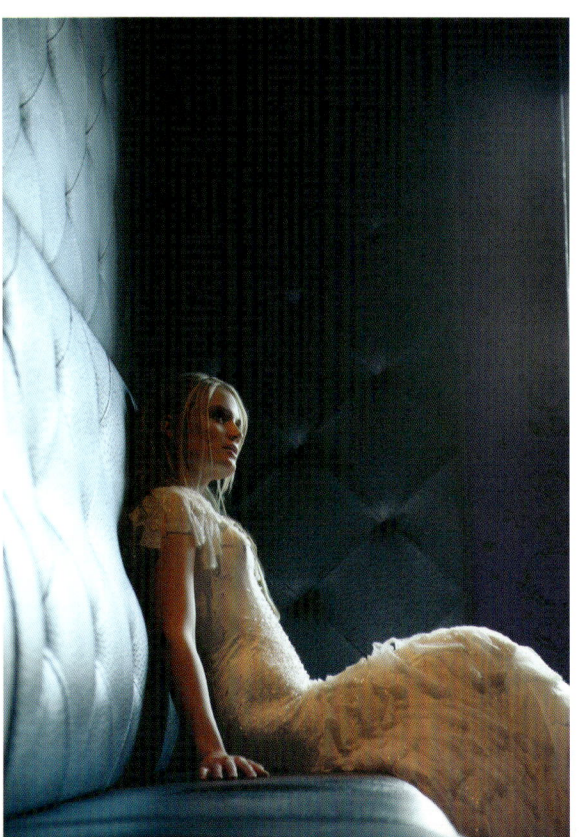
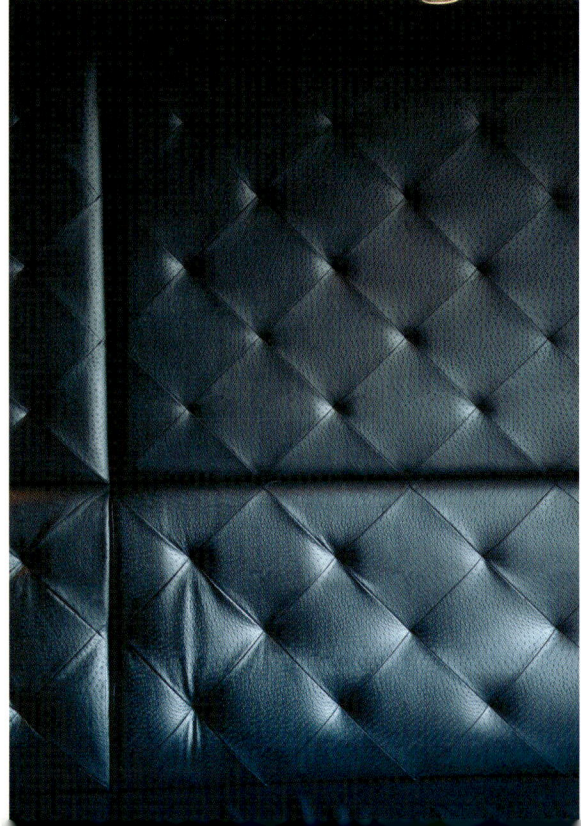

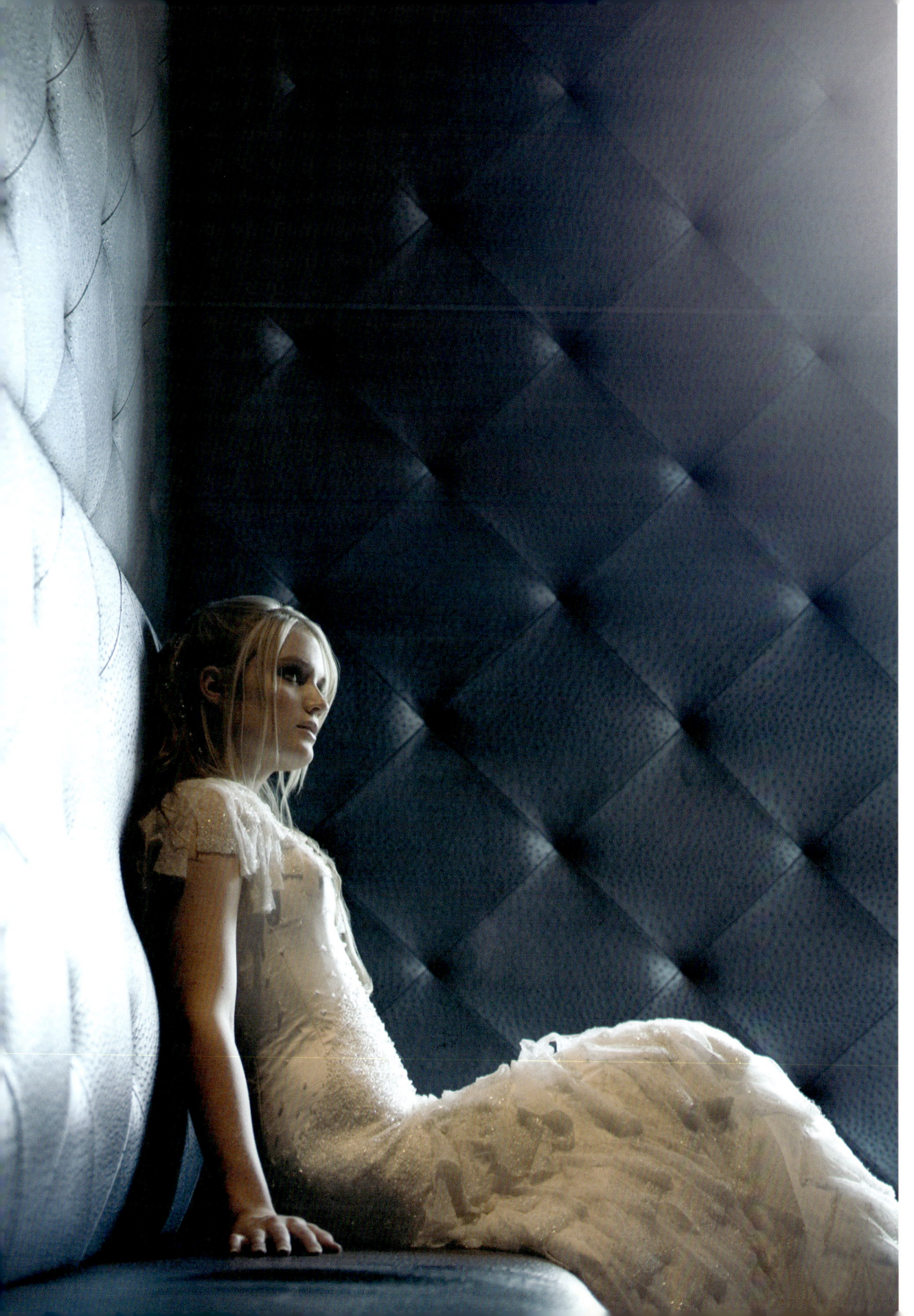

46. QUAINT AND PRETTY

Revisiting the 1950s

There seems to be a trend toward a 1950s décor and packaging aesthetic, which has traveled the globe. The look is reminiscent of a time when food was wholesome and homemade and people made time for their families. Several bridal magazines have picked up on this trend, and candy-stripes and beautifully iced cupcakes are popular.

This shot was made in a patisserie with 1950s-style design elements, like black & white checks and pastel stripes. The quaint, pretty backdrop was well suited to the bride's wedding theme.

> **QUICK LOOK**
>
> **CAMERA** Nikon D4
> **LENS** Nikkor 70–200mm f/2.8G ED VR II
> **MODE** M
> **ISO** 4000
> **SHUTTER** $^1/_{125}$
> **APERTURE** f/2.8
> **LIGHTING** Elinchrom Ranger RX

Lighting and Postproduction

In terms of lighting, I placed the Ranger RX portable strobe in the second room of the pastry shop and bounced the light off the ceiling, flooding the room with the light that you see in the background. I adjusted my exposure for her skin and dress, so the background became blown out.

No light came from in front of the bride (note that there is no catchlight in her eye); it bounced off the interior white walls only. Therefore, I had to use a wide aperture to get this shot.

I desaturated the image in postproduction to further enhance the pastel colors and old-fashioned atmosphere the patisserie created.

Left: An alternate pose. **Right:** The position of the strobe.

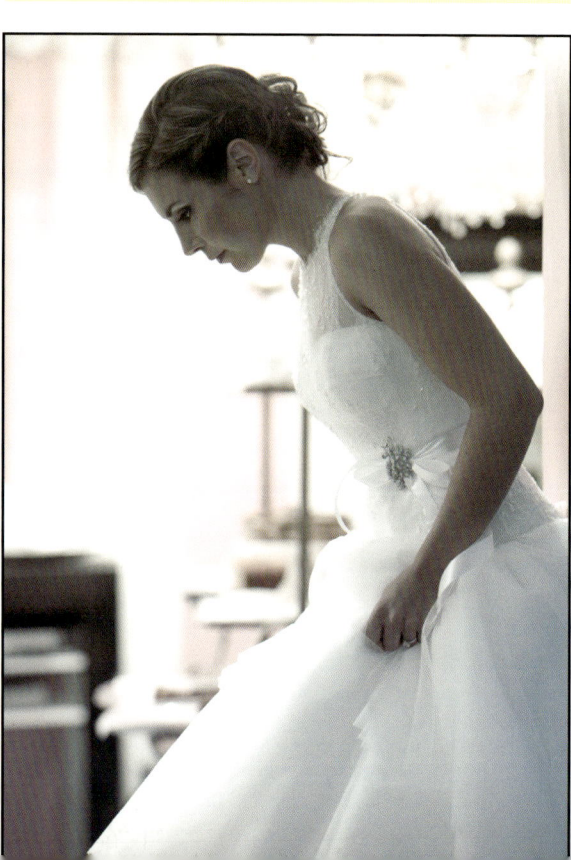
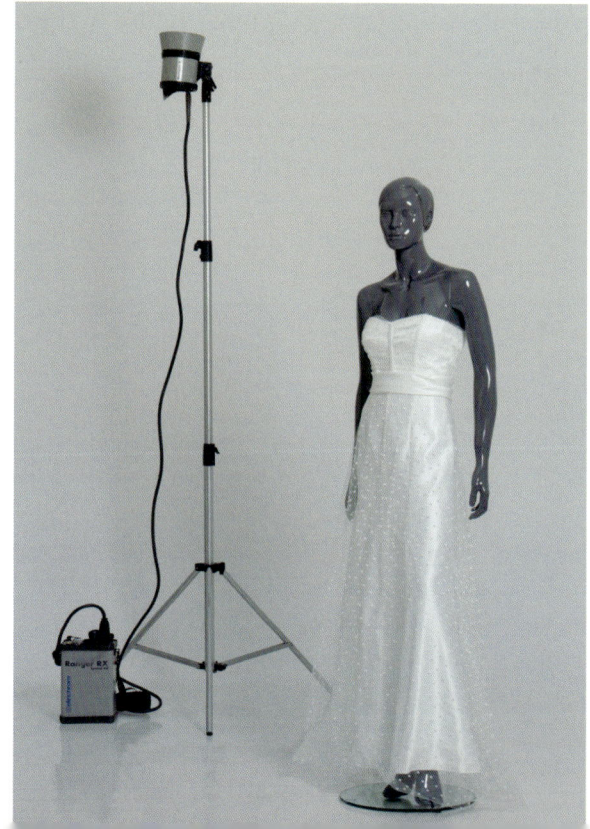

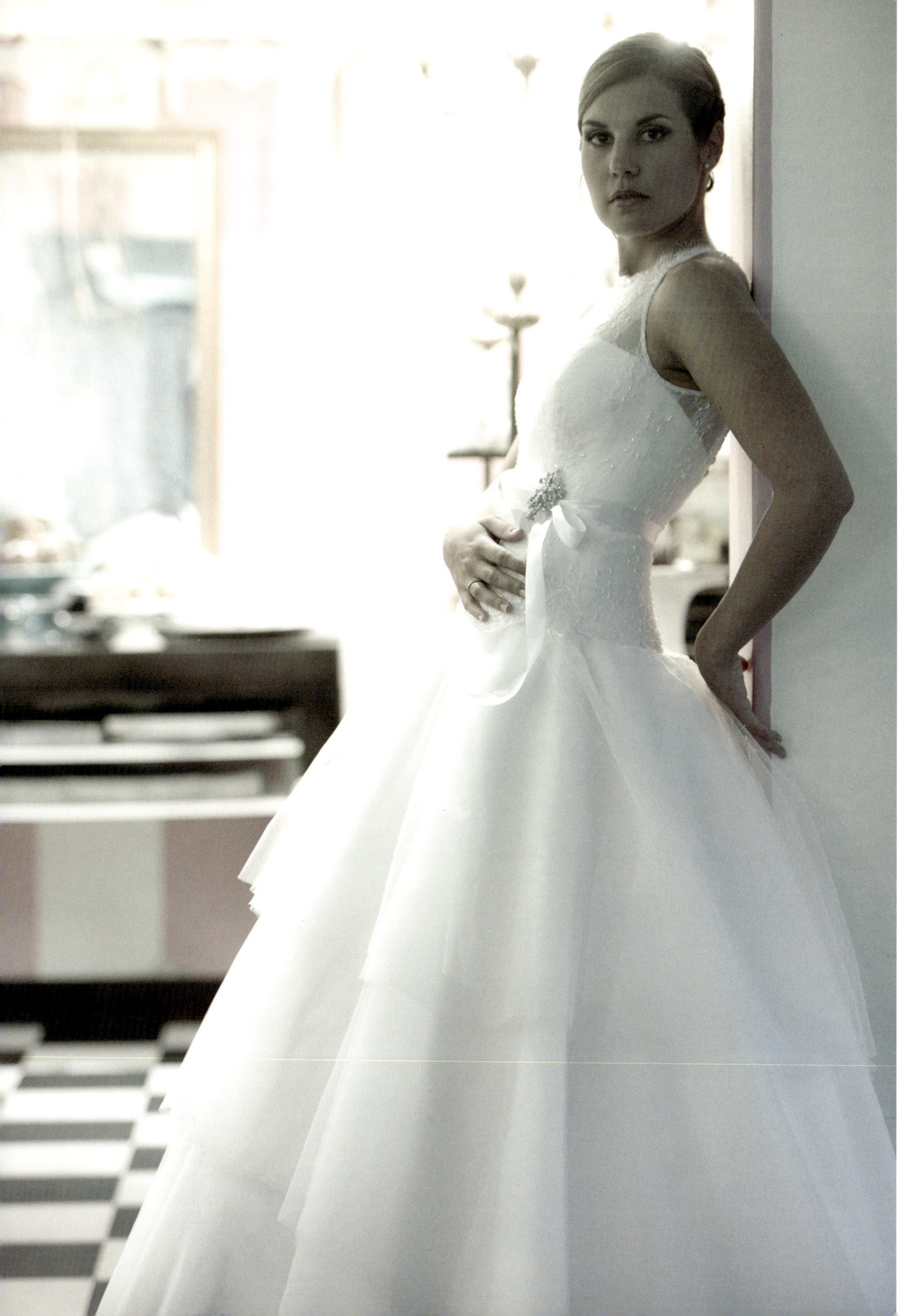

47. TRICKS OF THE TRADE

Camera Angle

For head-and-shoulders shots, I make sure that I keep the lens at eye level to avoid distortion of the head. Posing the bride slightly sideways to the camera produces a slimming effect; even if the bride is already slim, it is a good option, as it is a classically elegant pose. I tend to ask the bride to tilt her head down slightly and keep her eyes up to the camera. This creates an alluring effect that draws the viewer in.

Other than the images of the bride getting ready, which are generally taken in a photojournalistic style, the first posed images of the bride are these sort of portraits. At this stage, I always check for little details that will distract from the image (e.g., a stray hair across the face, lipstick on her teeth, or bad posture). Mention these issues to the bride in a polite way. After all, she is relying on you to take magnificent pictures and to make her look gorgeous. Touching up in post-production is an option, but it is extremely time-consuming.

The 5-in-1 Reflector

From this image, we can see how versatile the 5-in-1 reflector is at manipulating available light. In contrast to many of my images shown already, where the reflector is throwing light in from the opposite side of the available light, this time I had my assistant hold the reflector below the bride, bouncing the light upward, as you can see from the catchlight in her eyes. This allows for a bit of contrast in the shape and form of her face, but the 5-in-1 reflector really illuminates the subject and fills in any shadows that could lie underneath the bride's eyes.

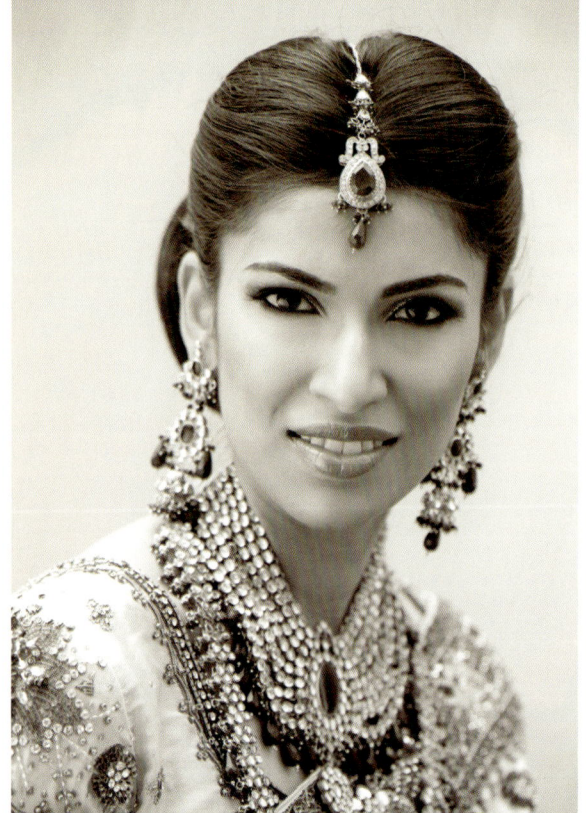

QUICK LOOK	
CAMERA	Nikon D4
LENS	Nikkor 70–200mm f/2.8G ED VR II
MODE	A
ISO	400
SHUTTER	$^1/_{125}$
APERTURE	f/2.8
LIGHTING	Lastolite 5-in-1 collapsible reflector

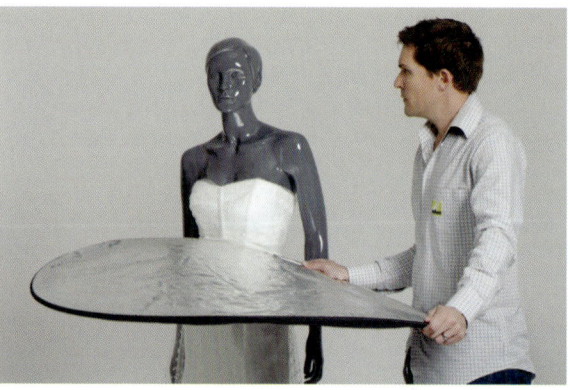

Left: A slight variation and sepia version of the shot. **Above:** The reflector position.

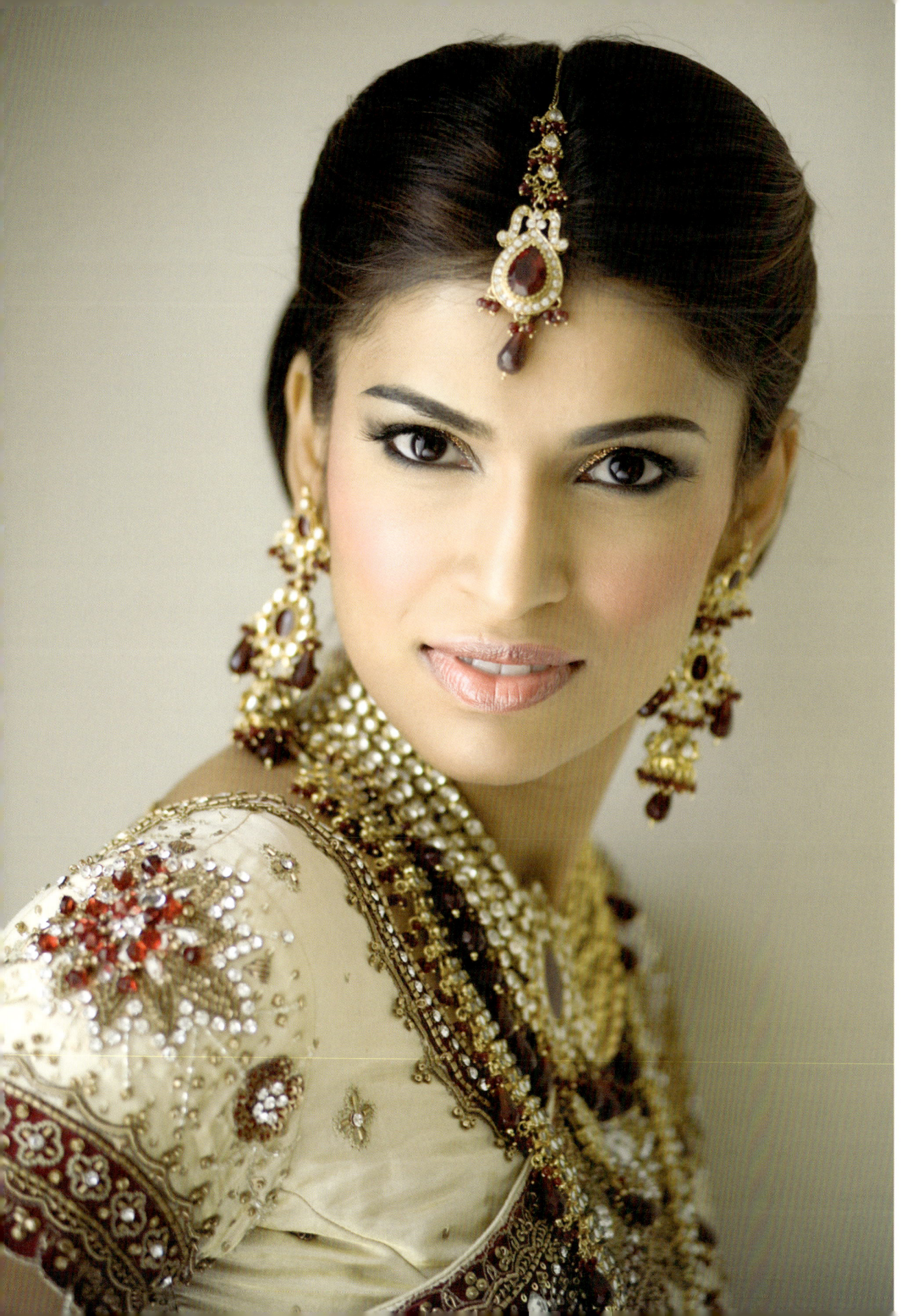

48. THE REAR VIEW

It's All in the Details

Brides go to an enormous amount of trouble, and these days, vast expense, to have the perfect dress for their wedding day. As the official photographer, it's important to get a full-length image of the dress, as well as the back of the dress, because often there is gorgeous detail there too. The designer or dressmaker is always grateful to get an image of the dress that they can use for their advertising or portfolio. It's also a great marketing tool for you, as having a great reputation amongst the other wedding suppliers is highly valuable. If an expert in the trade endorses you as the preferred photographer, a potential client will be more likely to book you.

The Setup

This rear-view image was made late in the afternoon and, as the session was held on the west coast of Africa, the sun was setting into the sea. I posed the bride on a large boulder and had her face the sea, looking out to the horizon. From my lower vantage point, the setting sun was at about chest height, and it created a stunning golden, halo-like glow around her. The reflection of the sun's light on the water made the sea look gilded and slightly shimmery, and the sky also took on a light golden hue. I illuminated her back with the Ranger RX power pack, using only a bare bulb as I wanted to get as much light onto her dress as possible, without softening the light with modifiers. The details on all the ruffles and the satin ribbon are now perfectly enhanced.

> ### QUICK LOOK
> **CAMERA** Nikon D3s
> **LENS** Nikkor 70–200mm f/2.8G ED VR II
> **MODE** M
> **ISO** 100
> **SHUTTER** $^1/_{250}$
> **APERTURE** f/22
> **LIGHTING** Elinchrom Ranger RX

Below: An alternate pose. **Right:** The strobe position.

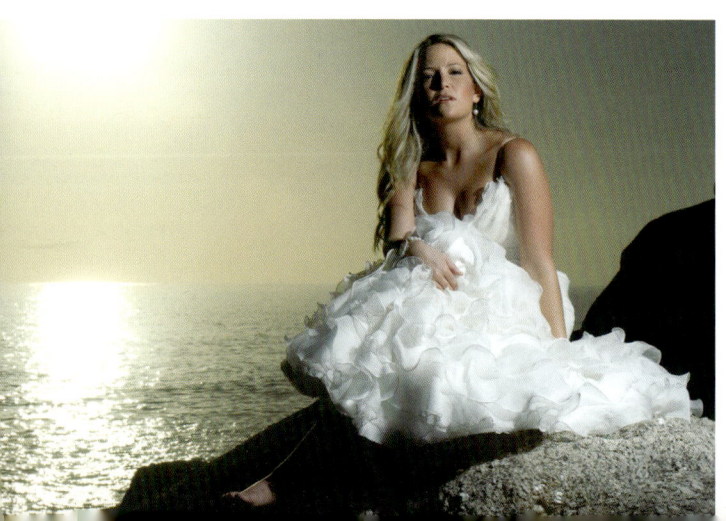

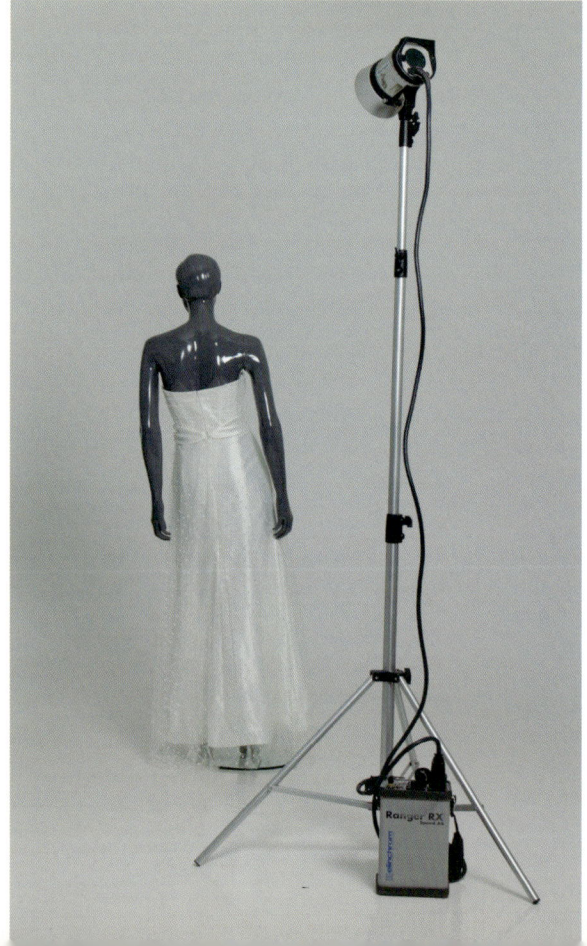

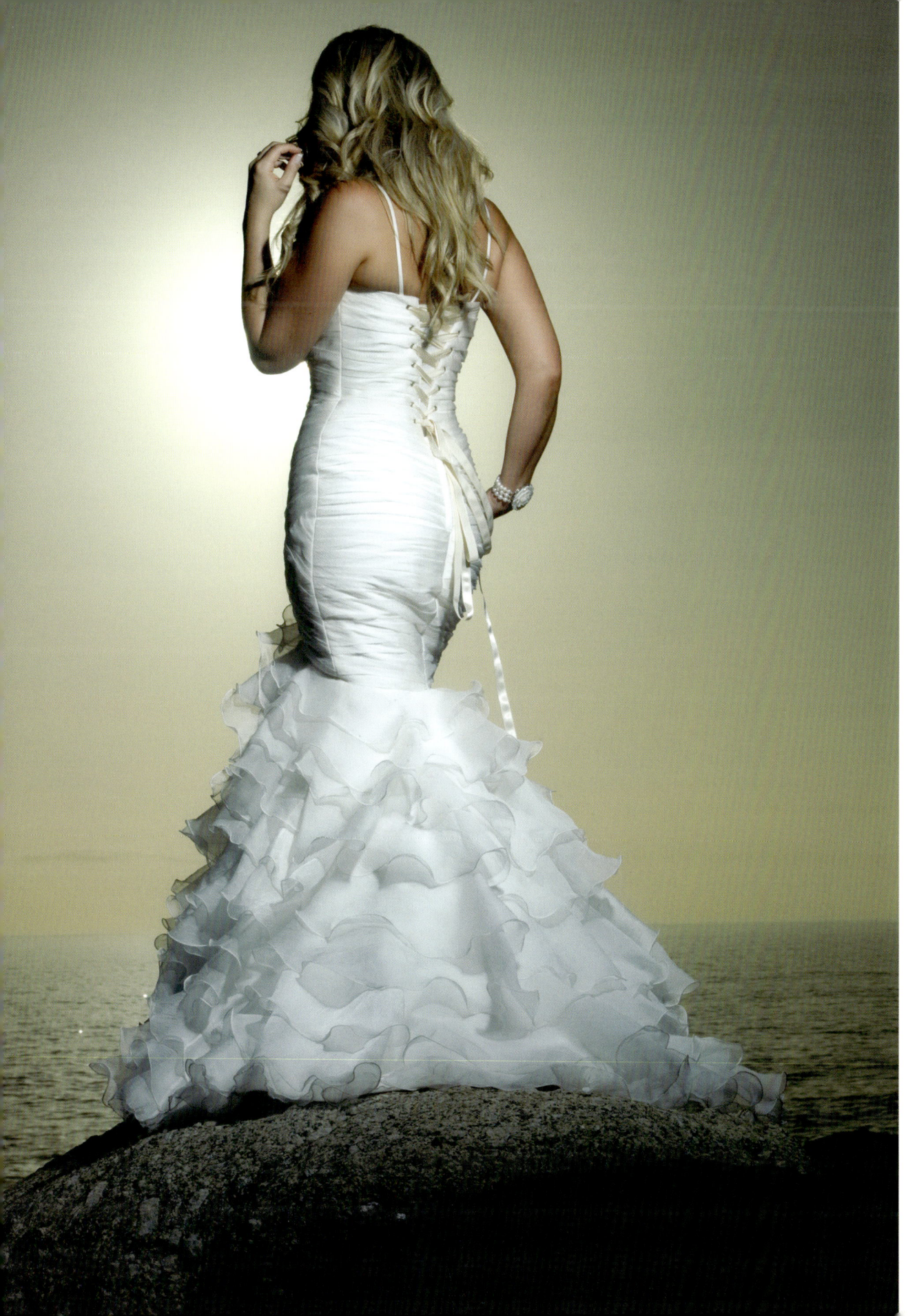

49. OLD HOLLYWOOD

Highlight and Shadow

The bride's beautiful dress and veil, classic French chignon hairstyle, and makeup reminded me of times gone by. There was an old Hollywood glamour and elegance that I wanted to capture to my best ability. Thinking of movie stars such as Marlene Dietrich, Mae West, and Greta Garbo, I set up my lighting to reproduce the black & white portraits typical of that era. Wanting plenty of tonal contrast, I had my assistant hold an LED light almost directly above and very close to the bride to accentuate the falloff, without illuminating the background too much.

I asked the bride to turn her face to a three-quarter position and lift her chin so she was looking directly into the light. This created great highlights and shadows on her face, resulting in a three-dimensional structure and resultant powerful elegance. The pose is self-assured and speaks of a woman who is very confident—a movie star!

The light captured all the crystal beading on the intricately detailed dress, so it shone in true Hollywood style. I love the way the strong lighting cast shadows from the lace detail on her chest.

Intensifying Contrast

I used Nik Software's Silver Efex Pro to convert the image to black & white and increased the contrast to produce an incredibly striking image.

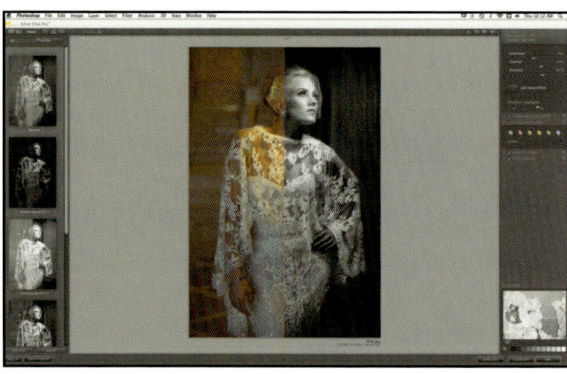

QUICK LOOK
CAMERA Nikon D4
LENS Nikkor 70-200mm f/2.8G ED VR II
MODE M
ISO 2000
SHUTTER $1/160$
APERTURE f/2.8
LIGHTING LED video light

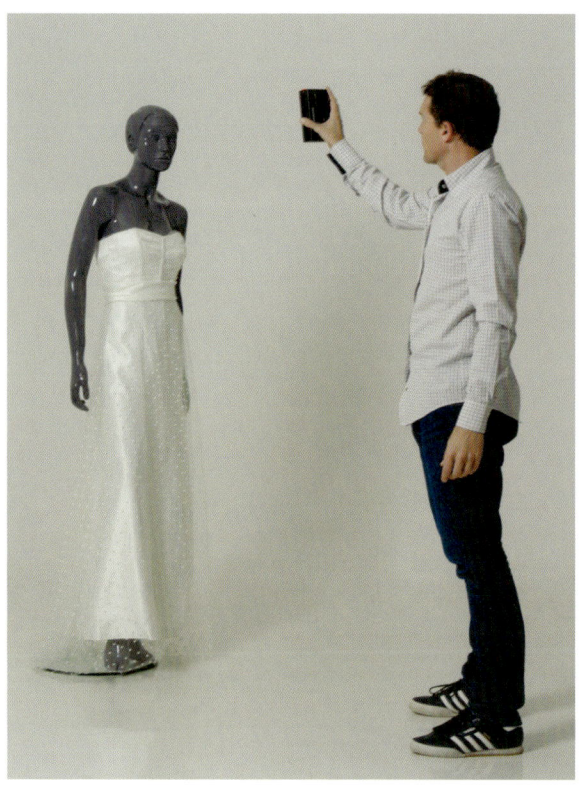

Above: Nik Software's Silver Efex Pro interface.
Right: The position of the LED lighting unit for this image.

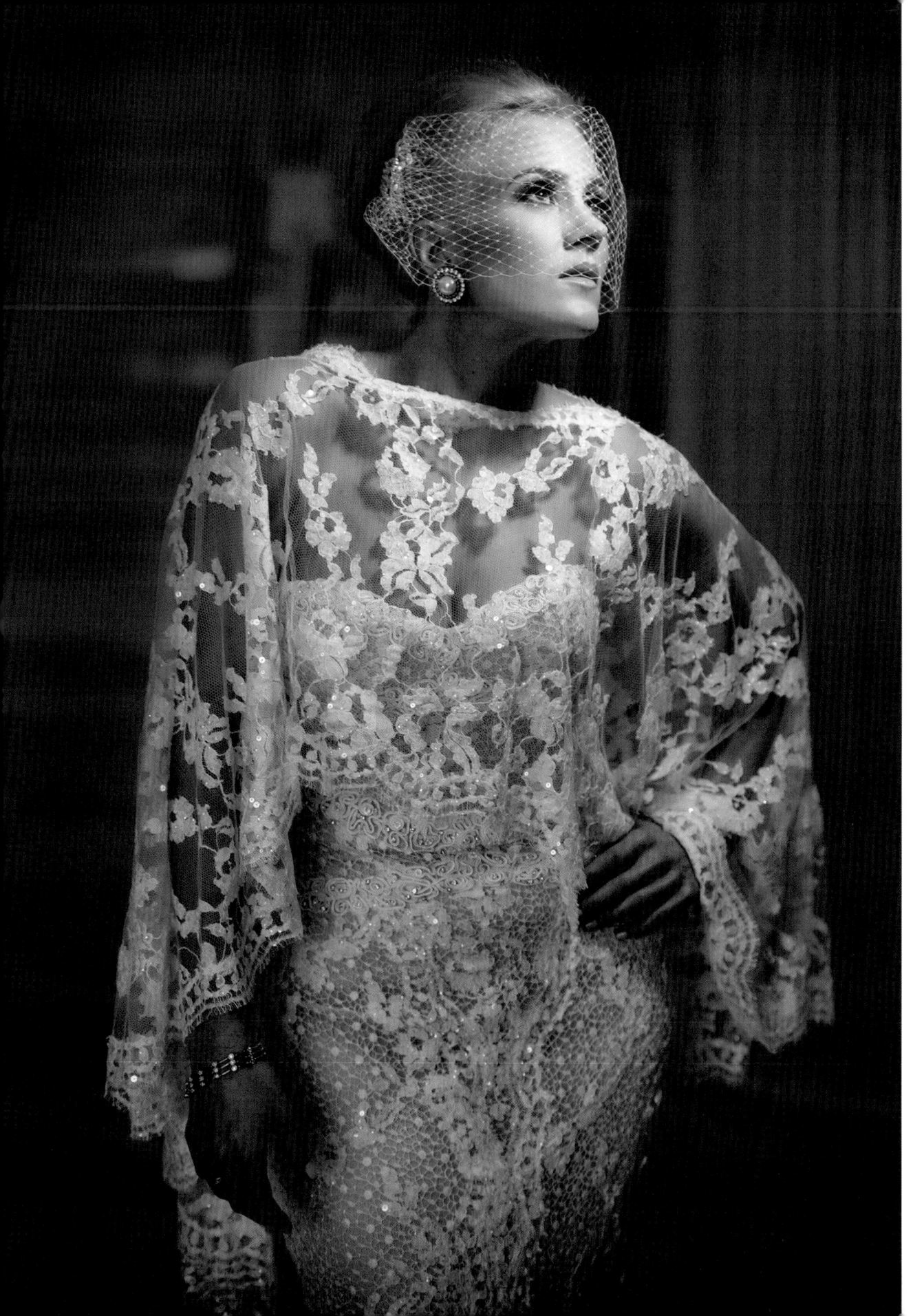

50. CHIAROSCURO

If you're familiar with Rembrandt's paintings or the work of other 17th and 18th century artists, you may know the term *chiaroscuro*. The word means "light-dark"; in this context, it refers to the clear tonal contrasts in the artwork. It is almost as if someone had shone a spotlight onto the subject, while the rest of the room remained dark. This gave the paintings a dramatic, theatrical look. The colors were very yellow and black, and the atmosphere created was moody and intriguing.

The bride's antique lace shawl reminded me of eras gone by. When I discovered the richly decorated, Victorian-inspired library at the reception venue, my mind went to the paintings of the old

Top: A group portrait made using the same setup. **Bottom:** The position of the LED.

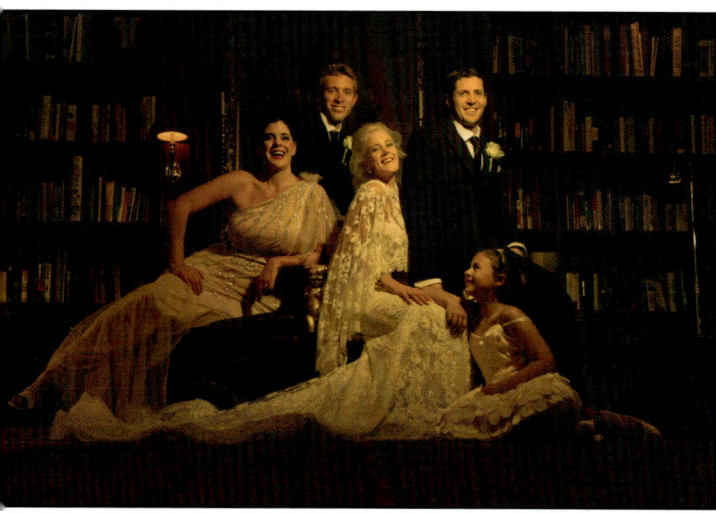

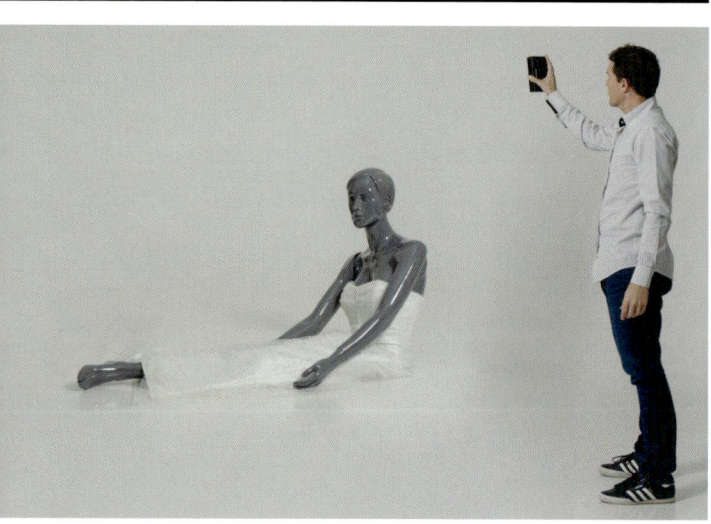

Dutch masters, and I knew that re-creating the chiaroscuro effect for the bridal portraits would be impactful and unusual.

Closing the doors and the heavy curtains to the library and switching off all lights, we created a room that was gorgeously dark and gloomy. My assistant held the LED to the bride's left and set it to create the warm, yellow chiaroscuro glow. I positioned the bride on the antique chair with the Baroque golden cherubs and had her turn her body to the left, pulling the train of her dress out to the right so that its incredible antique lace

and jeweled detail could be perfectly displayed. The positioning of the bride's head is demure and serene, and it speaks of an era where women were quietly aware of their sensuality.

QUICK LOOK

CAMERA	Nikon D4
LENS	Nikkor 24–70mm f/2.8G ED
MODE	A
ISO	2000
SHUTTER	$^1/_{125}$ – $^1/_3$ EV
APERTURE	f/4
LIGHTING	LED video light

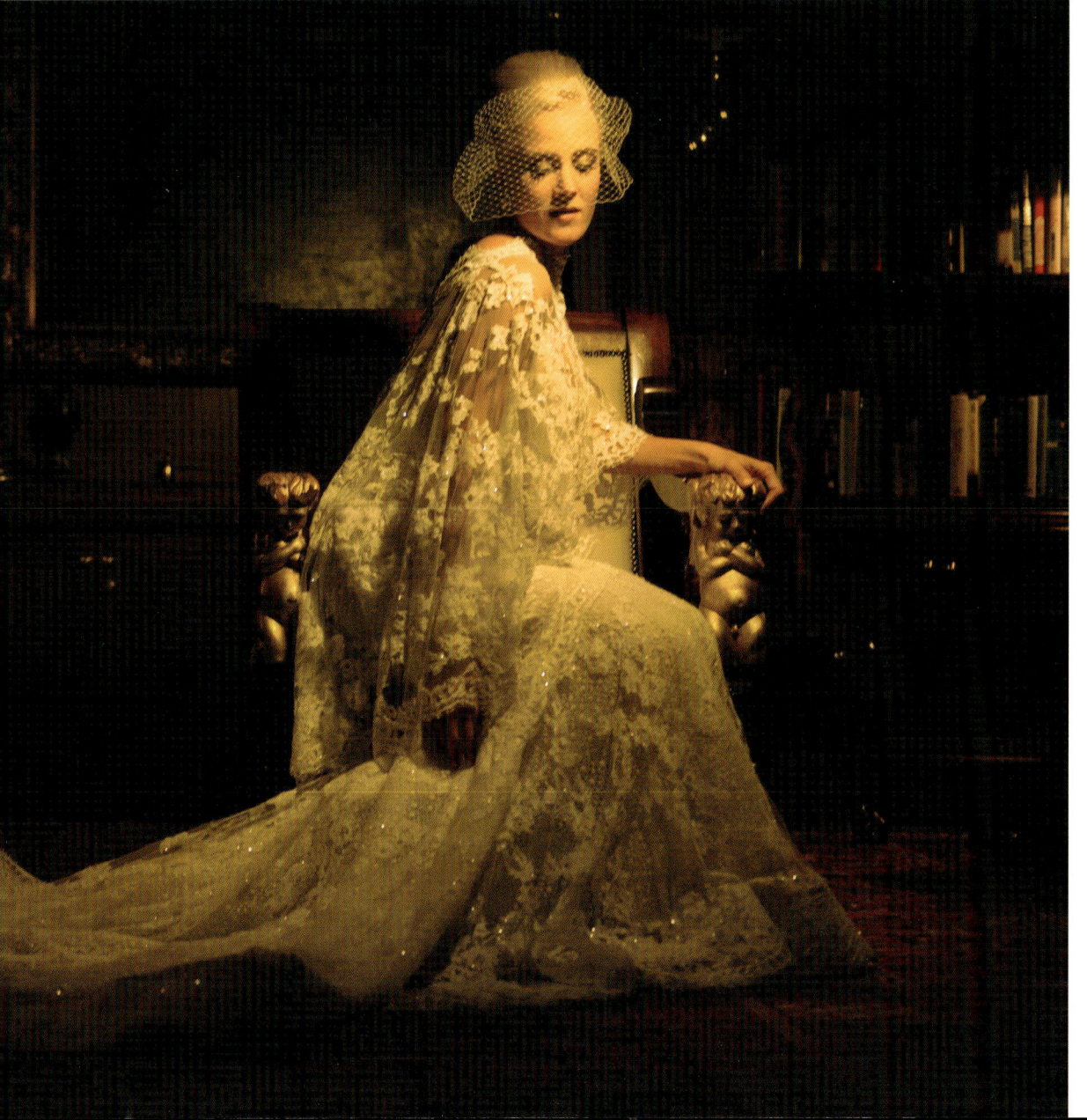

51. LOW LIGHT

Advancing Technologies

This image was created during one of my London wedding workshops, at about 10:30PM. The model was completely frontally illuminated by only a small LED flashlight, which just goes to show how amazing the technology of cameras is these days! At the time, I was still using the Nikon D3s, which has tremendous low-light capabilities. Obviously, my Nikon D4 has even better low-light capabilities, which makes my work as a professional photographer incredibly easy! In fact, the low-light capabilities of the new cameras have opened up a whole new avenue of

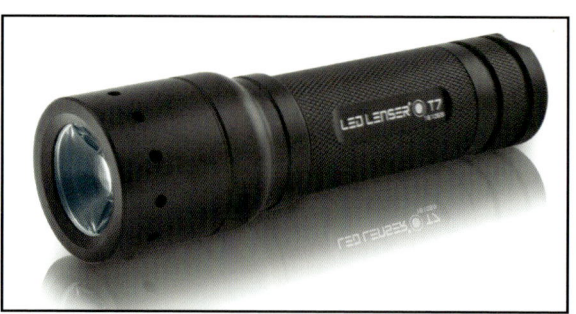

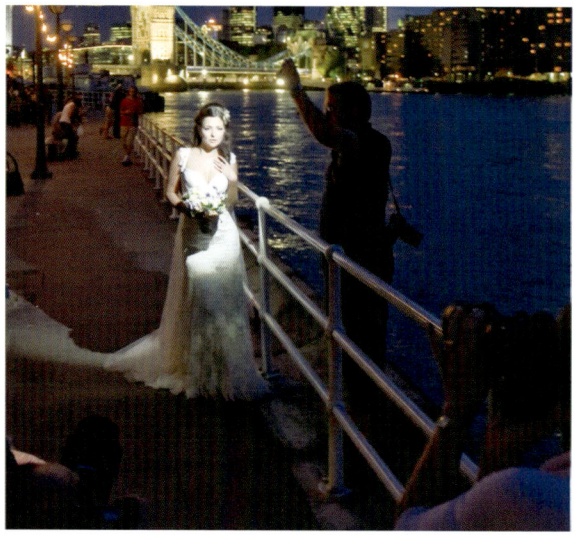

"after dark" photography that was not available when we were using film. Instead of low light being a challenge, it is now an opportunity to create magical images that were not possible before.

The wonderful thing about LED lighting is that you can place it anywhere you like, and you can see the results immediately. You can also have your assistant move backward or forward to manipulate the intensity of the light. The use of LED lighting with gels or off-camera flash can also be really effective.

I used the Ranger Quadra to backlight the bride. This created highlights in her hair. Because I was exposing for the ambient light, relative to the LED light falling on her face, I was able to capture the glow of Tower Bridge in the background.

Happily Ever After

You can add a lot of depth to your storybook by taking a bride and groom outside during or after the reception and finding a really nice area where ambient light can be used to create gorgeous, dreamlike images.

Top: The LED Lenser T7 flashlight. **Bottom:** The setup.

QUICK LOOK

CAMERA	Nikon D3s
LENS	Nikkor 70–200mm f/2.8G ED VR II
MODE	A
ISO	4000
SHUTTER	$^1/_{125}$
APERTURE	f/2.8
LIGHTING	LED Lenser T7 flashlight

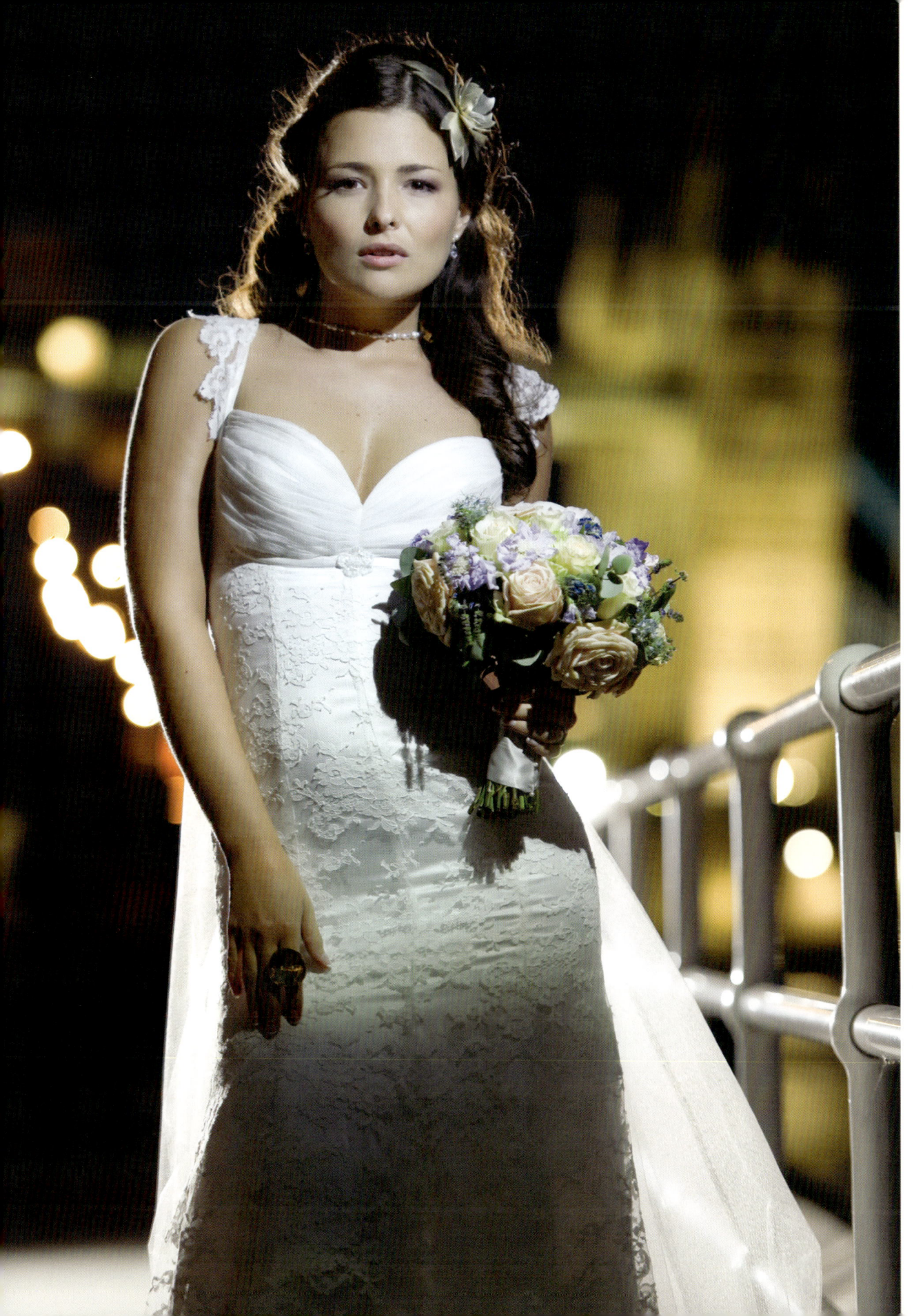

52. AN ANGELIC GLOW

Signature Style

I'm a big fan of backlighting when it comes to shooting with ambient light. More often than not, the backlighting is intense and very prevalent in my images. This has become a hallmark of my style, and couples that choose me as their wedding photographer are generally very drawn to these images in my portfolio.

This image was taken in late afternoon, in an expansive field where wheat had recently been harvested. The beautiful backlighting works really well in my opinion, creating a rim lighting that I find very pleasing. One of the rules of shooting this type of backlighting is to get the subject's shadow to point directly in front of her. This is the trick to getting that angelic glow that seems to encapsulate the bride. Here, I did not want to lose that contrast, so I chose not to illuminate her from the front. If you look at the supporting image, you will see that there is no catchlight in her eyes. I compensated for the contrast by increasing my exposure value.

Postproduction

In postproduction, I added a bit of interest by bringing in various filters using Nik Software's Color Efex Pro. I used their bicolor cast to create a little bit of depth by warming up the top right-hand corner, adding a slight brown cast. In the bottom-left corner I added a slight yellow cast.

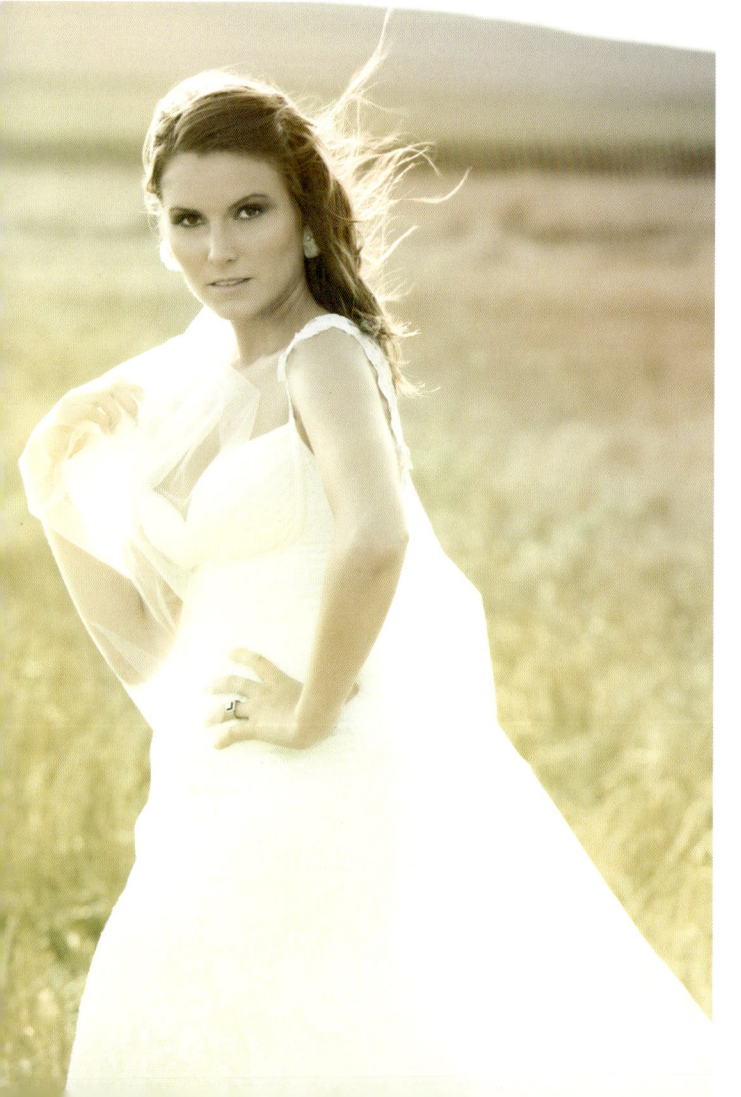

QUICK LOOK	
CAMERA	Nikon D3s
LENS	Nikkor 70–200mm f/2.8G ED VR II
MODE	A
ISO	100
SHUTTER	$^1/_{500}$ + $^2/_3$ EV
APERTURE	f/2.8
LIGHTING	No artificial light or modification

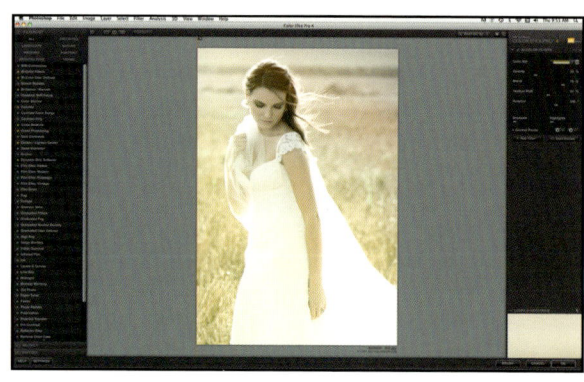

Left: An alternate pose from the session. **Above:** The Nik Software Color Efex Pro interface.

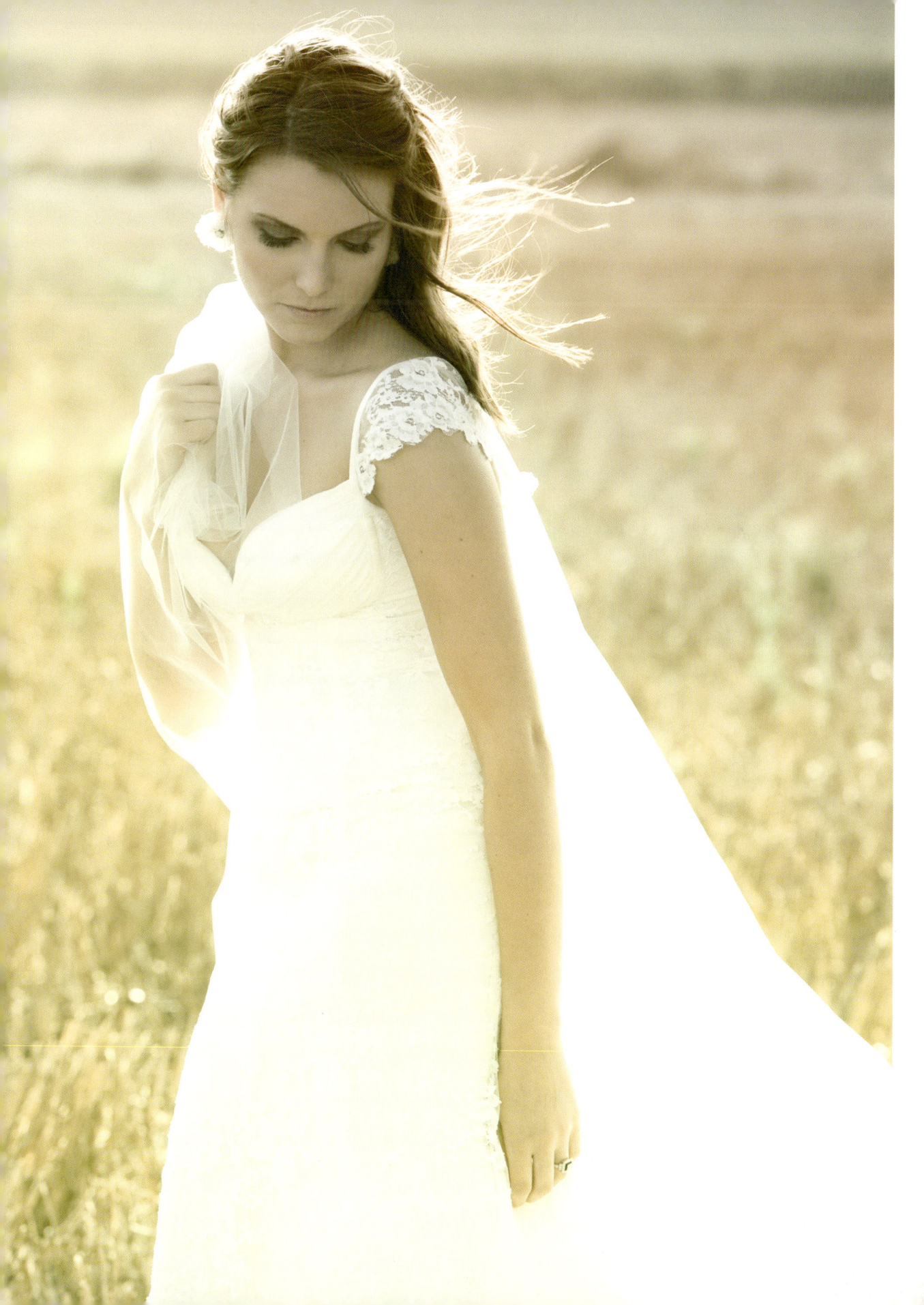

53. FASHION-INSPIRED SHOTS

My photographic style is very influenced by the fashion industry. I subscribe to all the best women's fashion magazines. There's a lot to be gleaned from looking at the fashion pages: wonderful innovative lighting techniques, trendy posing, and interesting postproduction effects. Granted, we won't always be working with girls that look like supermodels, but you'll be amazed at how stunning the portraits of even an "ordinary" bride can be when you give her a bit of encouragement and a sneak peak at the LCD so she can see how amazing she looks.

For this fashion-inspired image, I wanted a *Sex in the City* look. It seems as if the subject is on a rooftop, showing off her dress and "strutting her stuff." I had photographed the groom in a similar way; this lent continuity to the album.

This image was shot with a lot of flash, in a beauty dish, from the front. My aim was to make the sky as dark as possible to create a strong fashion look and feel. The side lighting was produced with the Ranger RX, which emphasized the texture in the fabric. This is an important approach to photographing clothing.

I used Nik Software's Viveza to embellish the form and shape of the clouds. I also removed the glass panels in the background.

Top: The image, before postproduction work.
Bottom: The position of the beauty dish.

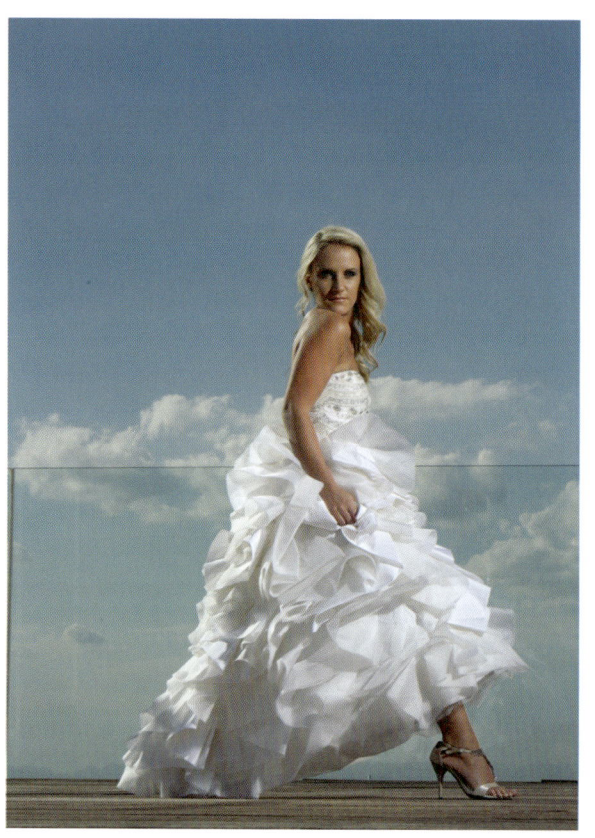

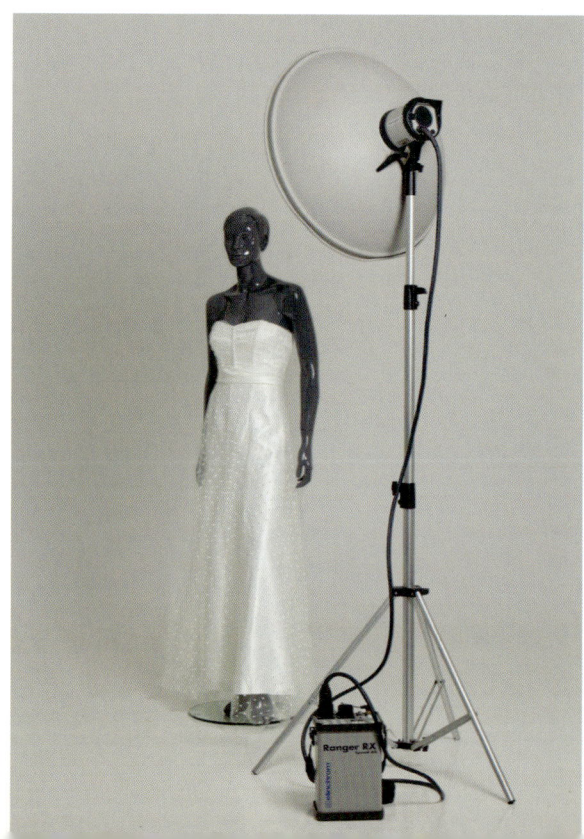

QUICK LOOK

CAMERA	Nikon D3s
LENS	Nikkor 70–200mm f/2.8G ED VR II
MODE	M
ISO	100
SHUTTER	$^1/_{250}$
APERTURE	f/22
LIGHTING	Elinchrom Ranger RX with beauty dish

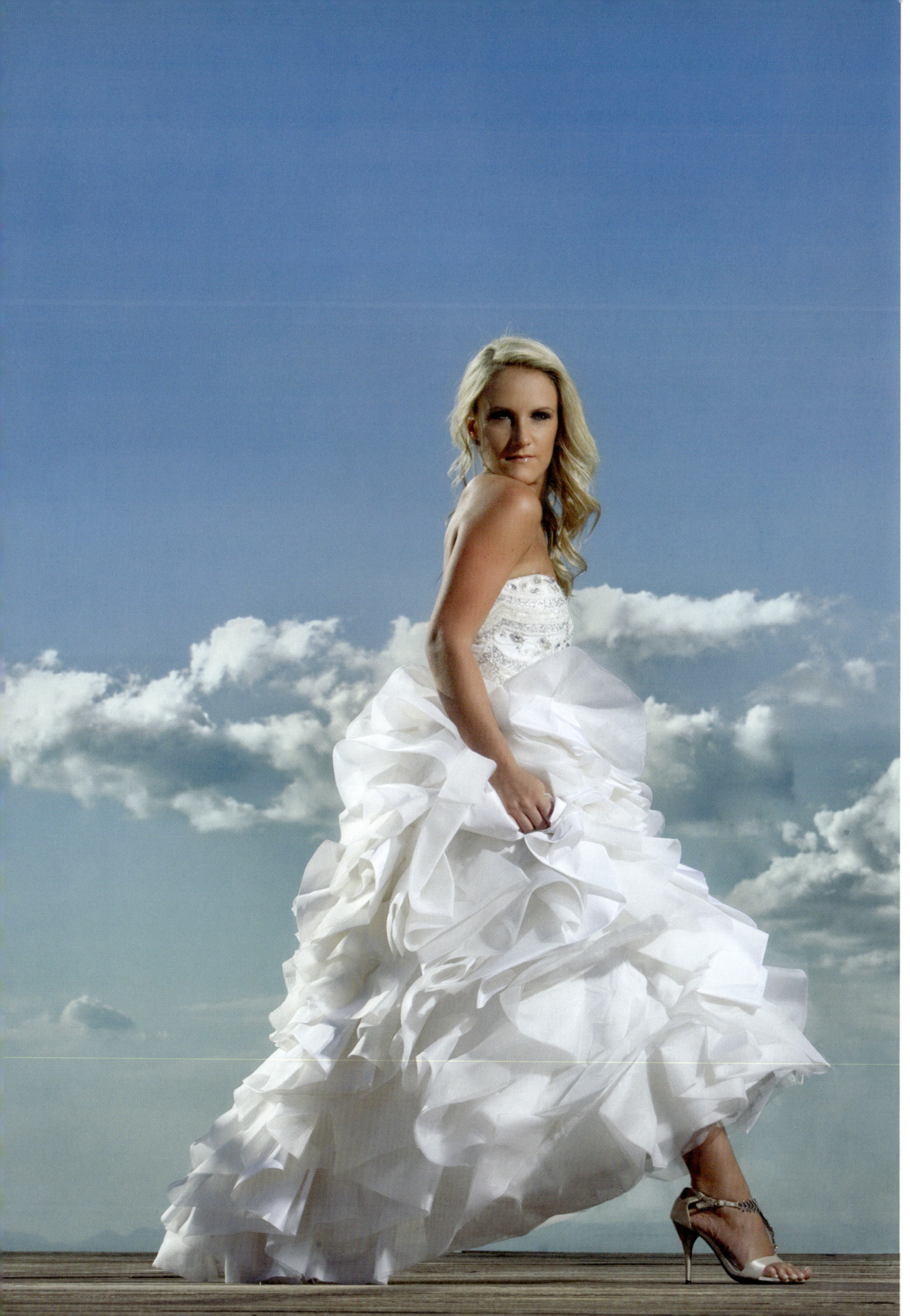

54. SCRIMS

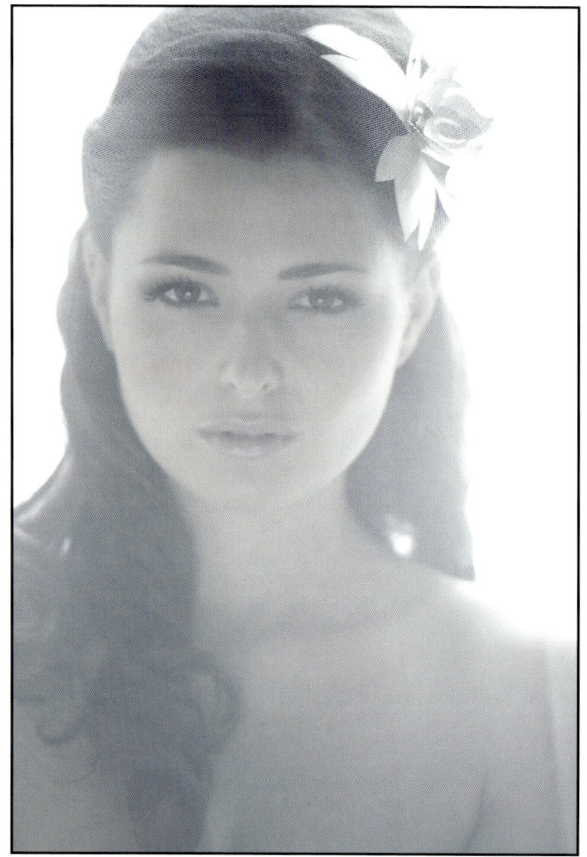

This head-and-shoulders portrait was created using the 5-in-1 reflector's scrim. Removing the reflective material, one is left with only the diffusion material—the scrim. Here, it was placed behind the bride along a nearby window to block plants and trees in the garden and create the perfect softbox surrounding the bride.

Top left: An alternate pose. **Bottom left:** The scrim position.

The subject wore an exquisite lace veil. I kept a small part of this lace detail from another exposure and added it in during postproduction. The rest of the image was blown out for effect.

The image is soft and intimate, and one has the impression that the bride is nude under the veil. Bare shoulder shots are sensual and feminine, and you must ask the bride to cover herself with a towel so that she feels comfortable while you shoot an intimate image such as this.

It is important to get many posing options in a certain location, or from a particular shot. I had the bride look in various directions. Each head movement produces a slightly different mood. For the profile shot, I increased the exposure by 1 stop to compensate for the heavy backlighting.

QUICK LOOK

CAMERA	Nikon D4
LENS	Nikkor 70–200mm f/2.8G ED VR II
MODE	A
ISO	800
SHUTTER	$^1/_{500}$ +1 EV
APERTURE	f/2.8
LIGHTING	Scrim behind the bride

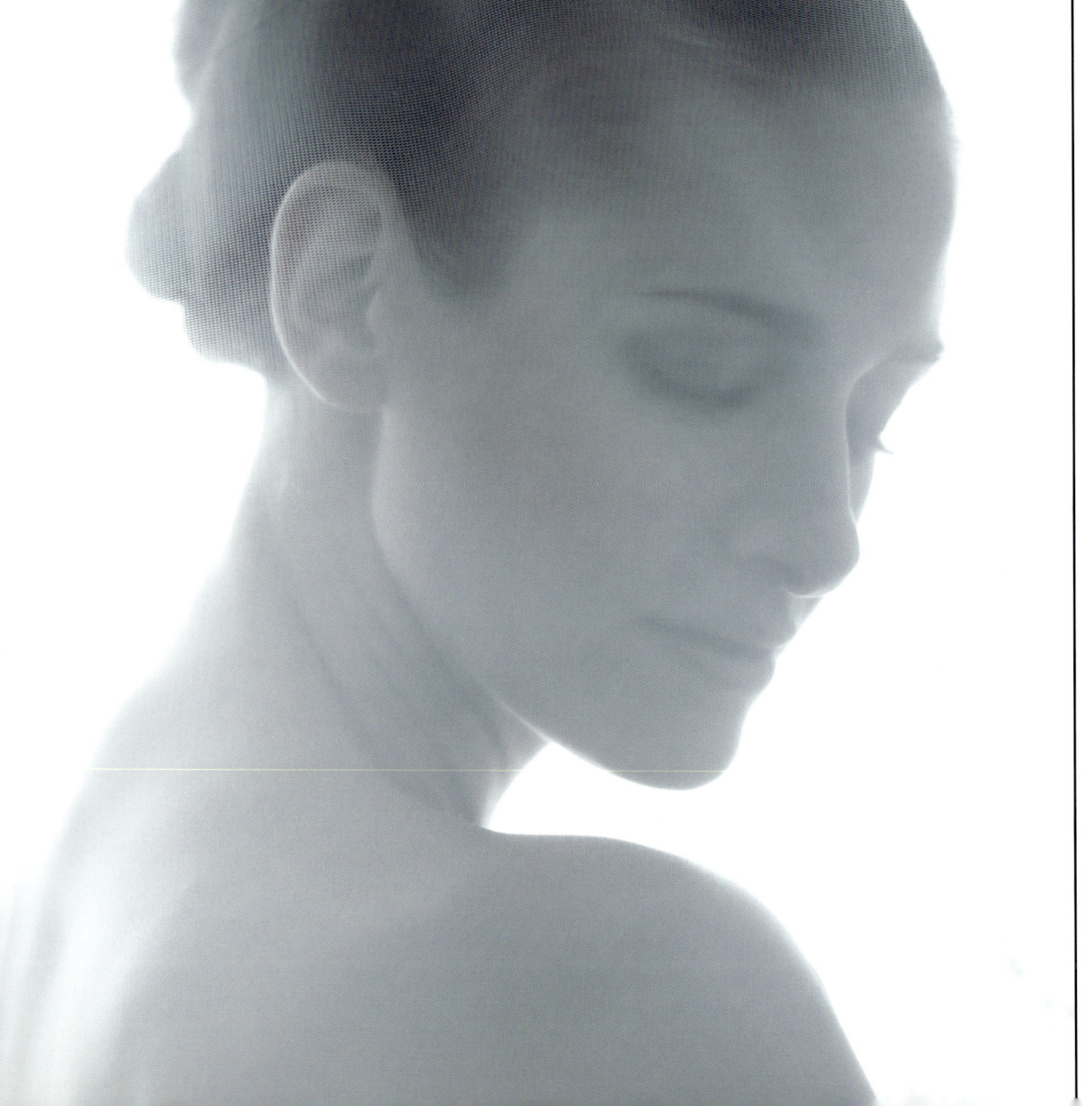

55. SPONTANEITY

Not So Formal

Formal portraits—images in which the bride looks composed, serene, and beautiful—have a high priority in my albums, but I love to balance them with shots that are not entirely formal.

This portrait of a bride captured in the midst of a laugh is an example of such an image. Portraits like these reveal an inner warmth and happiness and are always pleasing to viewers.

Lighting and Exposure

This image was created in the bride's apartment as she was getting ready. I closed the door to her bedroom and placed her in the hallway, pointing the external strobe, the Elinchrom Ranger Quadra, toward the door. This produced a wonderfully bright light source from behind the bride, and the light bounced off of all the white

Left: An alternate pose. **Right:** The flash position.

walls along the length of the passage. I love the way the light is enveloping her; it is lovely and soft because it was bounced off the bedroom door. If I had pointed the light directly at her, the background would have been dark because there would not have been any light landing on the bedroom door. As you can see, there is quite a bit of flare coming around her face, which I really like, as it gives the ethereal impression of a perfume ad. Because there was no light coming from the front, I had to increase my ISO so that the bride's skin was correctly exposed.

QUICK LOOK

CAMERA	Nikon D4
LENS	Nikkor 70–200mm f/2.8G ED VR II
MODE	A
ISO	2000
SHUTTER	$^1/_{160}$
APERTURE	f/2.8
LIGHTING	Elinchrom Ranger RX Quadra

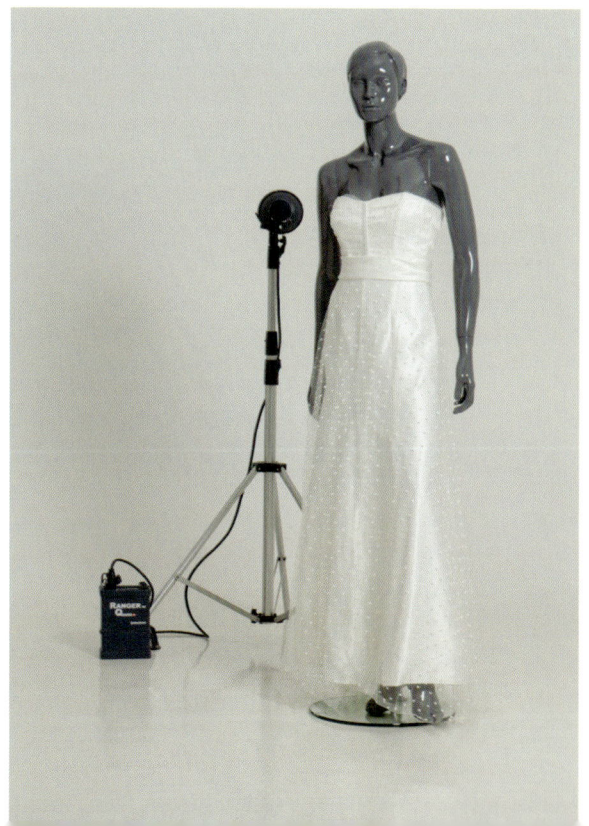

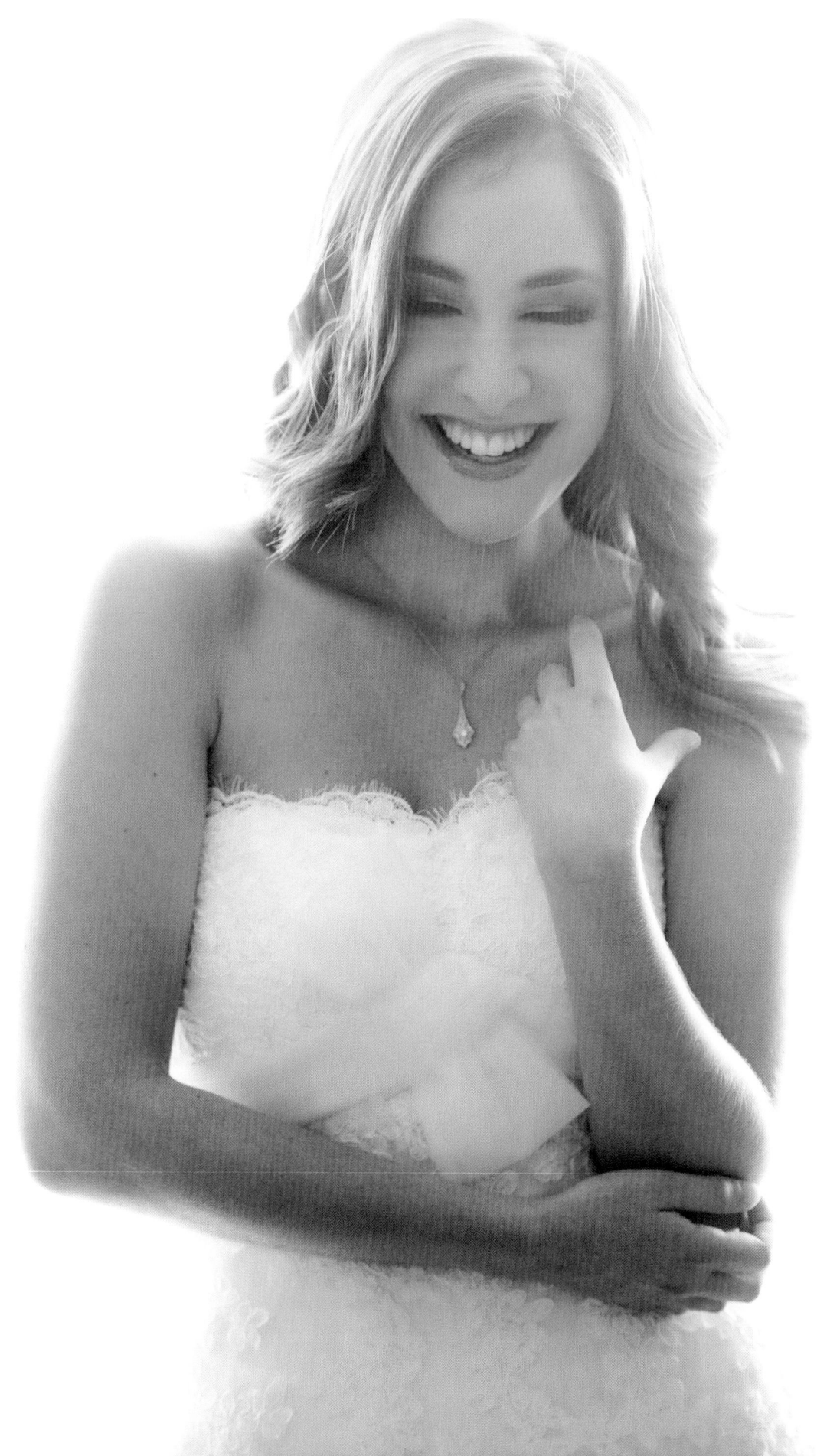

56. LUMINOUS

Déjà Vu

This image was shot in the same hallway as the previous image, using the same setup. The strobe was pointed toward the closed bedroom door, producing lots of bright light bouncing off the white walls of the long passage.

In the previous image, the bride was not touching the wall with any part of her body, and this gave the effect of the light wrapping around her. In this image, however, I positioned the bride so that she used the wall as a prop to lean against, resting just the top of her back near the shoulder blades and extending her body quite far so as to let a lot of light through behind her. This created an impression of depth in the image. This position also gave the bride's body an interesting, sultry shape that is very much inspired by the poses one would see in *Vogue, Vanity Fair,* or other upscale fashion glossies.

Left: The flash position. **Right:** An alternate pose.

The lighting technique I employed is also very much influenced by those high-end fashion magazines, where there is a huge trend toward backlighting and desaturated images, which have a rather magical, luminous feel.

A Second Image

In the supporting image (below left), the bride's pose is self-embracing, which I feel creates a perfume-ad feel. I once again exposed for the bride's true skin tone. The image was desaturated in post-production to emphasize the angelic mood and feel.

QUICK LOOK	
CAMERA	Nikon D4
LENS	Nikkor 70–200mm f/2.8G ED VR II
MODE	A
ISO	2000
SHUTTER	$^1/_{160}$
APERTURE	f/2.8
LIGHTING	Elinchrom Ranger RX Quadra

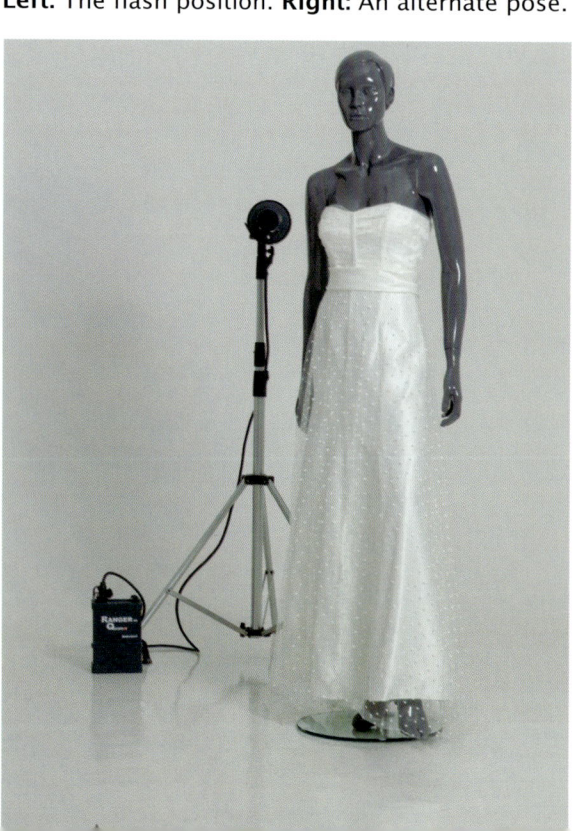

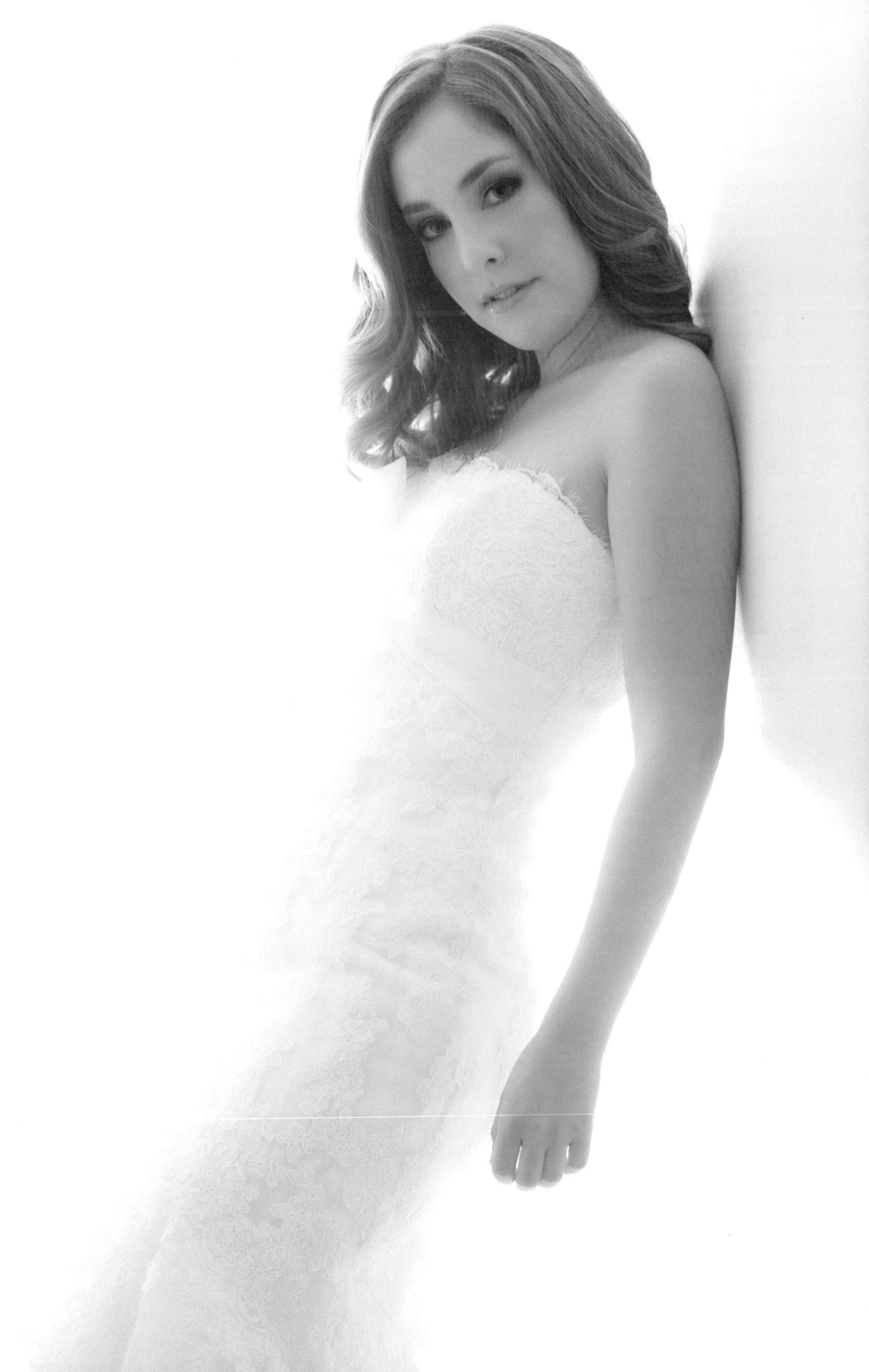

57. A WESTERN FEEL

Sometimes we look at an image and perceive color and texture in the background but are not sure what has created it. This image was made in a stable. The bride was standing in front of a beautiful white horse, which was there to provide a background of color, texture, and form only.

QUICK LOOK

CAMERA	Nikon D4
LENS	Nikkor 70–200mm f/2.8G ED VR II
MODE	A
ISO	200
SHUTTER	$^1/_{250}$ +$^2/_3$ EV
APERTURE	f/2.8
LIGHTING	Lastolite 5-in-1 collapsible reflector

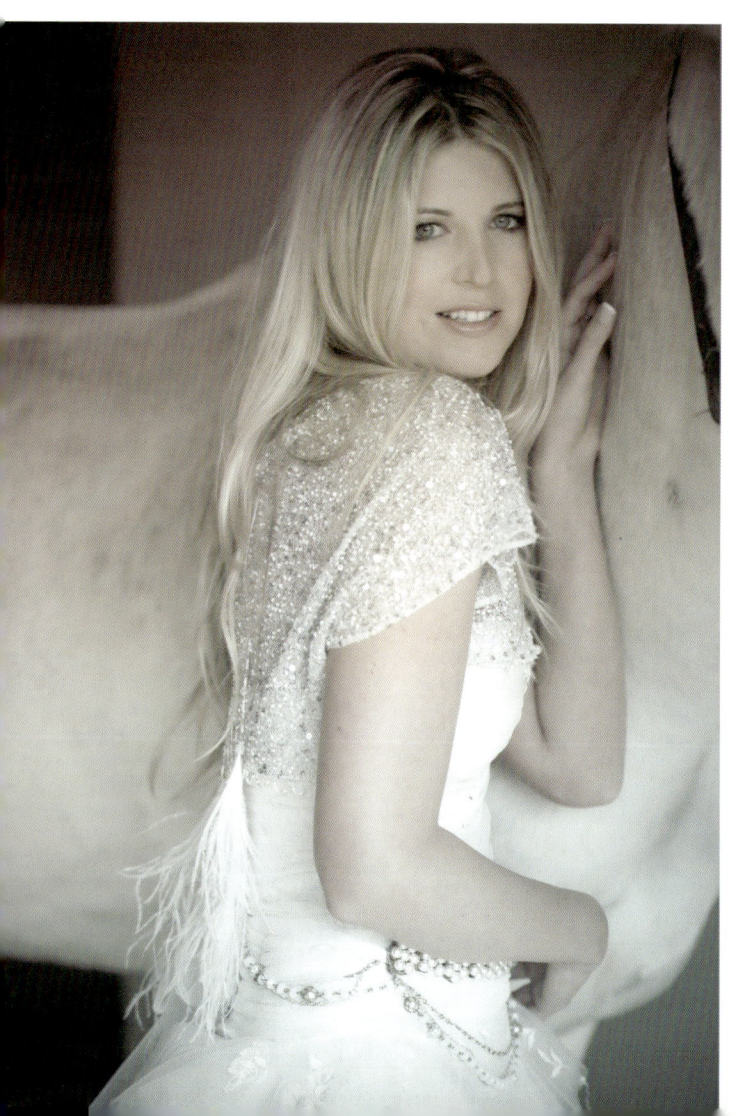

Pose and Lighting

In keeping with her loosely styled, long hair, the bride's pose was very relaxed and casual—she had one shoulder swung to the back, with her head straight-on and her gaze very direct to the camera.

This image was shot using only natural light, which came through the front door of the stables. There was a lot of white in the frame (the white horse and the wedding dress), so I had to overexpose the image by $^2/_3$ stop. The image was shot on f/2.8 to get the ideal shallow depth of field so that the horse is out of focus and is implied, not obvious, in the background.

Postproduction

The bride had a particular color scheme running through the wedding, and I took advantage of this by using the same colors in postproduction. Using Nik Software's Color Efex Pro, I added a bi-color cast, with a magenta hue coming from the top-left corner and a blue cast emanating from the bottom right-hand corner.

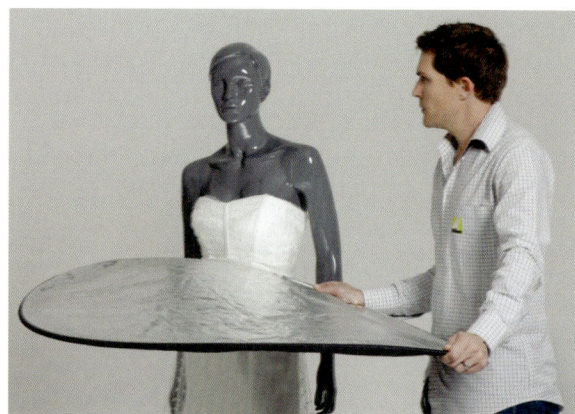

Left: An alternate pose. **Above:** The reflector position.

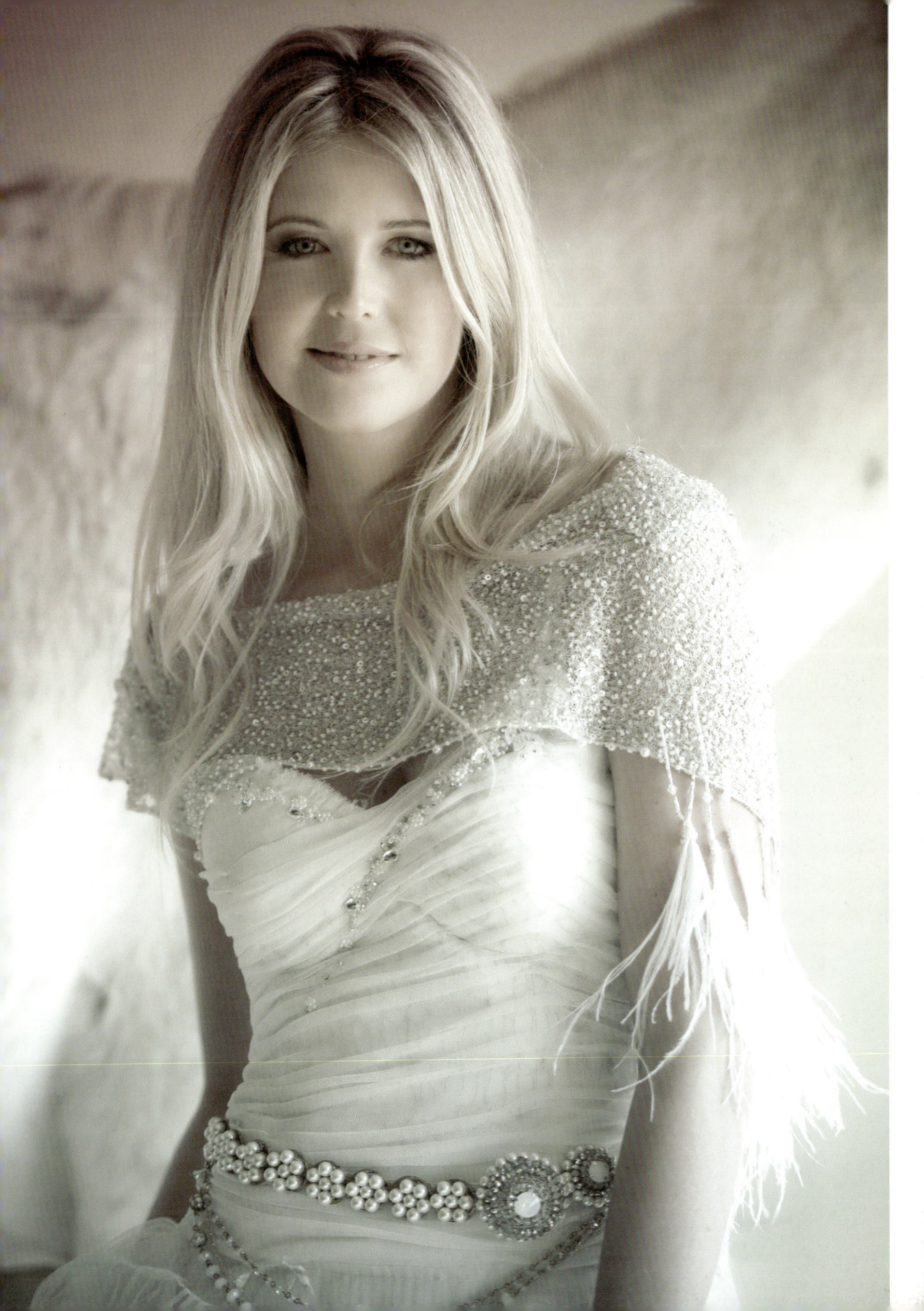

58. DROWN THE GOWN

The "day after" shoots tend to be adventurous these days, with many brides opting for a "drown the gown" session. I think it's a refreshing attitude, and it has allowed me to create some wonderfully creative wedding portraits, the likes of which I would never be able to shoot on the day of the wedding.

This image was shot in the early morning on the East Coast of Africa, where the sun rises over the ocean. The strong ambient backlighting highlighted the bride's shoulders and arms. With no ambient light falling onto the front of the bride, I illuminated this side with the Elinchrom Ranger RX. For a versatile method of use, I rigged my Manfrotto 680 monopod with a small spigot to attach the Ranger RX flash head, effectively turning it into a light stand. My assistant was then able to hold the system on his hip and move around freely to achieve optimal lighting. Wanting to freeze the action of the waves breaking over the rocks, I shot at $^{1}/_{250}$ second. Note how the frozen pattern of the breaking wave matches the lace detail on the bride's petticoat, and the billowing dress emulates the ripples of the water in the front. The light from the external strobe is balanced with the ambient light of the rising sun; therefore, it is not heavily underexposed in terms of the backlighting.

QUICK LOOK

CAMERA	Nikon D4
LENS	Nikkor 70–200mm f/2.8G ED VR II
MODE	M
ISO	100
SHUTTER	$^{1}/_{250}$
APERTURE	f/18
LIGHTING	Elinchrom Ranger RX

Left: Get your light test done, whilst the waves are out! **Right:** The strobe position.

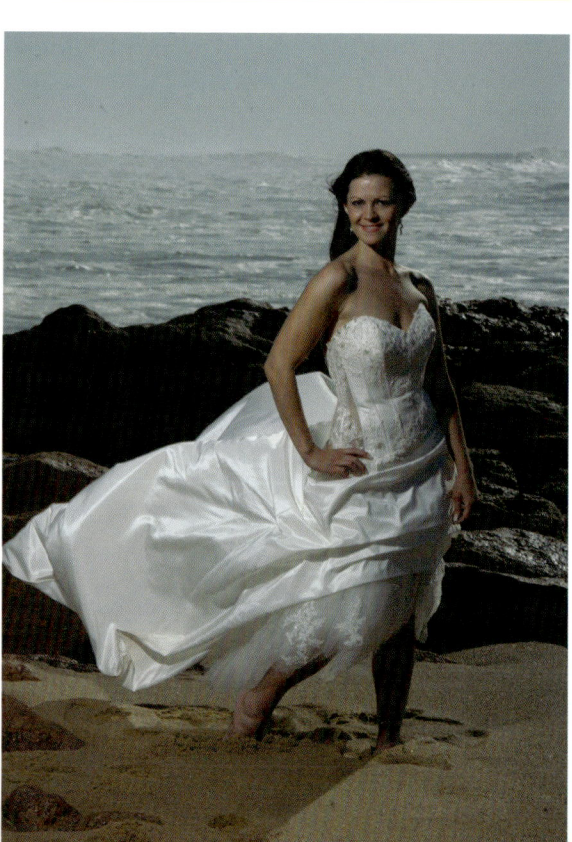
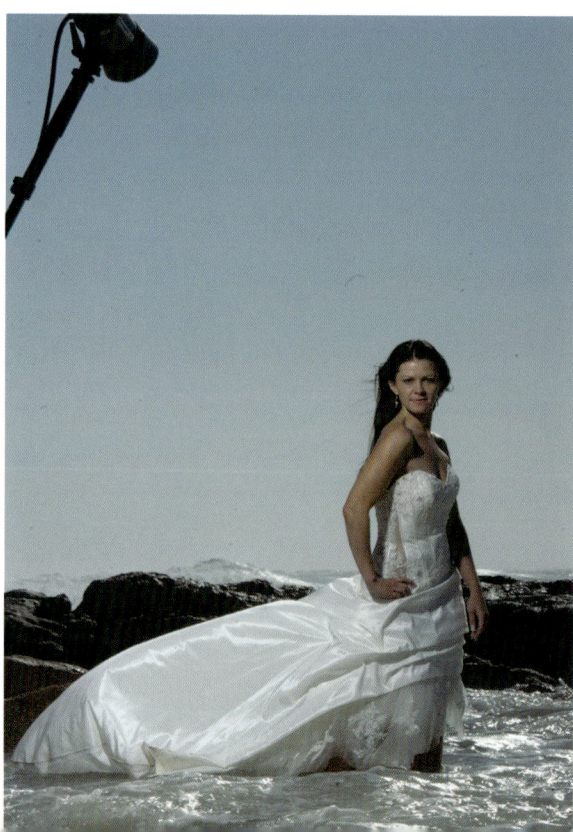

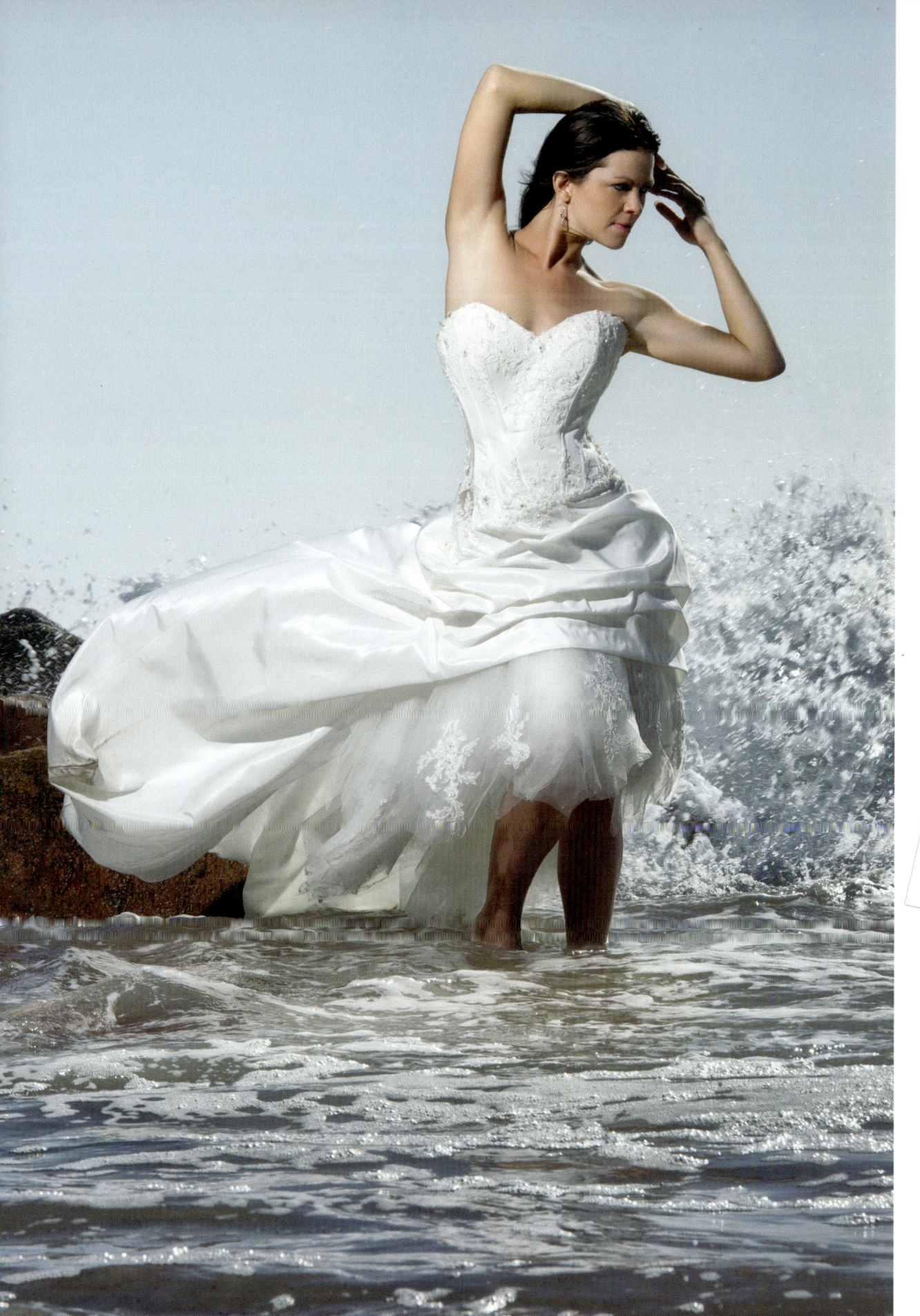

59. PERSPECTIVE

Flexibility

Using different perspectives when one is shooting produces a greater variety of portraits, which makes the wedding album that much more interesting. When it comes to getting all the angles and perspectives that I want, I have to resort to being rather flexible. Whether it be lying flat on the dusty floor or climbing high onto a small ledge, I don't worry about how I may look, as long as I get the shot. Lying down for this image, I was able to pick up on the reflection of the bride's dress in the shiny marble tiles of the patio at her parents' home. The angle of view also gives us a lovely full-length portrait, showing off the dress to its full potential.

The wind was blowing slightly, which lifted the veil just enough to give the shot a bit of movement, and the bride's positioning of her arm and hand-holding the veil added to the elegance of the image.

Bounced Light

The lighting was completely ambient. I never had to manipulate the lighting in any way whatsoever. This was due to the white shiny marble floors, the clean white wall behind her, and the very bright sunlight that bounced off these highly reflective surfaces. Even though the bride was posed in the shade on a patio, the reflective light falling on her provided sufficient illumination.

QUICK LOOK

CAMERA	Nikon D4
LENS	Nikkor 70–200mm f/2.8G ED VR II
MODE	A
ISO	100
SHUTTER	$^1/_{250}$
APERTURE	f/2.8
LIGHTING	No artificial light or manipulation

Left and right: Two alternate poses.

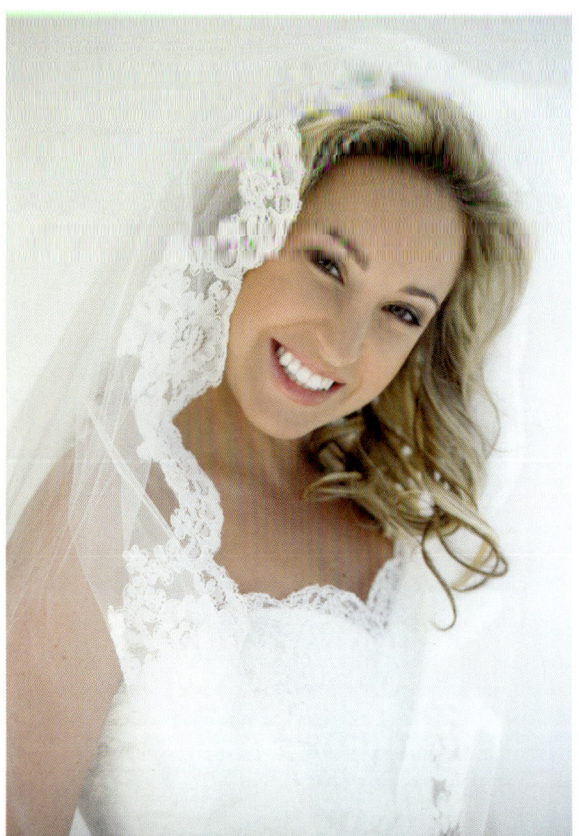

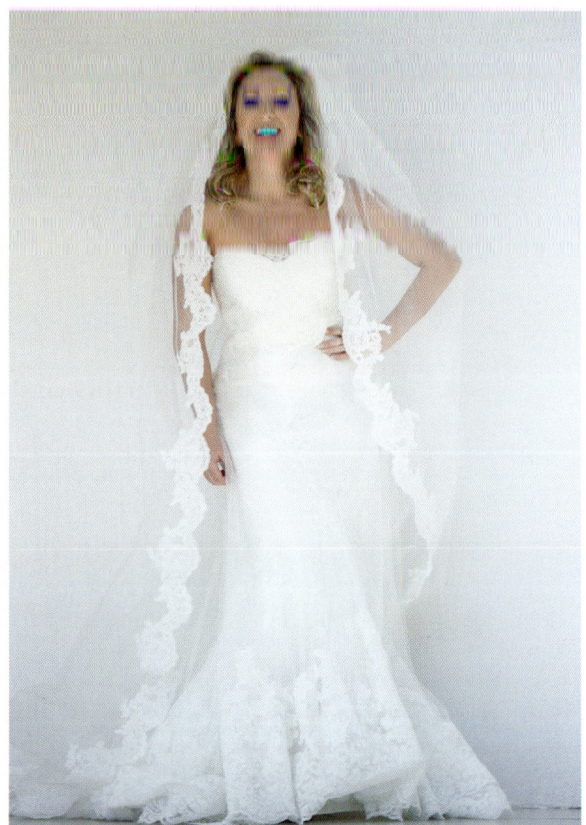

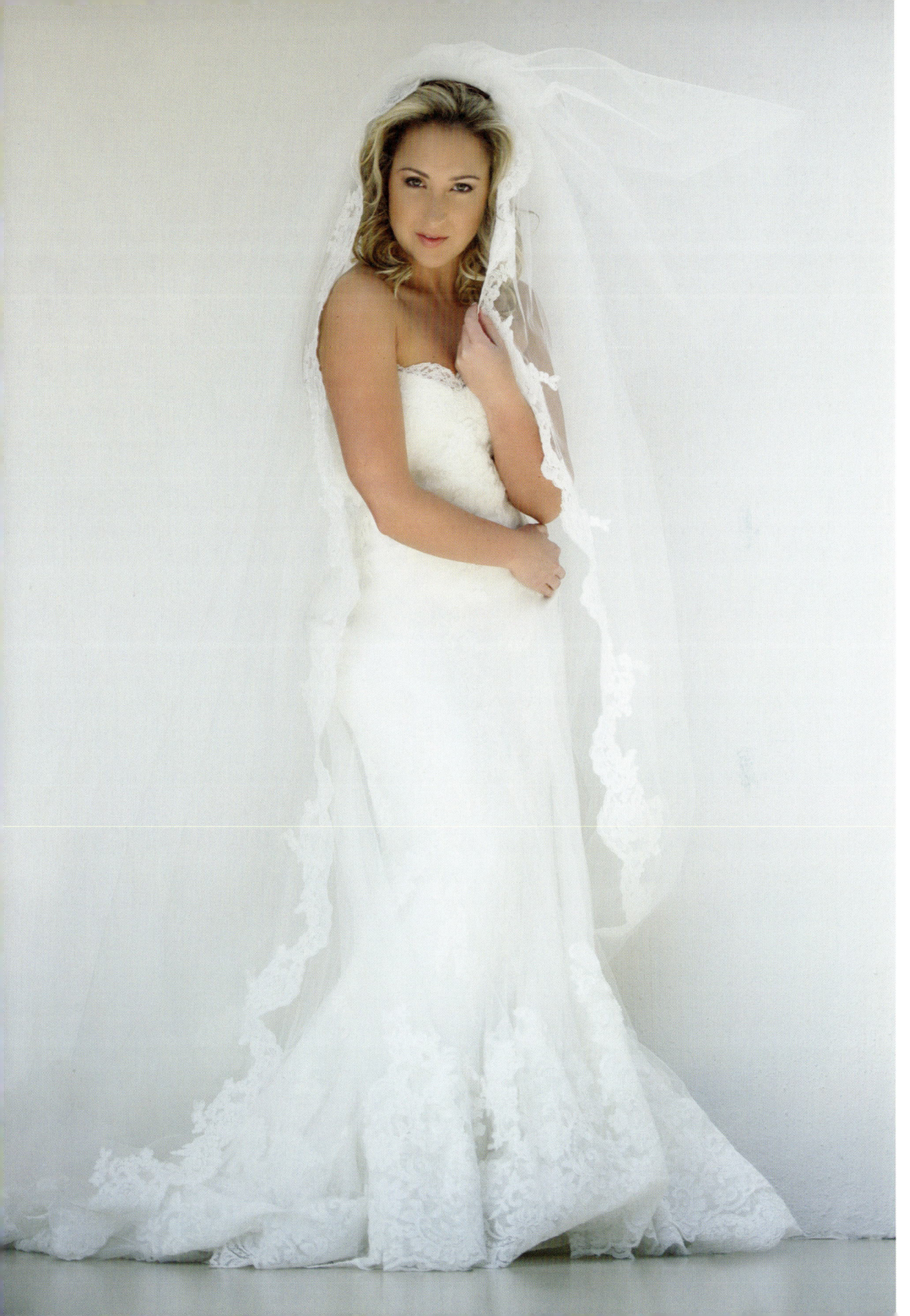

60. AN URBAN SCENE

Location

I love a location that offers a strong contrast to the bridal innocence and elegance. It adds an edge to the photos, and they certainly have a modern editorial look and feel to them.

This area of town made us a bit nervous, but with a large group of men in the bridal party keeping a lookout, we managed to get the shots that we were after. I loved the concrete and steel masculinity of the flyovers. I also loved the urban feel of the colorful graffiti; the bright colors made an excellent contrast to the bride's white dress.

Lighting

I placed the Elinchrom Ranger RX behind the bride to provide the bright backlighting that highlighted her veil. I like the way that the external strobe created lines of shadows and highlights in the foreground.

My assistant held the 5-in-1 reflector to the bride's right and bounced some of the strobe light back onto her from the front, as you can see from the highlight on the bride's cheek, which adds a bit of form to her face.

Composition

I positioned the bride under a flyover and pulled her veil out to follow the arch of the bridge, creating two curved parallel lines. These were made more obvious by the ambient light catching the side of the bridge—light that matches the intensity of the illumination on the veil.

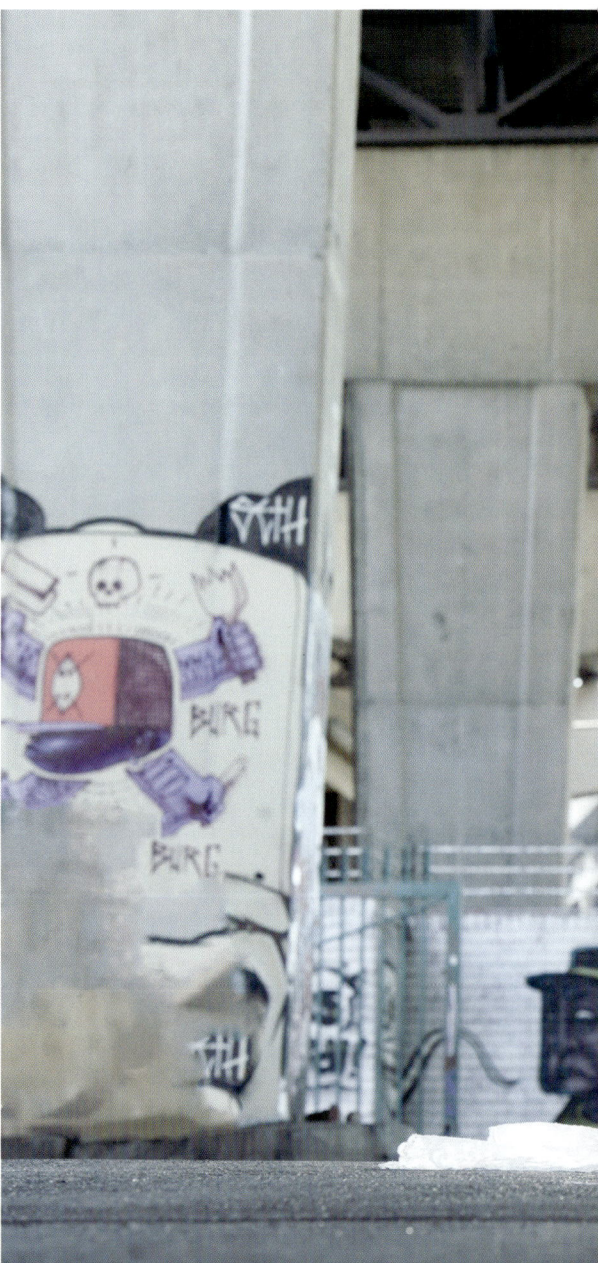

> **QUICK LOOK**
> **CAMERA** Nikon D4
> **LENS** Nikkor 70–200mm f/2.8G ED VR II
> **MODE** M
> **ISO** 800
> **SHUTTER** $^1/_{160}$
> **APERTURE** f/9
> **LIGHTING** Elinchrom Ranger RX and Lastolite 5-in-1 reflector

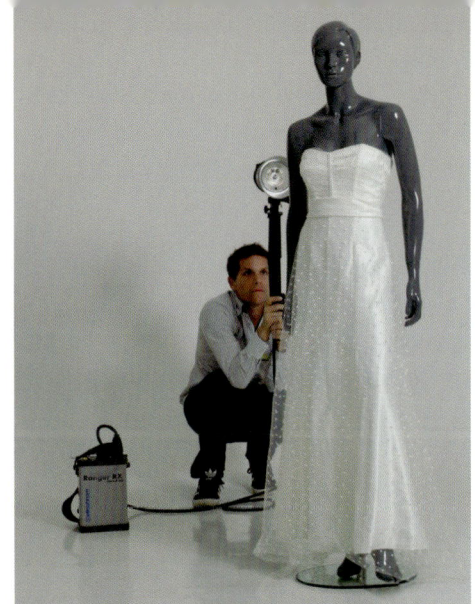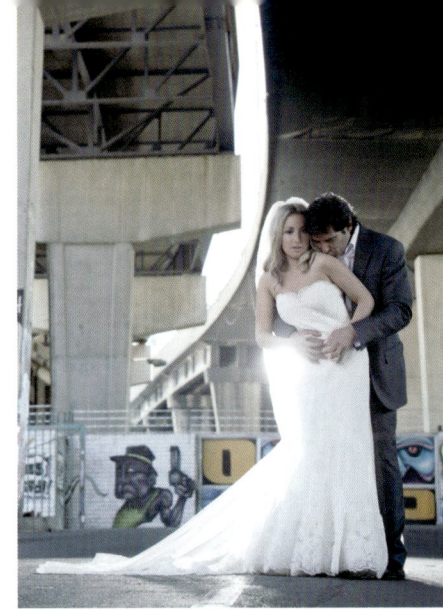

Right: The strobe position. **Far right:** An image of the bridal couple made at the same location.

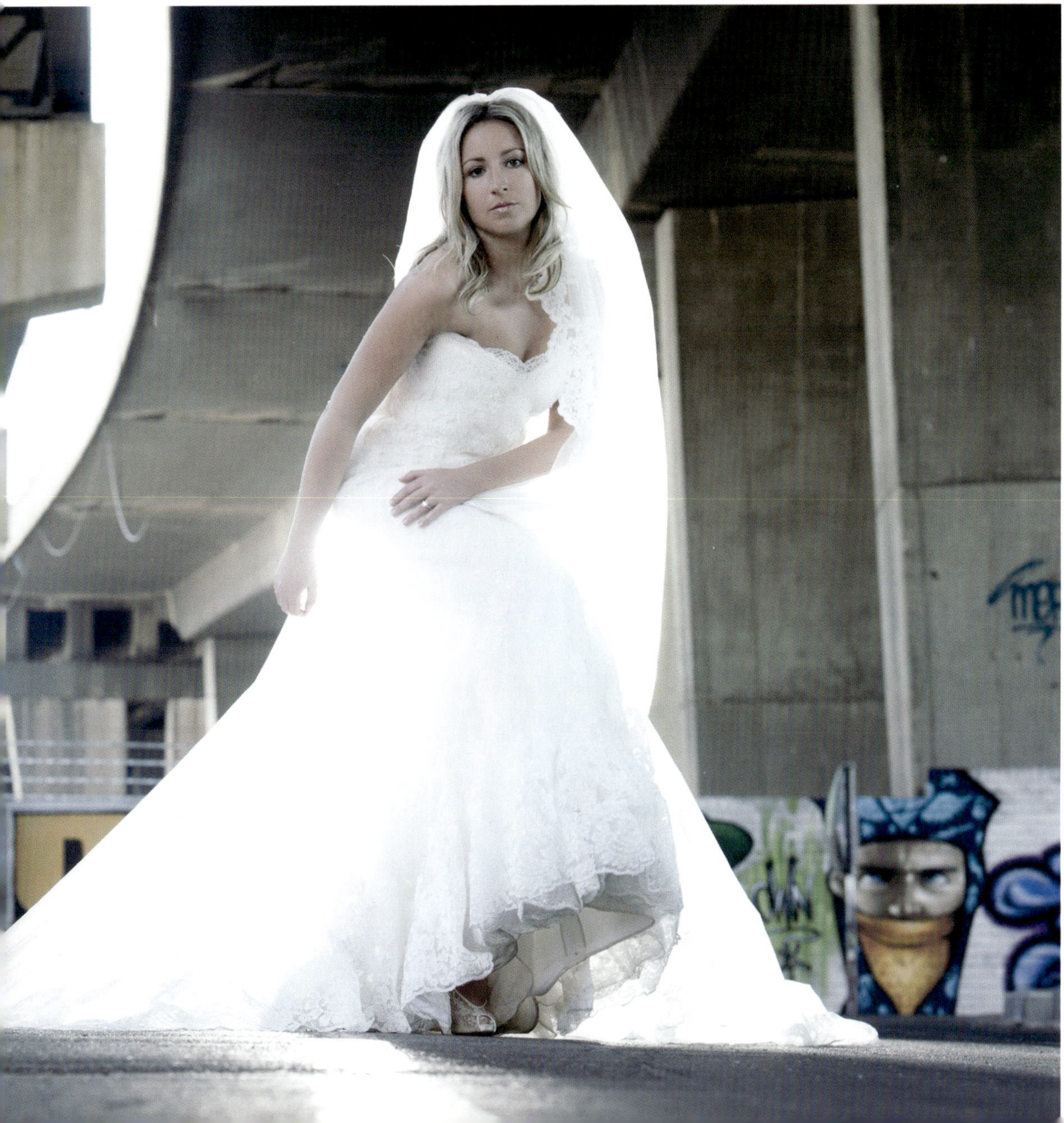

61. SULTRY

This image was shot at midday in a rough part of town. As you can see from the strong highlights on the subject's shoulder and coming through her hair, the light was harsh.

While I was shooting, someone came out of the building we were standing next to and opened a security gate. I decided to shoot through the metal structure with a Nikkor 85mm 1.4 G lens wide open at f/1.4. The bars of the gate are so out of focus that you can't quite see what is creating the flare circles and the shadowed lines falling on the bride's dress. The wide aperture gave me the ideal separation between the foreground and background and also created a hazy backdrop that adds depth and interest to the shot.

I asked the bride to give me a sultry, moody pose, which I felt was in keeping with the location. As a result, she looks sexy and empowered.

There was no manipulation of the light from the front. I exposed purely for her skin tone, and because of the harsh sunlight, there are strong highlights along her arms.

I used Nik Software's Color Efex Pro to add a purple color cast in the top right-hand corner of the image, and a pastel pink cast was introduced in the bottom left-hand corner.

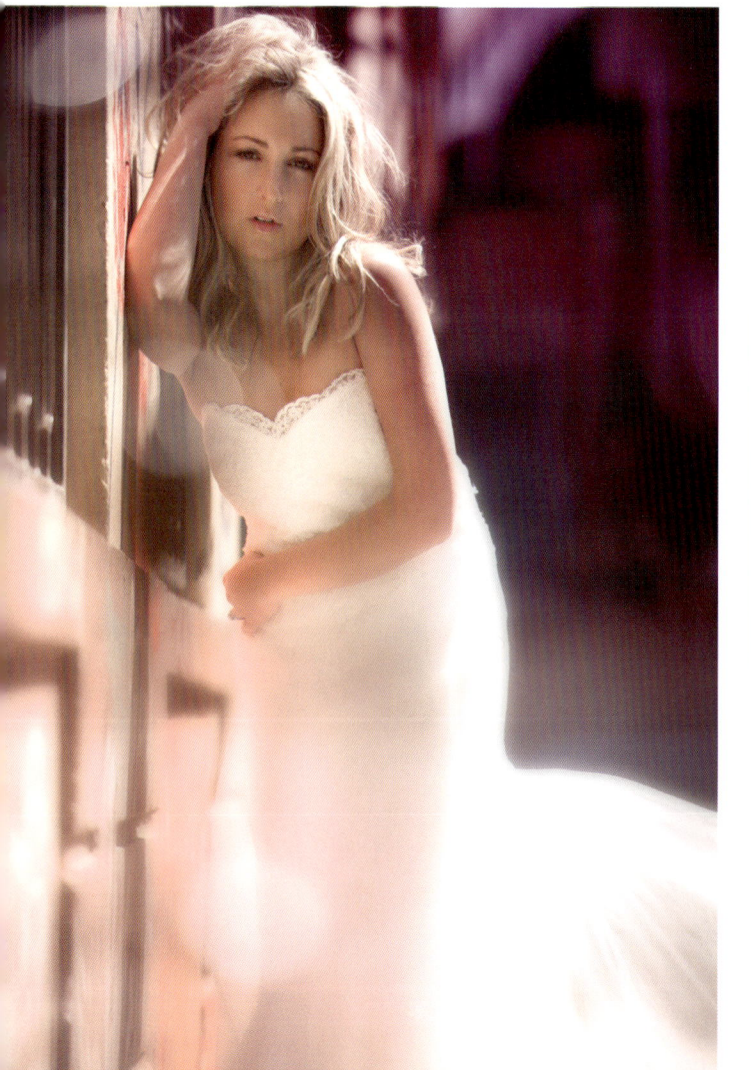

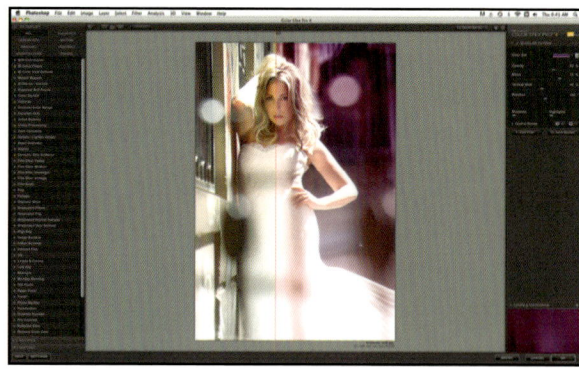

QUICK LOOK	
CAMERA	Nikon D4
LENS	Nikkor 85mm f/1.4G
MODE	A
ISO	100
SHUTTER	$^1/_{500}$ +1$^2/_3$EV
APERTURE	f/1.4
LIGHTING	No artificial light or manipulation

Left: An alternate pose. **Above:** This screen shot provides a glimpse of the image before the color effects were fully in place.

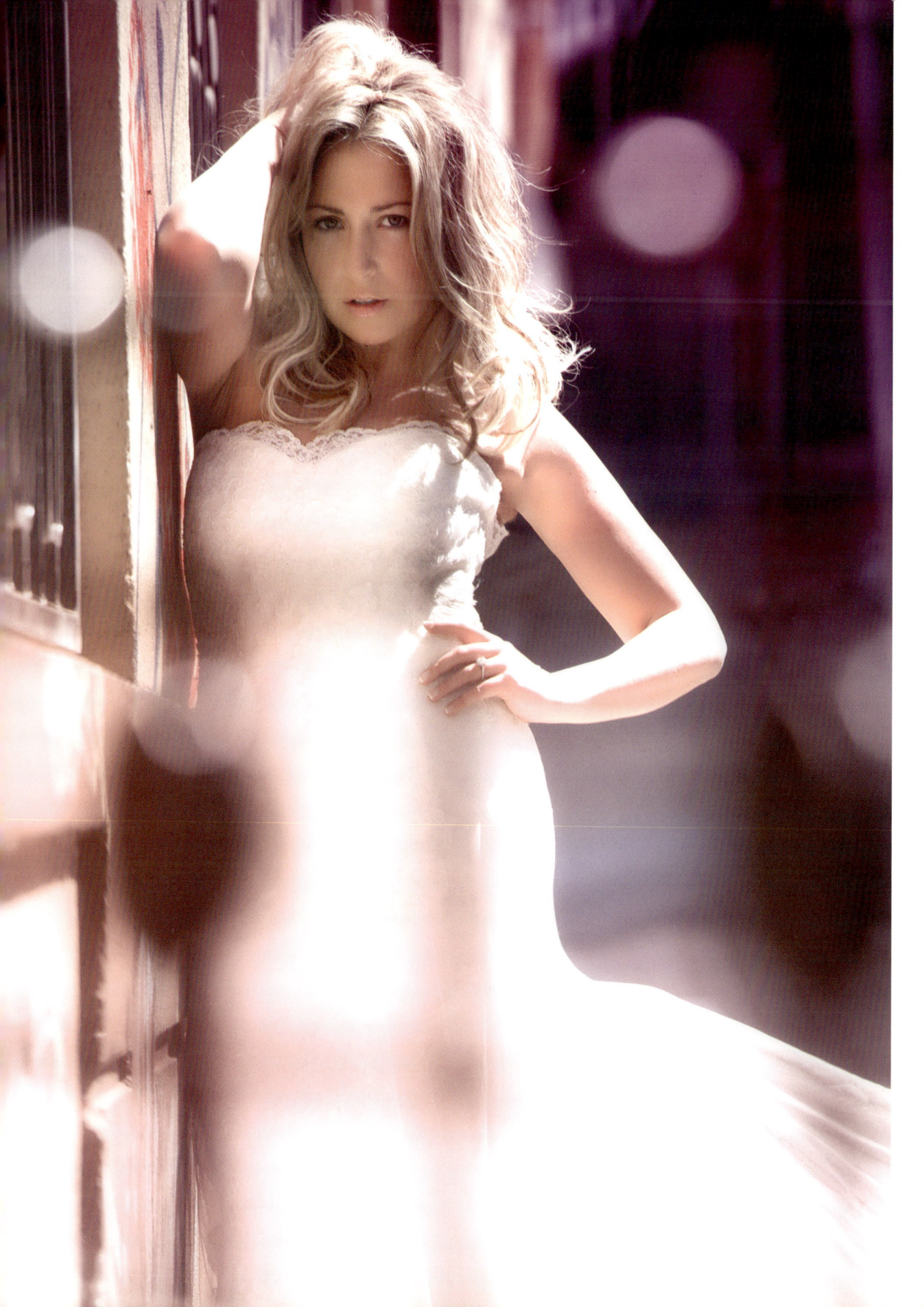

62. EXAGGERATED POSES

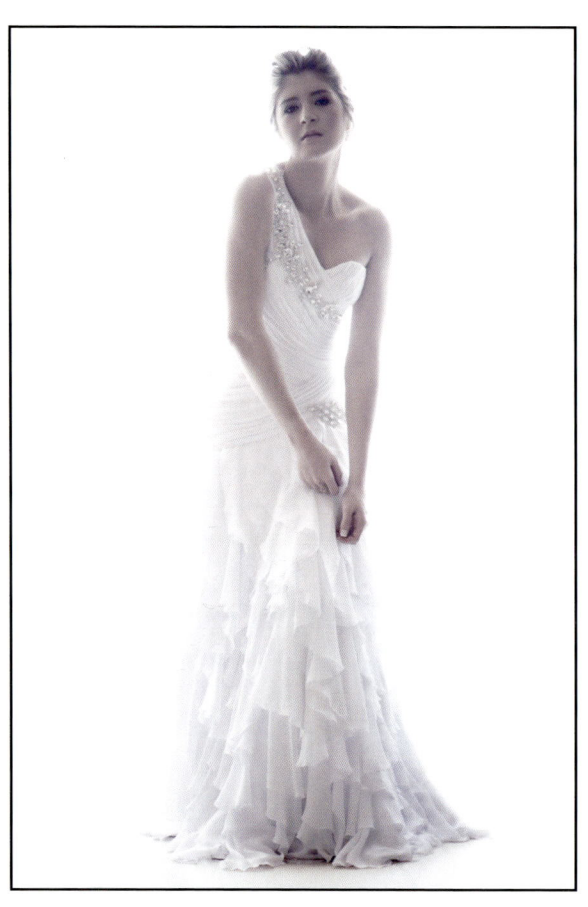

A Modern Trend

I try to get a variety of full-length poses. Often, this comes down to making small changes in the subject's body position. Here, I asked the bride to drop her left shoulder substantially. This gave the body a lot of shape and interest. I then asked her to bend her right knee so that it crossed in front of her left knee. This made the pose a lot more comfortable and raised her right hip, creating a sensual S-shaped curve to her body. These very exaggerated poses are very much a modern trend. I find them appealing.

The shot was made in front of a white net curtain, with the ambient light flooding in from the sliding door behind. I used an 85mm f/1.4 lens wide open, overexposing the image by three stops. It was very dark inside the room, but I needed to keep the contrast so I could completely blow out what was behind the bride.

Postproduction

I desaturated the image in postproduction and added a slight pink color cast to it.

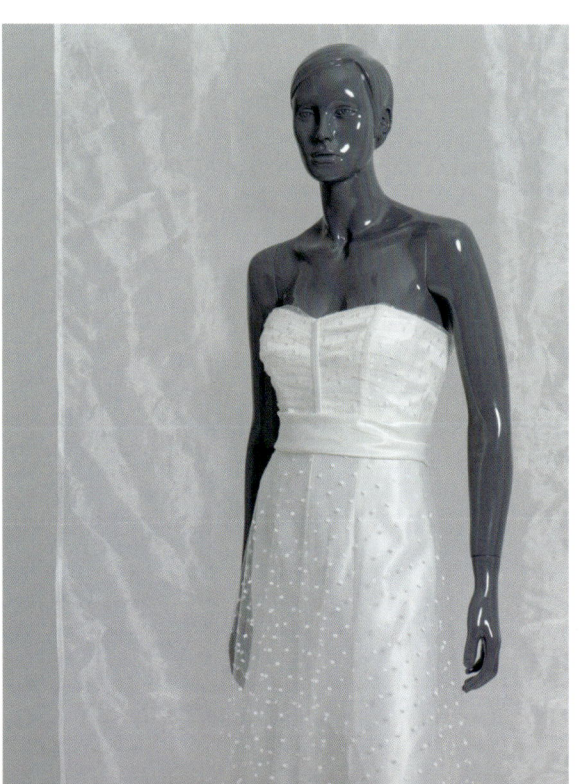

QUICK LOOK	
CAMERA	Nikon D4
LENS	Nikkor 85mm f/1.4G
MODE	A
ISO	800
SHUTTER	$^1/_{200}$ +3EV
APERTURE	f/1.4
LIGHTING	No additional lighting or manipulation

Top: Another dramatic pose. **Bottom:** The light-diffusing fabric position.

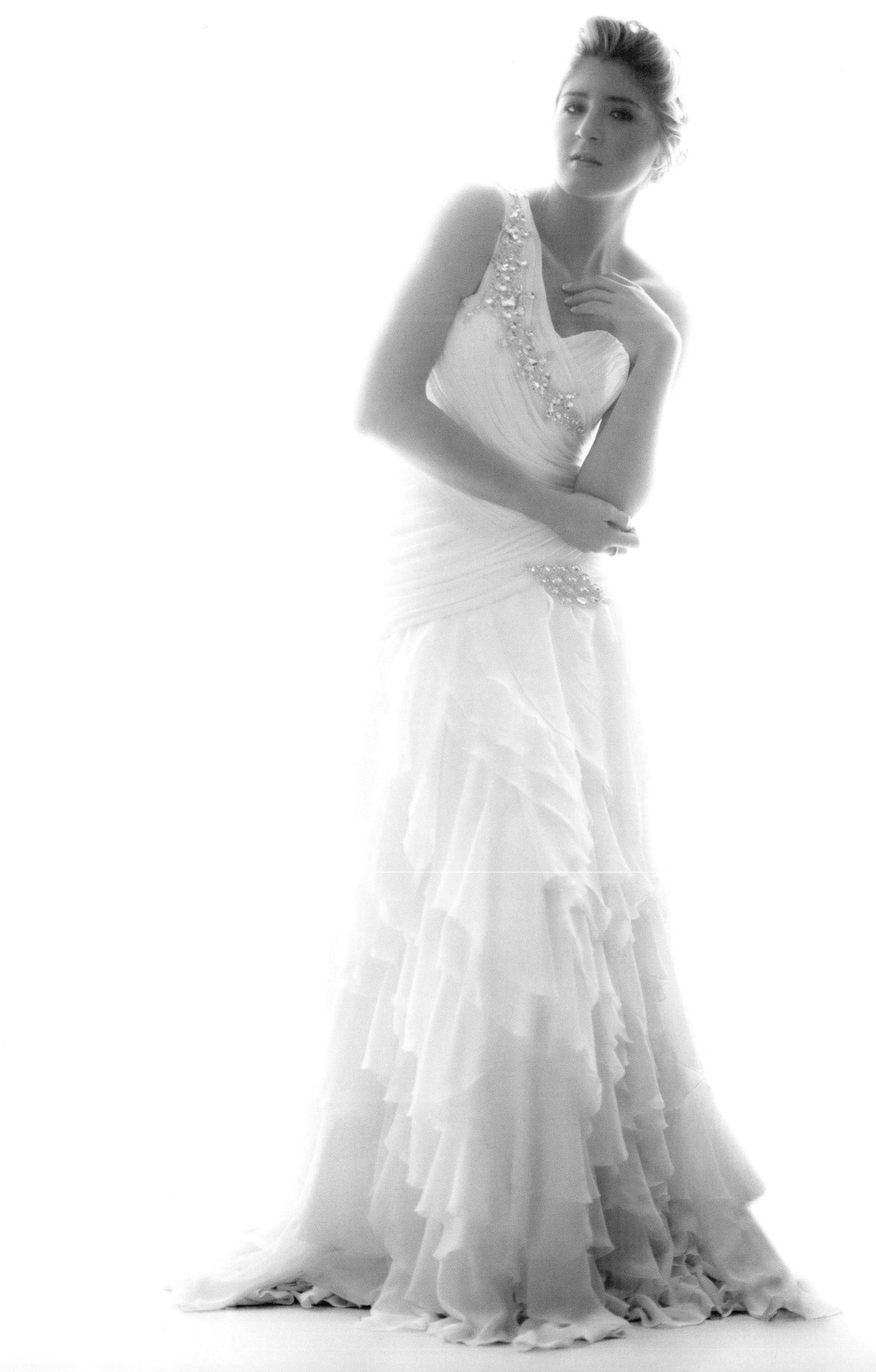

63. STRIKING SETTINGS

The Warehouse

Some locations deserve to dominate an image. Whether it be a large expanse of sky, a sand dune, a field of flowers, or an interesting building, you can create a highly effective image by placing your subject on a rule-of-thirds line with a lot of dominant space around or in front of her. This will only be successful if the background is not too busy; if it is, it will draw attention away from the subject, and the image will lose its impact.

This old warehouse was so appealing that even the decrepit, rusty steps leading to a loading area didn't deter me from getting the shot! I tested the old staircase to ensure it was safe, then positioned the bride to the right of the round window. As luck would have it, there was also a pool of ambient light, falling onto the bride from above, like a spotlight.

My assistant held a 5-in-1 reflector close to the bride to illuminate her from the front and soften the harsh shadows from the overhead light. The brick wall was dark, so the camera's matrix metering system assumed that it needed to add light to the exposure. Therefore, I had to override the exposure by two stops. Nothing was lost in the highlights, but the bricks became darker.

Composition

I positioned the bride at the intersection of the lower third and left hand third of the image. I really like the way she pops out of the image due to the very dark dominant space around her.

Left: The groom was brought into position for an additional look. **Below:** The reflector position.

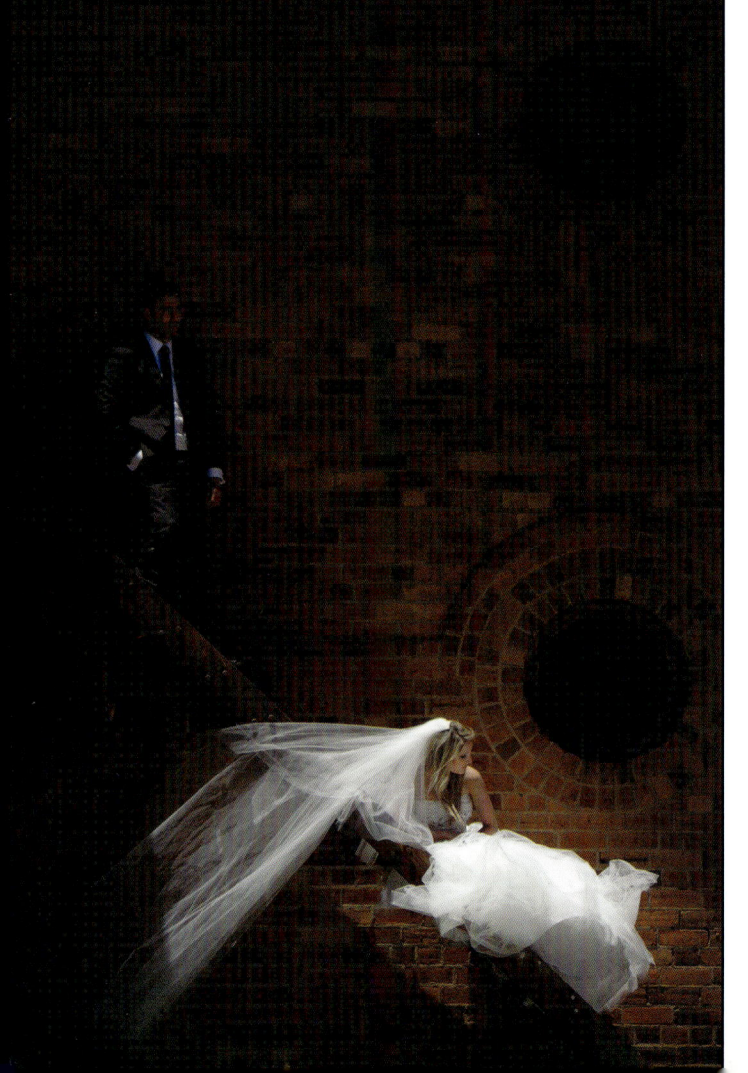

QUICK LOOK	
CAMERA	Nikon D4
LENS	Nikkor 70–200mm f/2.8G ED VR II
MODE	A
ISO	100
SHUTTER	$^1/_{3200}$ –2EV
APERTURE	f/2.8
LIGHTING	Lastolite 5-in-1 collapsible reflector

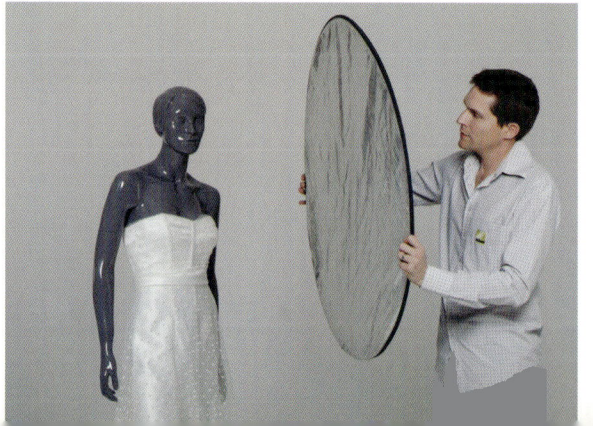

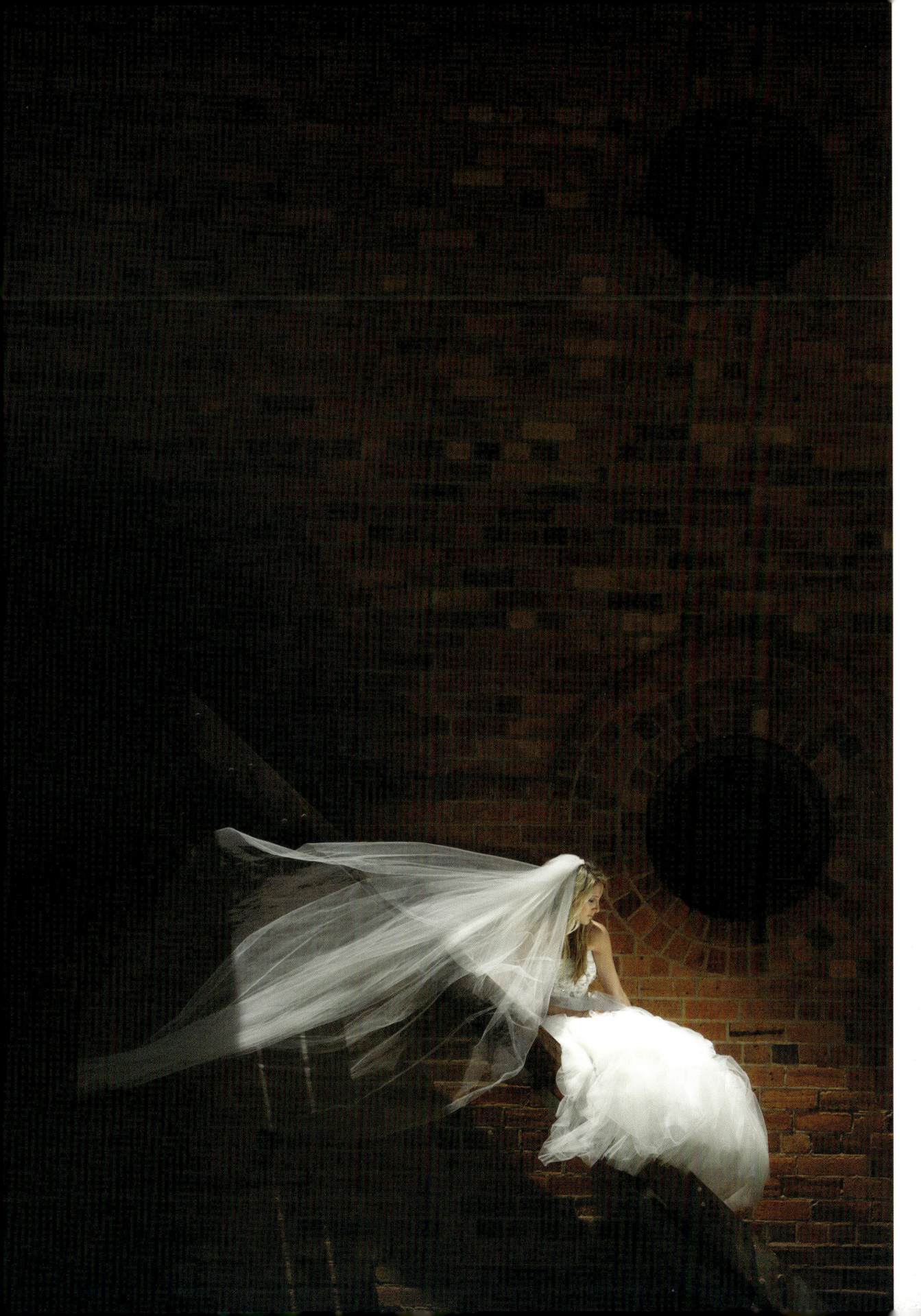

64. FAIRY LIGHTS

This shot was made during one of my wedding workshops. It was made in the evening, not far from my studio. The trees were wrapped in fairy lights for the Christmas season. Wanting to demonstrate just how great the Nikon D4 works in low light, I positioned the bride between the LED fairy-light lit trees, which provided a magical backdrop. There were lots of tiny LED lights around the bride, but there was no light falling on her, so I used an LED video light to illuminate the bride slightly from the front. I didn't want to use a flash because it would have been a different color temperature than the fairy lights.

Standing next to a tree, I shot very close to the fairy lights to get these big, round flares coming into the front of the image, which tied in compositionally to the smaller flares coming from the lights in the trees behind the bride.

Left: An alternate presentation. **Right:** The placement of the LED light.

Postproduction

I used Nik Software's Color Efex Pro to warm up the image and create the mood I was after.

Another Look

The alternate pose shown below was shot a little wider. I asked my assistant to lift the veil behind the bride to create the illusion that it was blowing in the wind. Note the large spray of light on the right-hand side of the image; this was created by a stream of cars driving past as we were shooting the portrait.

QUICK LOOK

CAMERA	Nikon D4
LENS	Nikkor 85mm f/1.4G
MODE	M
ISO	4000
SHUTTER	$^1/_{80}$
APERTURE	f/2
LIGHTING	LED video light

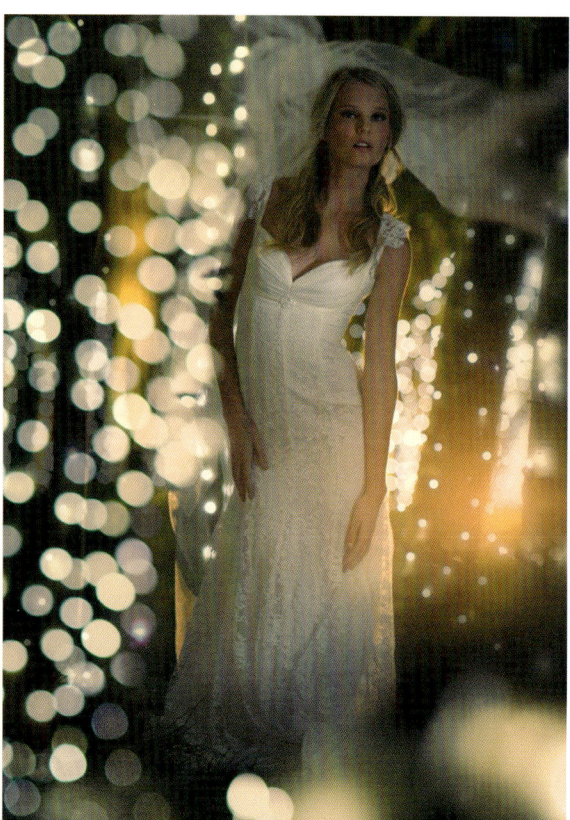

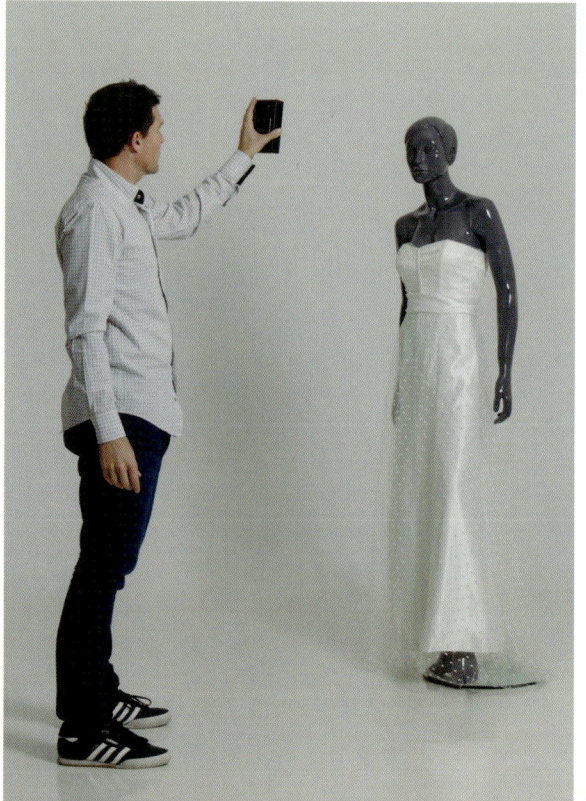

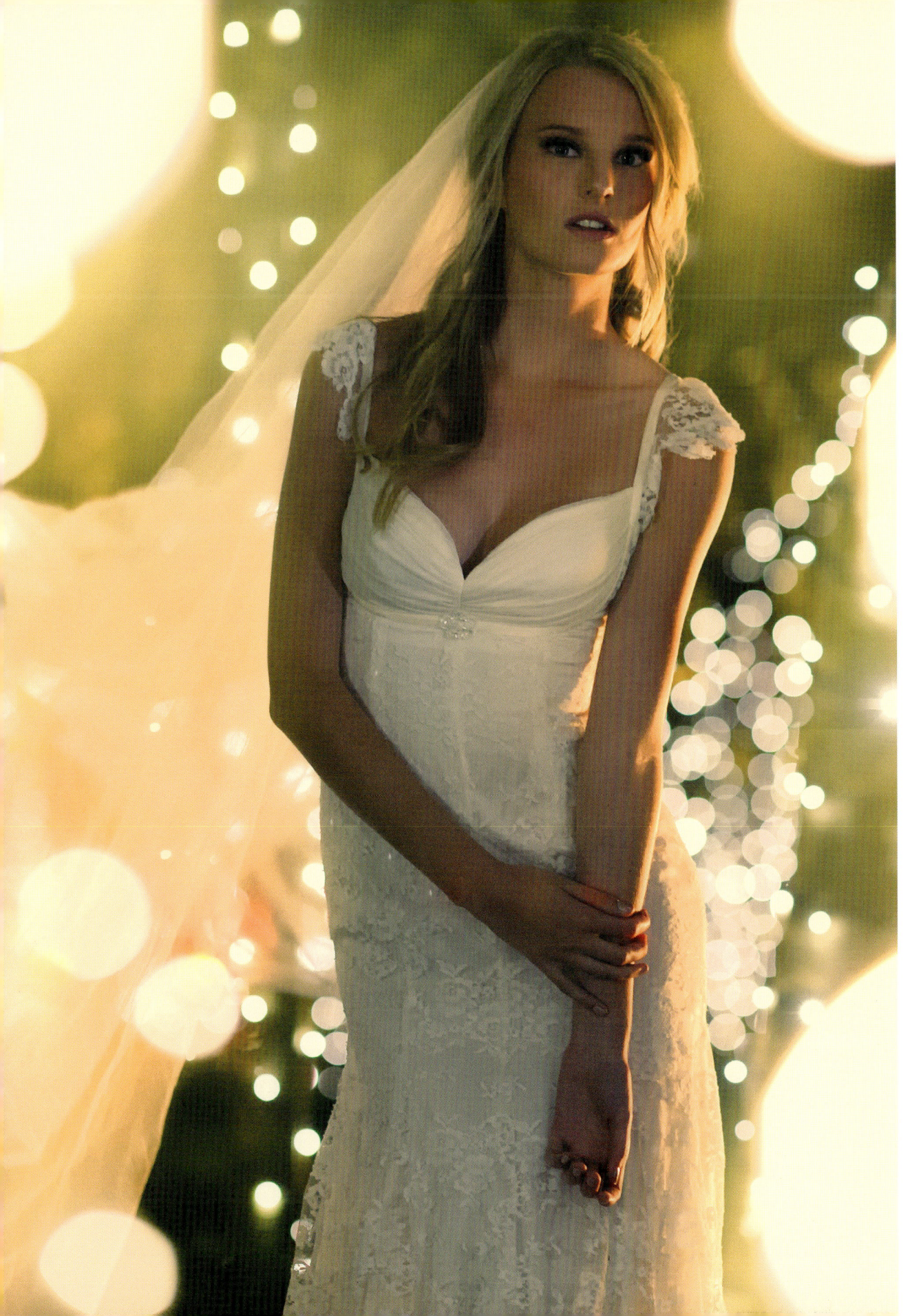

65. DISCRETELY SENSUAL

Strive for Consistency

You will have noticed that I use similar techniques for many of my bridal portraits. I probably have five or six approaches that I feel really work for me, and these have become synonymous with my style of photography. I strongly believe that, as a professional photographer, it is extremely important that you maintain a certain consistency in your work and don't change your style too radically over a short period of time. Always introduce new techniques slowly, so that you evolve over a period of time; after all, your client has booked you on the merit of your port-

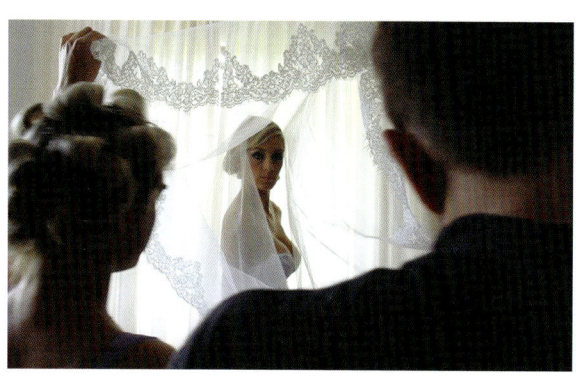

folio, and she will expect to see some of the same images in her own wedding album.

Having a few tried and trusted techniques gives me the confidence to know that I can create the perfect image in practically any given situation. If I were trying to shoot in a different style and technique for every wedding, I'd be a nervous wreck, and I'd never be able to perform to the best of my ability. Instead, I try something new for one or two images. If this works for me, then I incorporate these techniques into my style. This is how I evolve as a photographer.

A Blended Approach

In this image, I have combined two of my favorite techniques—using a net curtain to create a softbox effect behind the bride and producing the tunnel effect with the veil. With the heavy backlighting behind the bride, it is necessary for me to overexpose; here, that was by 1 stop at $^{1}/_{160}$ second. I shoot these sort of images before the bride is fully clothed, asking her to use her veil to cover her chest so that she looks bare but discreetly sensual.

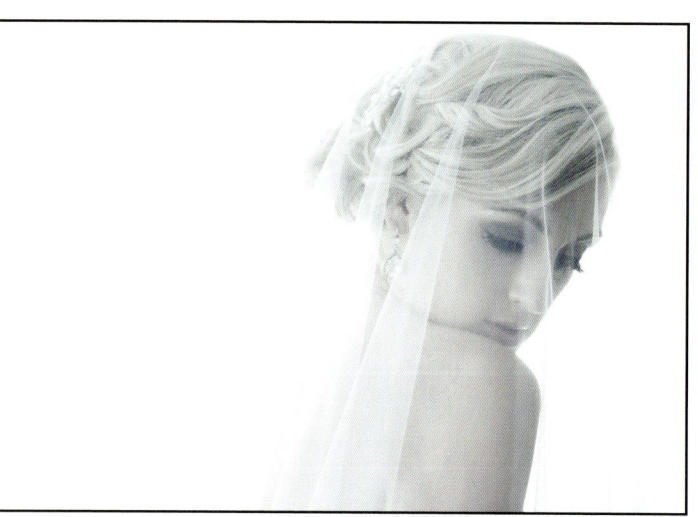

QUICK LOOK	
CAMERA	Nikon D4
LENS	Nikkor 70–200mm f/2.8G ED VR II
MODE	A
ISO	800
SHUTTER	$^{1}/_{160}$ +1EV
APERTURE	f/2.8
LIGHTING	Lastolite 5-in-1 collapsible reflector

Top: A setup shot for an alternate pose. **Bottom:** The final alternate image.

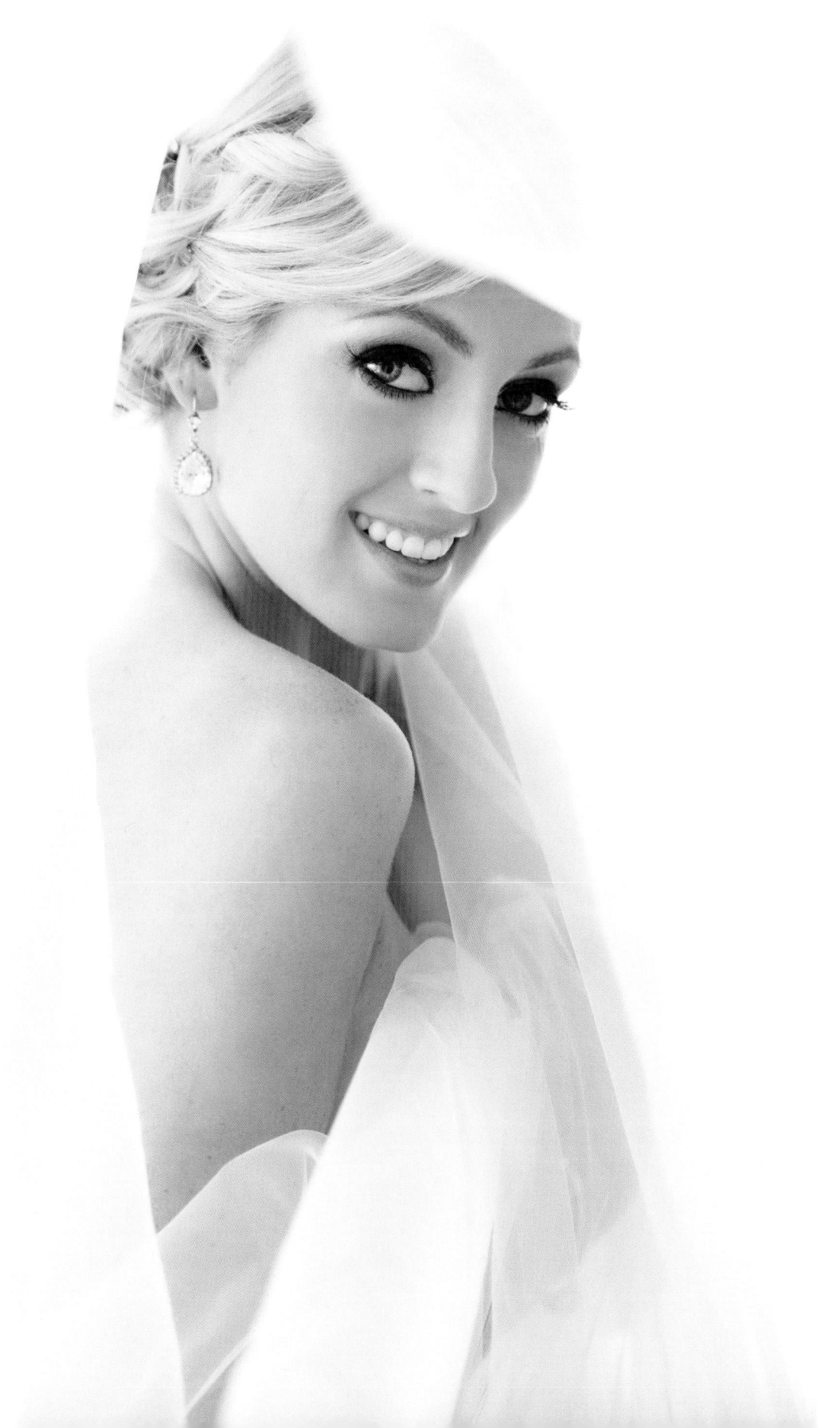

66. POSING REPERTOIRE

It is important to have a repertoire of smaller poses within the basic pose. These would be things such as: tilt your head down to look at the floor; bring your bouquet to your chest; put your left arm on your hip; and lean against the wall and turn your head toward the camera. Always have a plan. If you look as if you have run out of ideas, the bride will lose confidence in your ability to direct her. In turn, she will lose confidence in herself, and ultimately, the images will suffer.

This shot was made in the corner of the bedroom where the bride was getting ready. I like to pose the bride near a corner. I ask her to lean her shoulders against the closer wall and push her hips out to the side. This accentuates her body shape, creating a beautiful S-shaped curve to her frame.

Top right: The reflector position. **Bottom left and right:** Two alternative poses.

As you can see from the supporting images below, there are a number of options that can stem from the starting pose and placement.

> ### QUICK LOOK
> | | |
> |---|---|
> | **CAMERA** | Nikon D4 |
> | **LENS** | Nikkor 70–200mm f/2.8G ED VR II |
> | **MODE** | A |
> | **ISO** | 500 |
> | **SHUTTER** | $^1/_{250}$ |
> | **APERTURE** | f/2.8 |
> | **LIGHTING** | Lastolite 5-in-1 collapsible reflector |

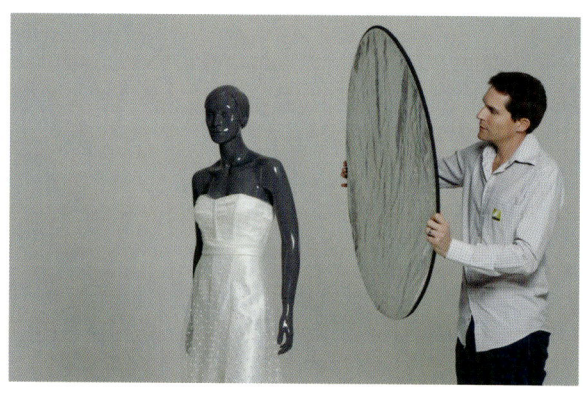

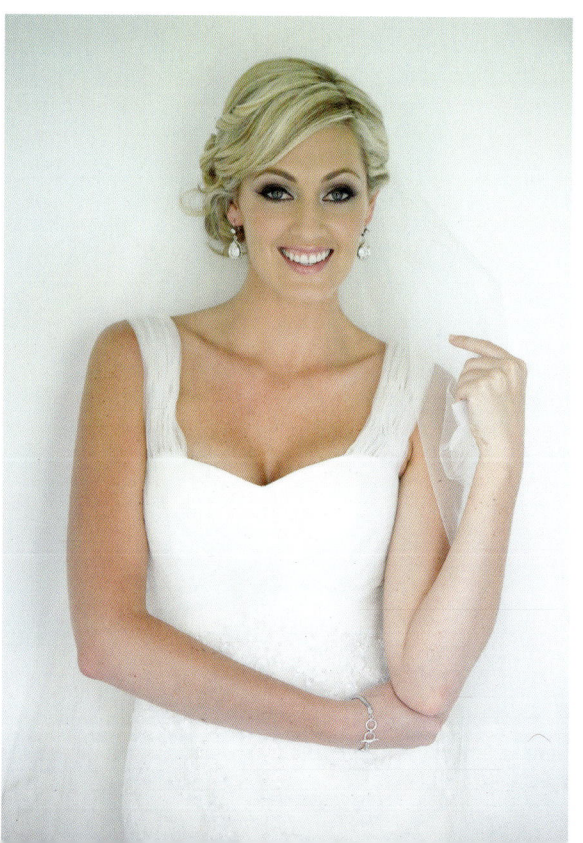

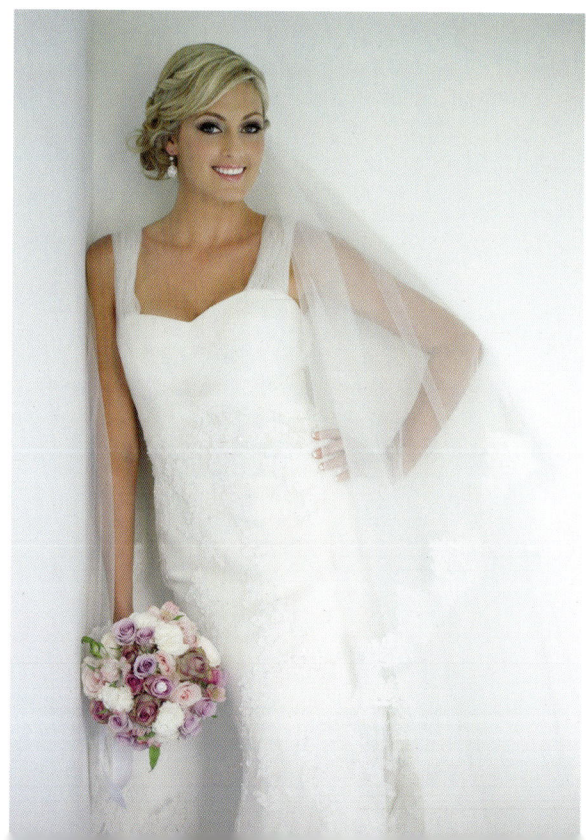

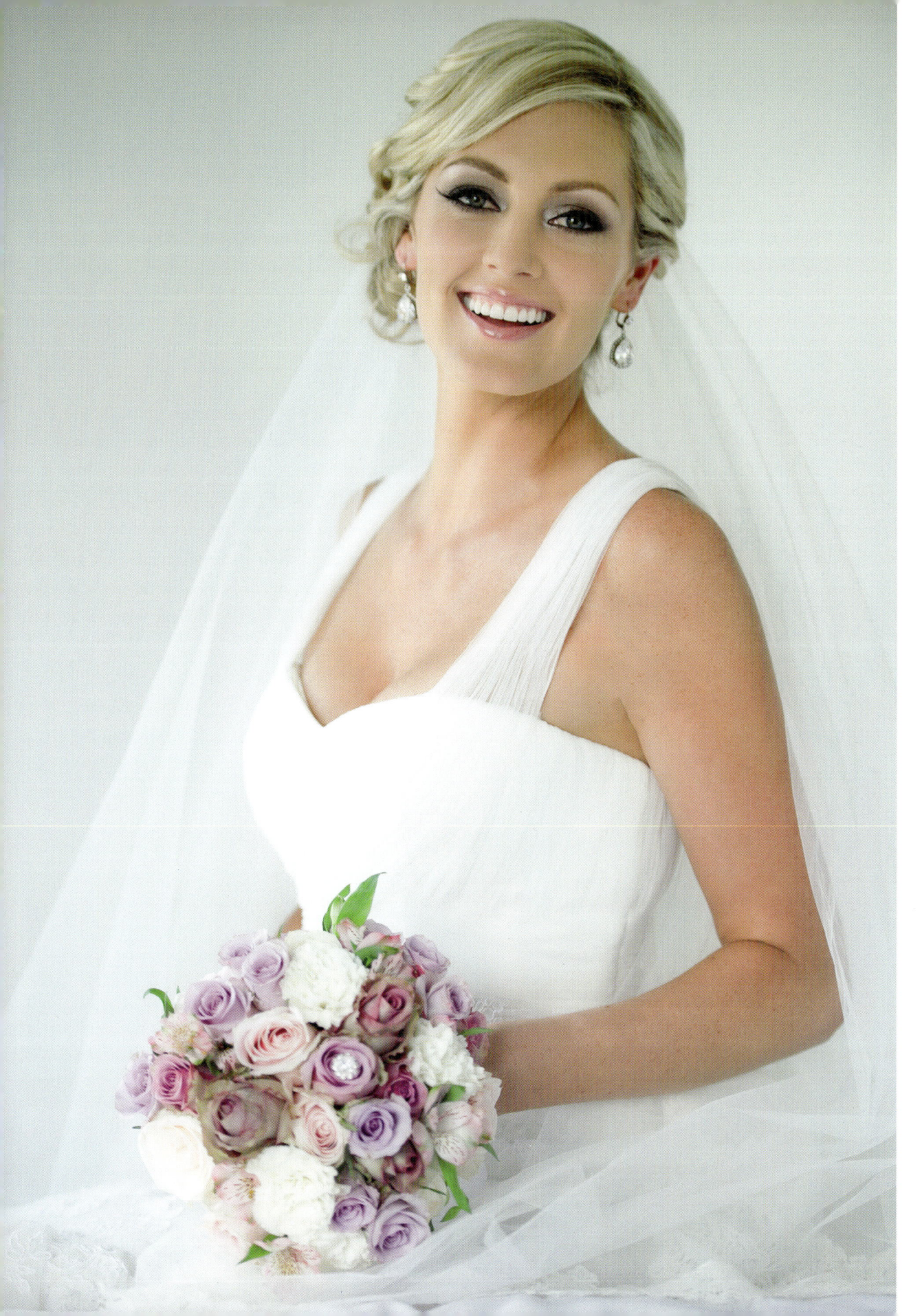

67. A BIRD'S-EYE VIEW

This image was produced during one of my "drown the gown" sessions. I stood on a step-ladder to get a bird's-eye view of the bride, who was floating in a pool below me. This was one of the first shots of the session, and she had just pushed herself away from the wall, while keeping her head above water so as not to wet her hair.

QUICK LOOK

CAMERA	Nikon D4
LENS	Nikkor 24–70mm f/2.8G ED
MODE	M
ISO	100
SHUTTER	$^1/_{200}$
APERTURE	f/8
LIGHTING	Elinchrom Ranger RX Quadra

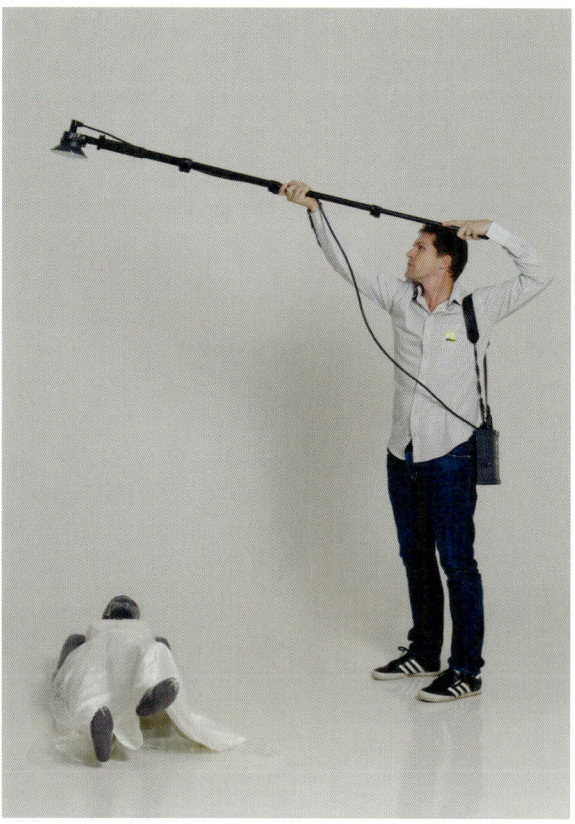

Getting Results

To ensure that this was a striking image, it was lit with an Elinchrom Ranger Quadra, which my assistant held just above the bride using a Manfrotto 680B monopod as a light stand. Unlike a light stand, the monopod gave the assistant the flexibility to move the strobe almost horizontally over the pool to perfectly light the bride.

It's best to get the sturdiest monopod possible with the smallest number of sections, and one that has the shortest length when collapsed for easy portability. If you've never used a monopod and are unsure whether it will be a valuable tool, I suggest you get a sturdy Manfrotto aluminium one (e.g., the 681B or 680B). I'm sure that you'll find it's a worthwhile investment.

Intensifying the Color

The dark-blue hue of the water was due to it being a dark, charcoal-colored swimming pool, but I used Nik Software's Viveza 2 to intensify the color, giving it a rich, royal-blue feel that envelops the bride like satin.

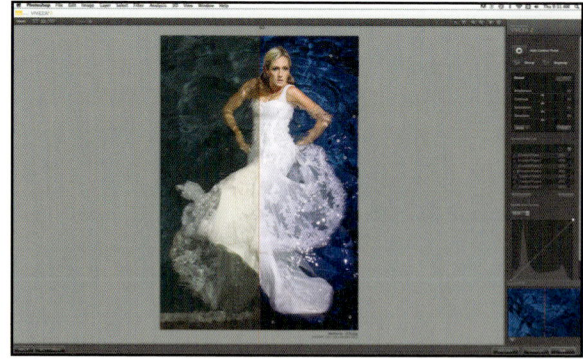

Left: The position of the strobe. **Above:** The image with and without enhanced color.

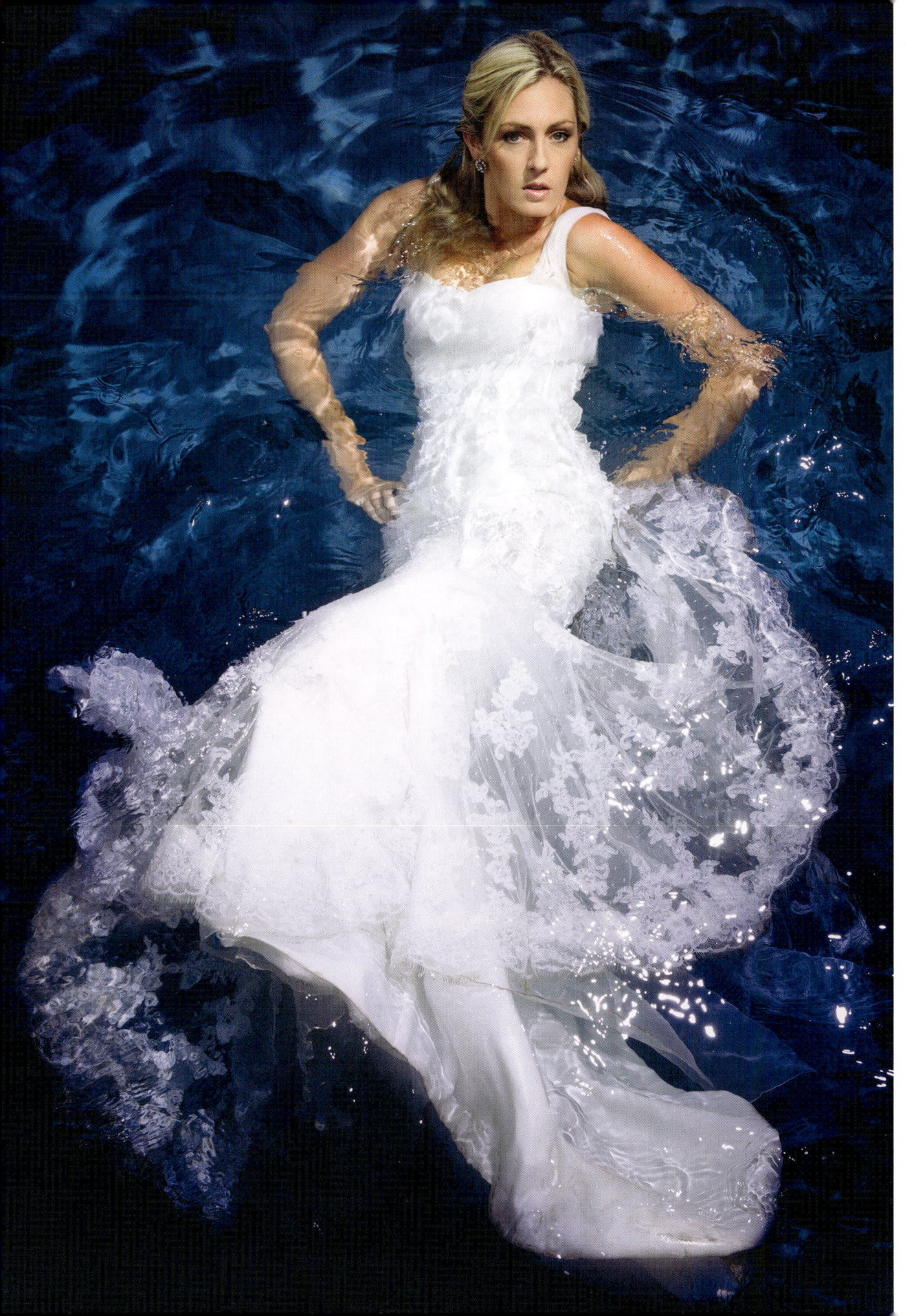

68. WARMTH AND ELEGANCE

For a wedding where the bride is not wearing white, using LED lighting can help retain the garment's warmth of color. With these lights, one can usually adjust the color temperature, making them warmer or cooler.

This image was made in an old building that was restored to its former glory. I posed the bride on a staircase with rich burgundy carpet and a dark wooden balustrade. My assistant was behind her and to her right with an LED set to an almost tungsten glow. The light created an intense warm highlight on the bride's cheek that gave her face a beautifully chiselled three-dimensional look. The blue highlight on her hair was caused by the daylight pouring through a stained-glass window at the top of the staircase; it added a lovely touch. My main light was the LED, held above the bride and to her left. It was set at a warm temperature, giving me rich, royal, opu-

lent colors that enhanced the gold jewelry and the gold trim on the sari. It also enhanced the lighter wood on the staircase and made it look almost like gold—a wonderful complement to the trim on the bride's garment.

I think that the obscurity of the background fooled the camera into thinking there wasn't enough light, and I found that the bride was overexposed when I shot the image without any exposure value compensation. I then used aperture priority and underexposed it by one stop. I shot this on 4000 ISO at $1/160$ second.

QUICK LOOK

CAMERA	Nikon D4
LENS	Nikkor 24–70mm f/2.8G ED
MODE	A
ISO	4000
SHUTTER	$1/160$ –1EV
APERTURE	f/2.8
LIGHTING	Two LED video lights

Left: An alternate pose. **Below:** The position of the LED lighting units.

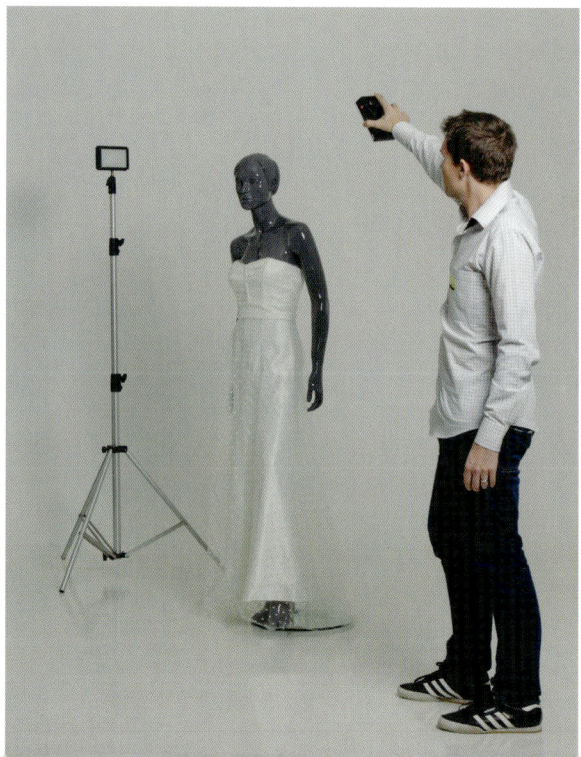

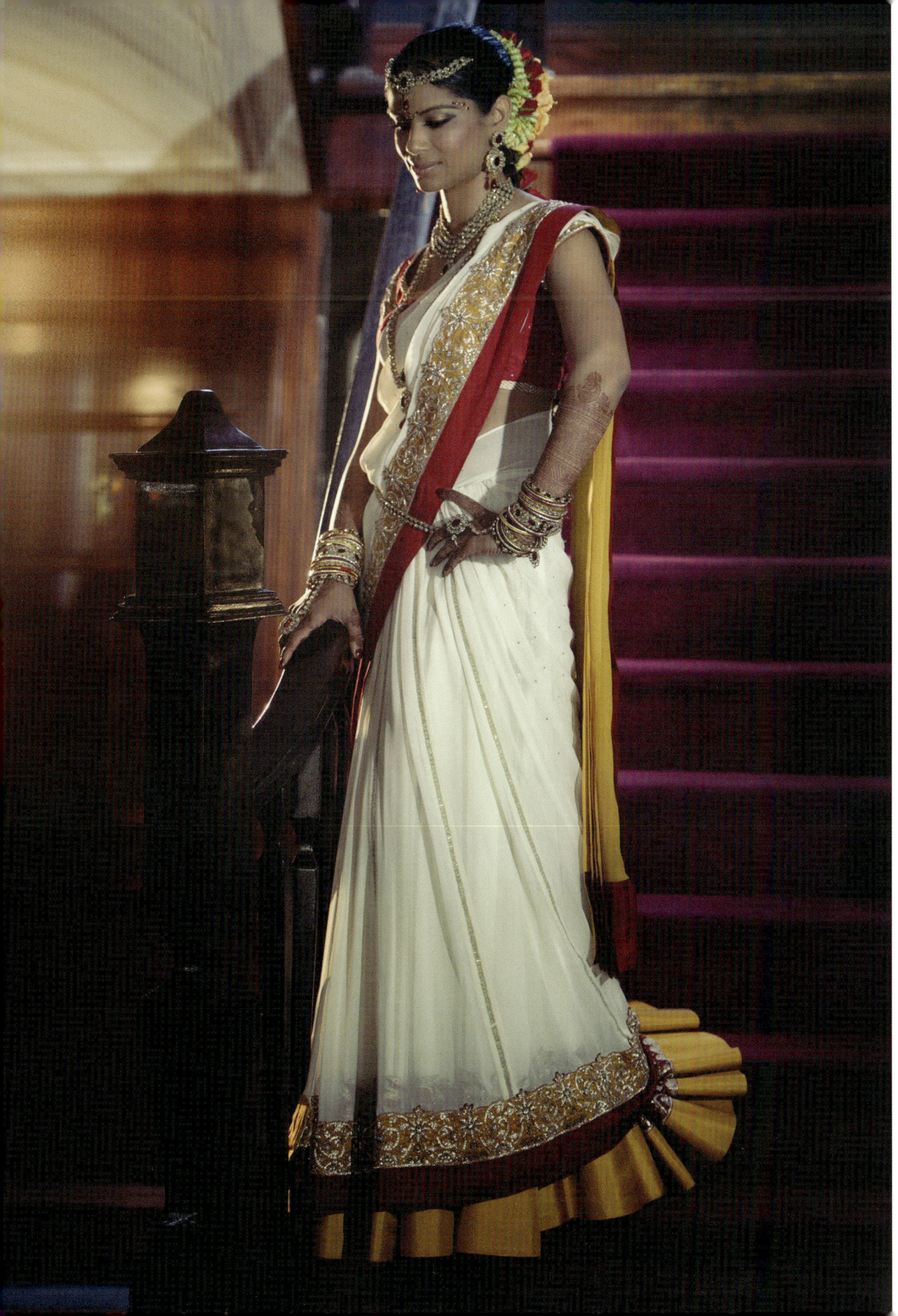

69. BALLERINA

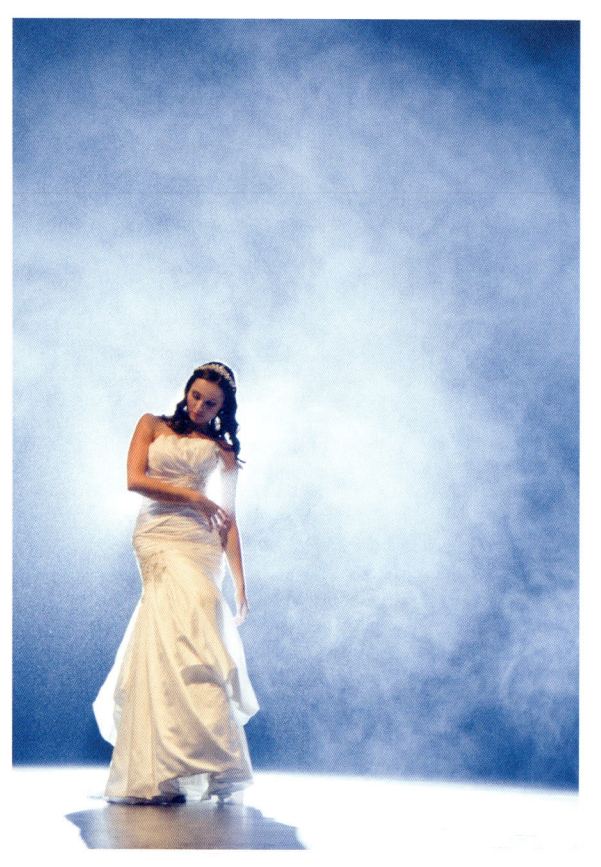

In the Spotlight

There are instances in which the couple's hobbies or careers can make for some stunning portraits, and these images can really enhance the look and feel of the album. This bride had had a long career in dancing, and she wanted to incorporate her love for ballet into her wedding portraits.

We went to the local theater and put on some stage lighting, a spotlight, which was extremely orange in terms of my white balance. I had to balance specifically for this orange stage lighting in order to get true skin tones on my bride. My assistant was just beyond the spotlight in the darkness of the stage, and using my very small LED camping flashlight, the Lenser T7, he threw some talcum powder up in the air and illuminated it with this flashlight, producing a dramatic and theatrical effect, which suited the bride, who was absolutely thrilled with the portraits.

Exposure

Because there was a lot of darkness in the background, I had to shoot it two stops underexposed. In the supporting image, you can see how the light from the LED flashlight created flare and added to the incredible theatrical mood of the image.

Top: An alternate pose. **Bottom:** The flashlight position.

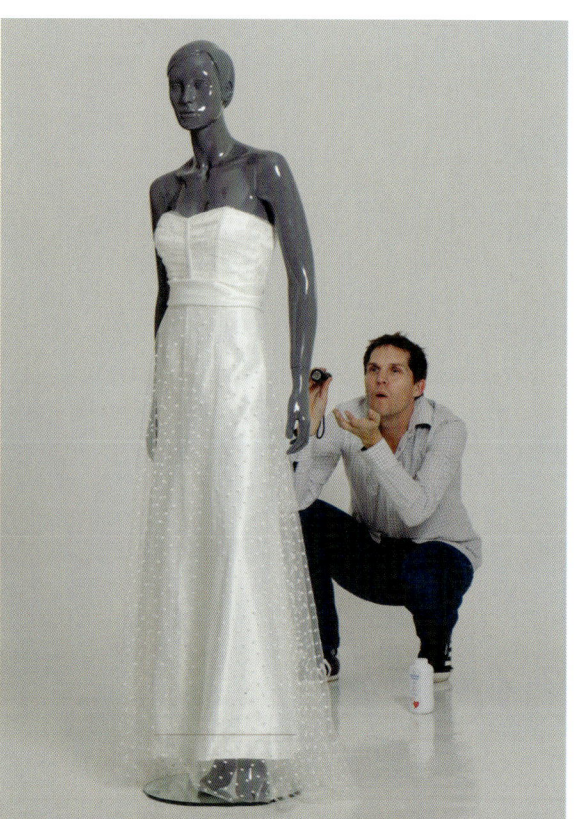

QUICK LOOK

CAMERA	Nikon D4
LENS	Nikkor 70–200mm f/2.8G ED VR II
MODE	A
ISO	800
SHUTTER	$^1/_{100}$ –2EV
APERTURE	f/2.8
LIGHTING	Stage lighting and Lenser T7 LED flashlight

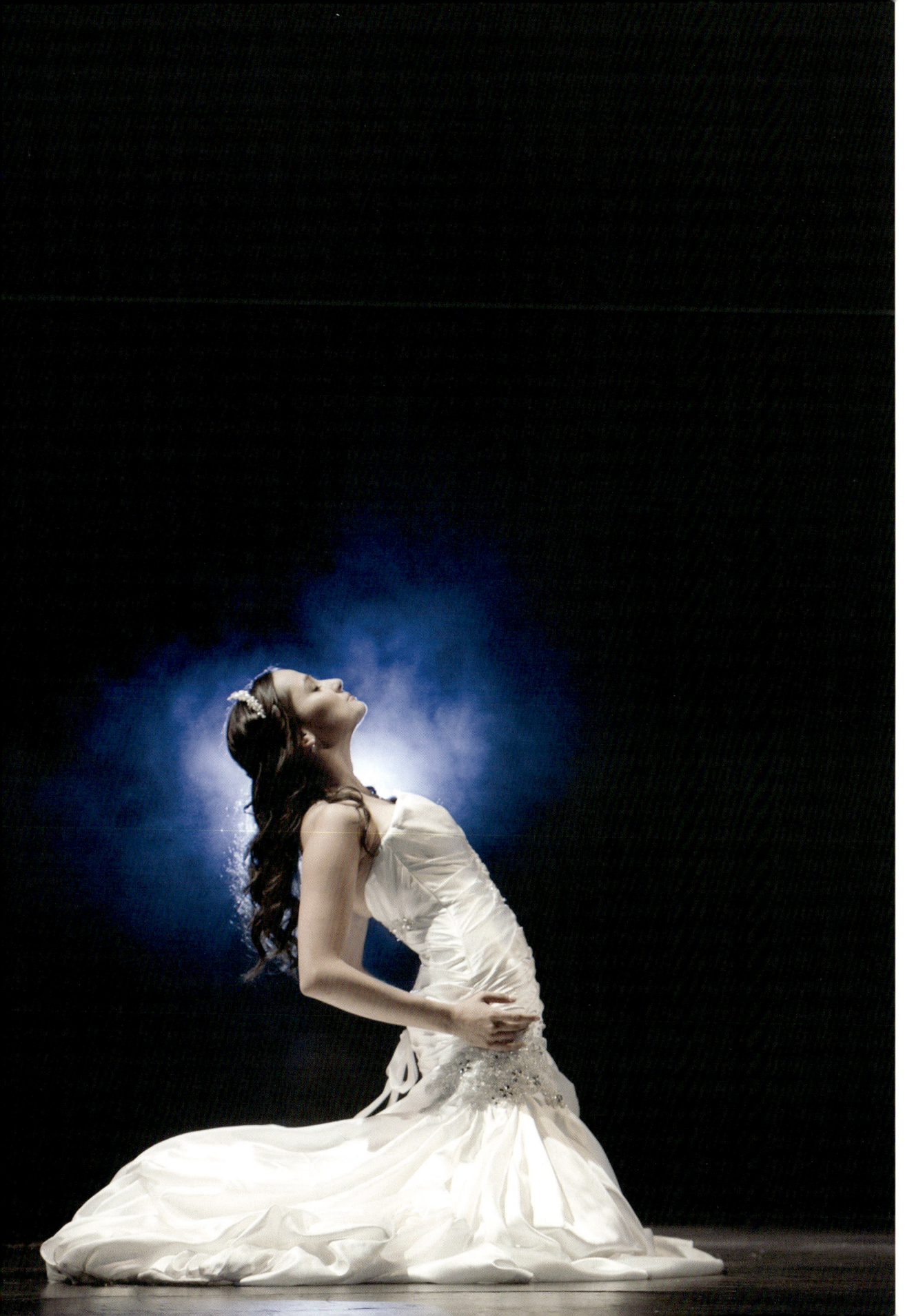

70. A FASHION-INSPIRED SHOOT

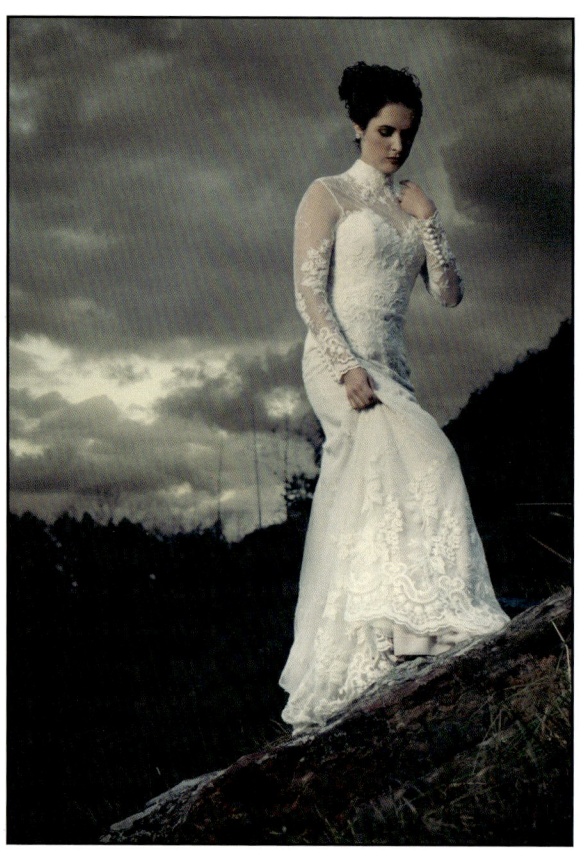

These post-wedding portraits were inspired by a fashion shoot in *Vogue* that was possibly shot in the Scottish highlands. The Scottish highlands may have been a tall order for tropical Durban where we live, but I knew of a rocky valley not far from the bride's house that would give us the same atmosphere. The other snag was that I needed really moody, stormy skies, and in Durban, the winters are generally very mild, with clear blue skies. Not to be deterred, I arranged to shoot in the late afternoon when I knew the valley would be in shade, and I had a number of stormy sky pictures that I'd taken previously, which I knew I could use in postproduction.

We used the Elinchrom Ranger RX portable flash with the octabox light modifier to create beautiful, even light. This we set up on the Manfrotto 680B monopod, and I had my assistant elevate the softbox high over the bride. I made

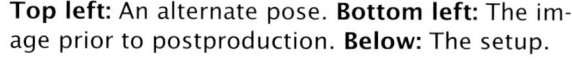

Top left: An alternate pose. **Bottom left:** The image prior to postproduction. **Below:** The setup.

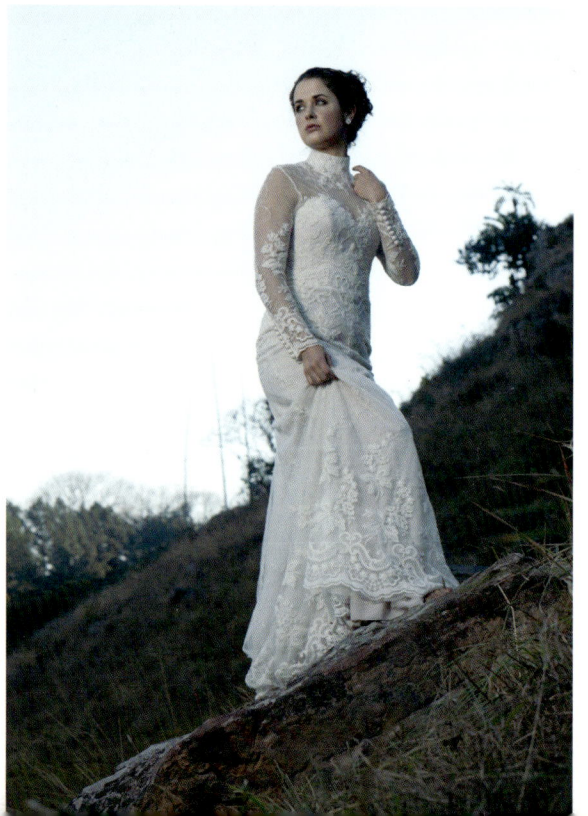

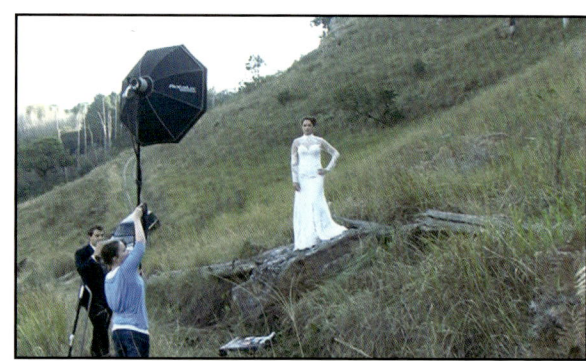

QUICK LOOK

CAMERA Nikon D4
LENS Nikkor 85mm f/1.4G
MODE M
ISO 160
SHUTTER $^1/_{200}$
APERTURE f/11
LIGHTING Elinchrom Ranger RX

sure that I had clean lines in the background, so that it was no hassle to drop in the stormy sky in postproduction. Having done this, my digital artist then used Color Efex Pro to further enhance the mood and color of the cloudy skies, making it look particularly brooding.

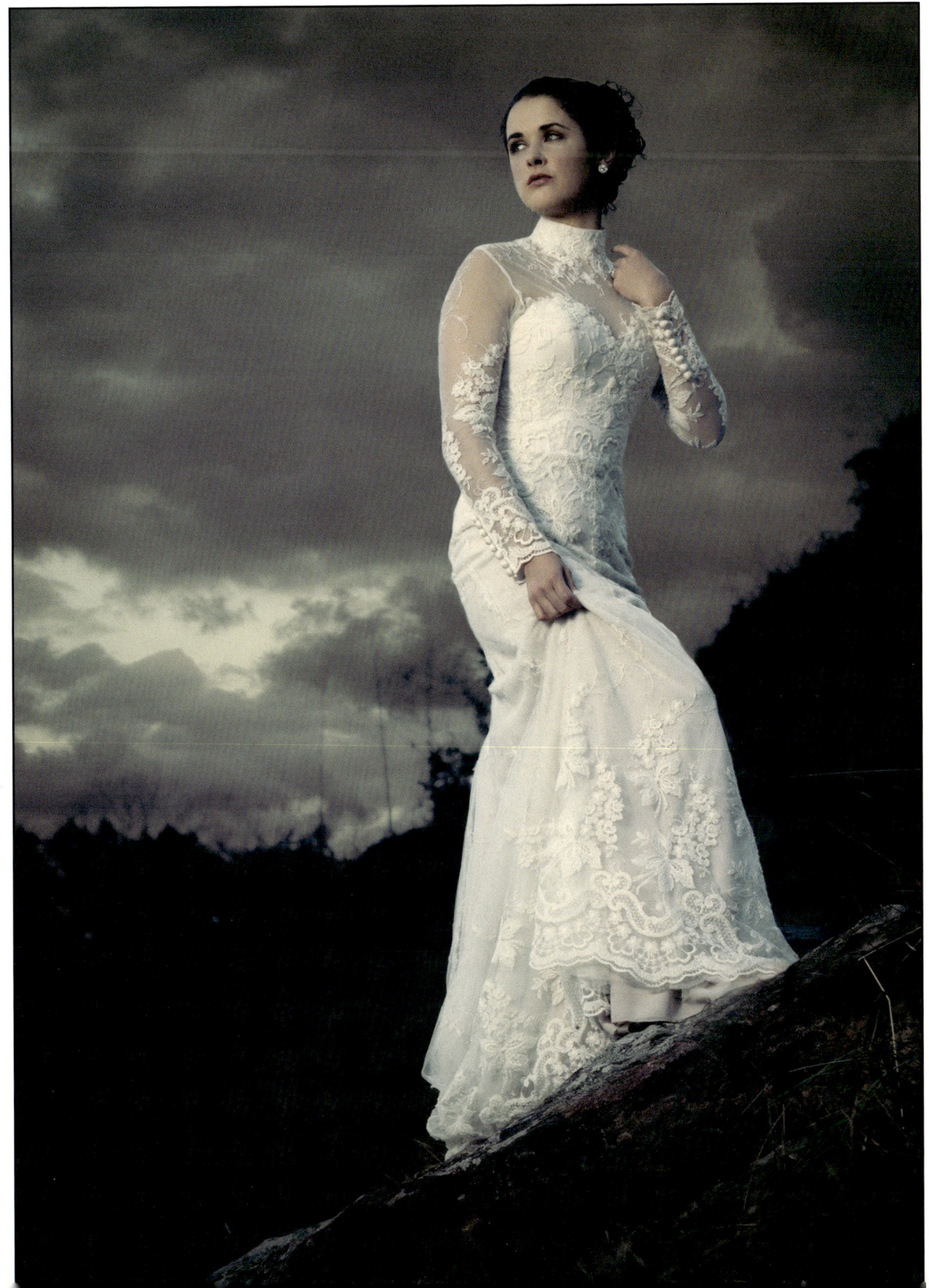

71. A SENSUAL SHOT

When it comes to assessing your clients' wants and needs, you need to be a bit of a psychologist! It's important that you learn to read the different personality types that you come into contact with. This is why a pre-wedding meeting is so valuable—you have a chance to get to know your clients before the big day. I usually have a meeting that lasts an hour or so, and in that time I have a pretty good idea as to what they will like or dislike when it comes to the photography. Some clients are more reserved and formal, others are extroverted and will be happy to push the envelope a bit in terms of posing.

This particular bride was quite an extrovert and was very comfortable shooting what would probably be termed a risqué portrait. The dress was a fabulous Vera Wang design, and this was an atypical way of showing off the dress. The bride was lying on the bare wooden floor below a stair-case, and I was four or five meters above her on the balcony. Posed completely naked with one leg wrapped sensually over the dress, the bride holds the voluptuous gown close to her body, in a possessive, "love affair" kind of way! This is the kind of image the dress designer could use for a magazine ad: it is very sexy and shows the dress off beautifully, but in an extraordinary way.

The image was lit only with available light.

QUICK LOOK

CAMERA	Nikon D4
LENS	Nikkor 24–70mm f/2.8G ED
MODE	A
ISO	4000
SHUTTER	$^1/_{100}$
APERTURE	f/2.8
LIGHTING	Unmanipulated available light only

Left: An alternate pose. **Right:** The image before postproduction.

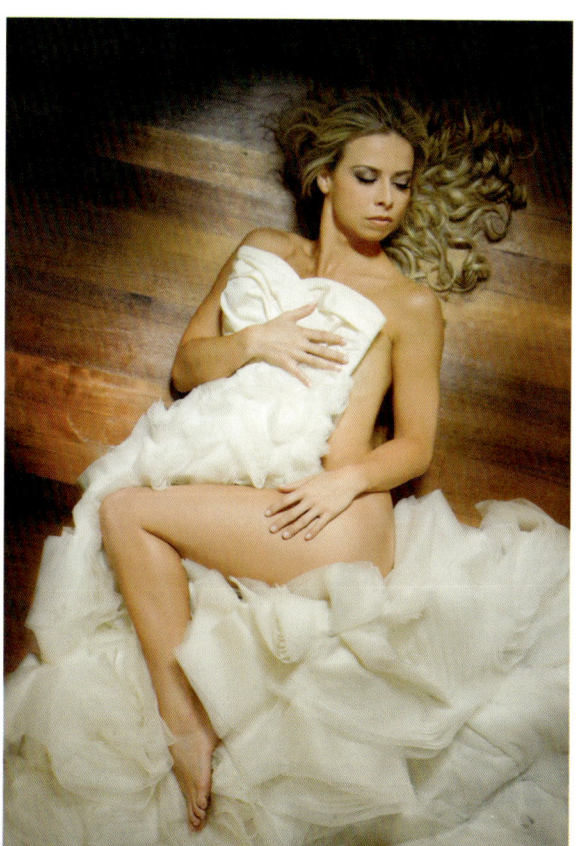
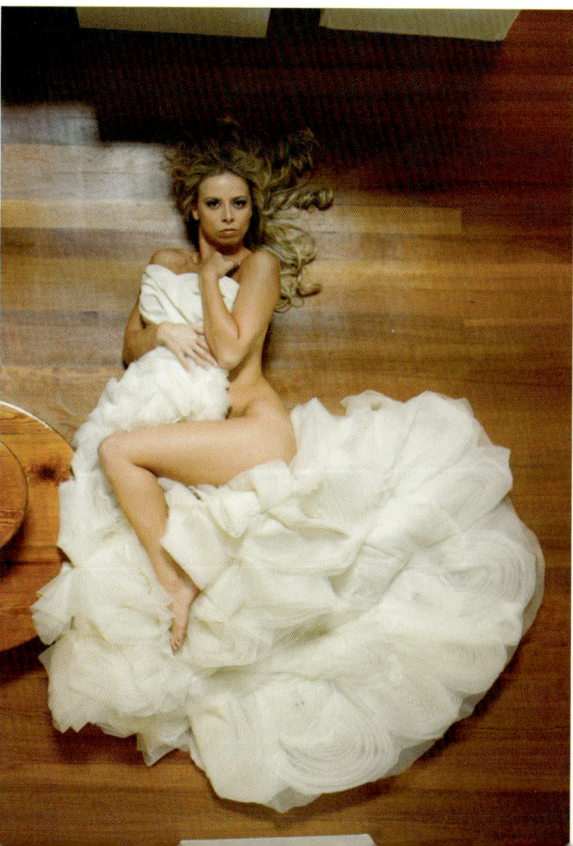

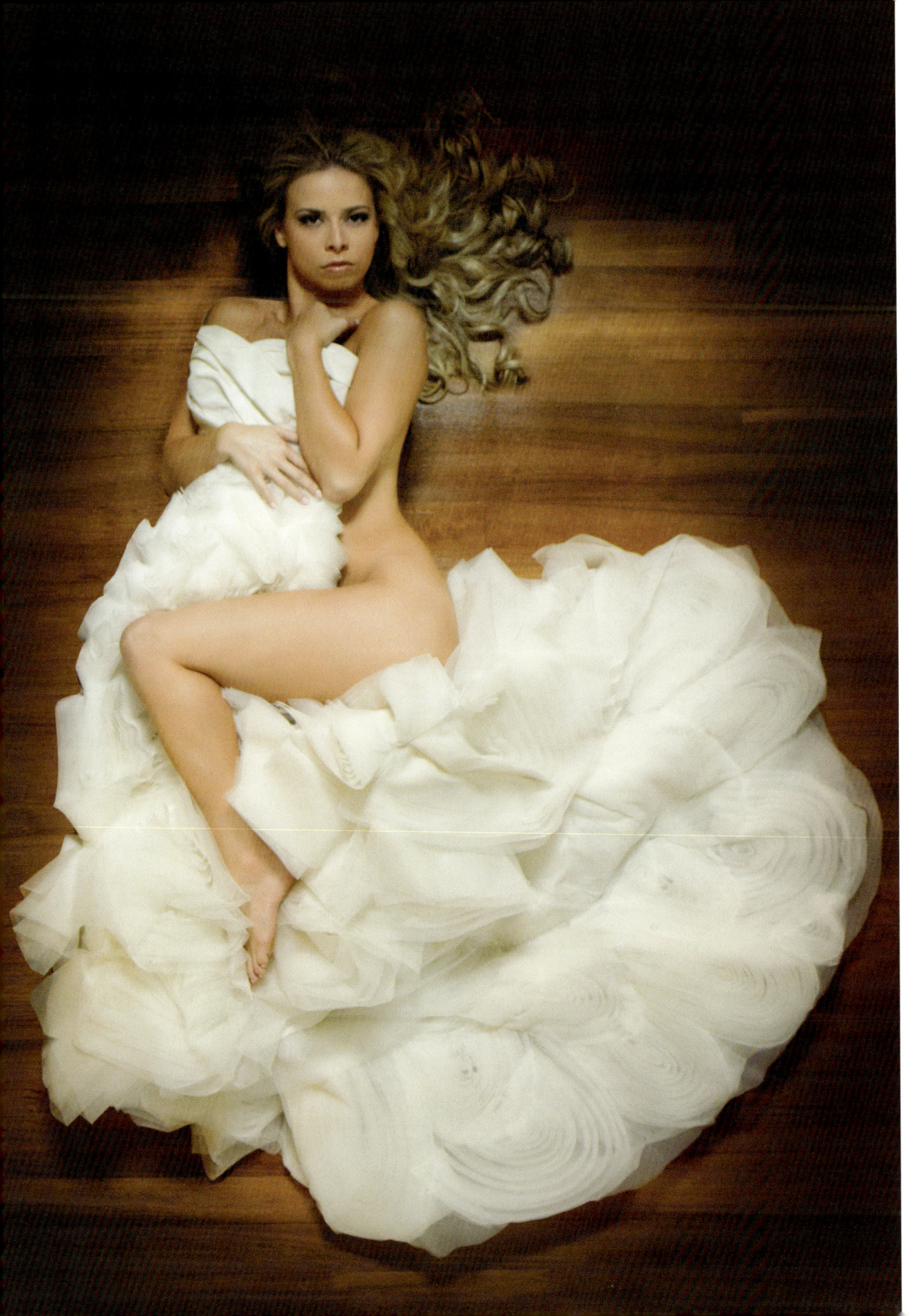

72. AN UNCONVENTIONAL APPROACH

One of South Africa's top fashion photographers, Jacques Weyers, often holds a large crystal bead just to the side of the lens, catching only a corner or shooting through it entirely to create a portrait. I'm inspired by Jacques' work, and I've followed a lot of his techniques to try and emulate the high-fashion look I aspire to attain in my images. I have tried this technique with crystal wine glasses, soda bottles, perfume bottles and the like, always getting interesting, diverse results. You can never predict the outcome of the image, so every photograph is unique.

Here, I held a CD near the lens. The colors that were reflected off this CD created little rainbow flares across the image, transforming the image into something completely magical. Combined with the ornate mother-of-pearl inlaid Indian or Balinese cupboard door, the image has a fairy-tale quality to it, almost as if the bride were a princess in an elaborately decorated castle.

The lighting was ambient, coming through a window. My assistant bounced the natural light back onto the bride with the 5-in-1 reflector.

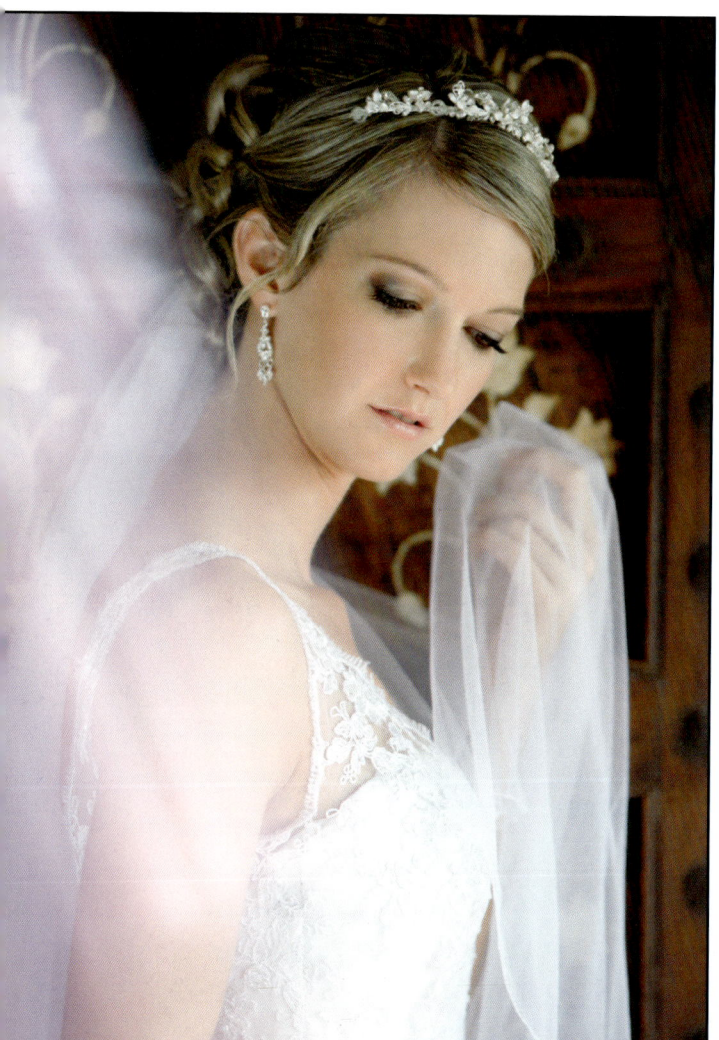

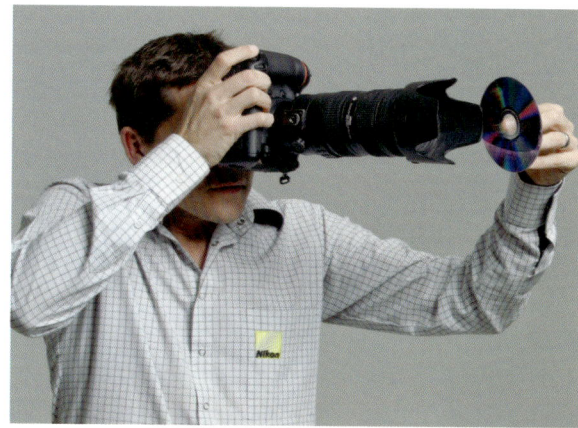

Above: The rainbow flares in the facing-page image were created by shooting with a CD placed right by the edge of the lens. **Left:** An alternate image from the session, made by shooting through a drinking glass.

QUICK LOOK	
CAMERA	Nikon D4
LENS	Nikkor 70–200mm f/2.8G ED VR II
MODE	A
ISO	800
SHUTTER	$^1/_{100}$
APERTURE	f/2.8
LIGHTING	Lastolite 5-in-1 collapsible reflector

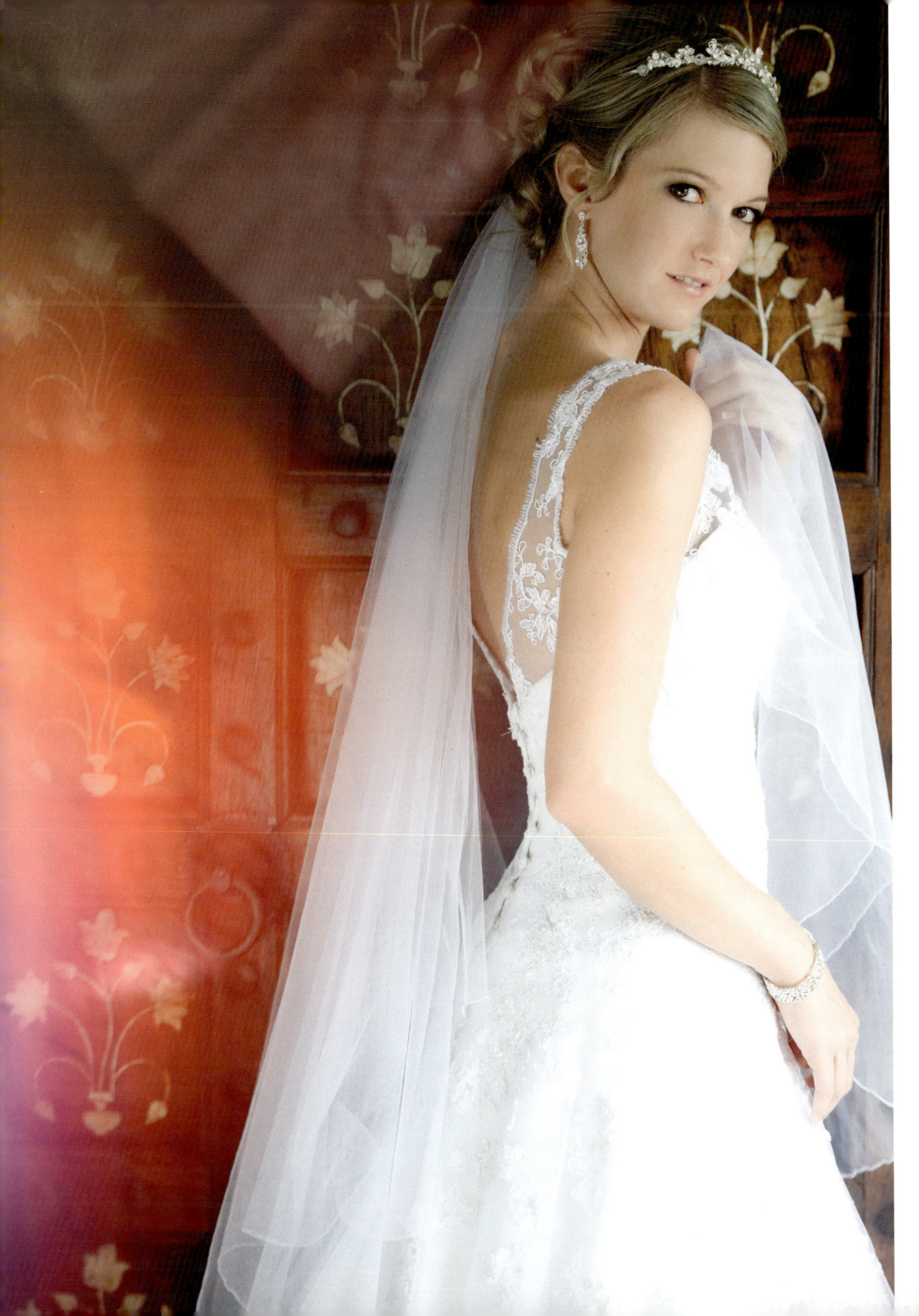

73. WARMTH AND AMBIENCE

This is one of my favorite images, inspired by a fashion shoot that appeared in *Harper's Bazaar* (July 2012). The shoot was photographed by Camilla Akrans. I really like her work, and I love the atmosphere that she created—there was a lot of warmth and tone in her backlighting.

I was able to emulate the same lighting and ambience in the images I shot, which I obviously combined into a single composite portrait for the bride's album. I love the contrasting expressions. In one shot, she is fully dressed, contemplative and serene; in the other, she was captured in a lovely gentle laugh with closed eyes.

The images were shot against a window. I overexposed the shot by two stops to blow out the very distracting background. The lighting was ambient and intense, as you can see from the pose where the light is shining on her back.

I used Nik Software's Color Efex Pro to warm up the image to emulate the red or orange glow of the *Harper's Bazaar* shoot.

Left: The setting. **Bottom left and right:** The images used in the final composite portrait.

QUICK LOOK	
CAMERA	Nikon D4
LENS	Nikkor 70–200mm f/2.8G ED VR II
MODE	A
ISO	1000
SHUTTER	$^{1}/_{500}$ +2EV
APERTURE	f/2.8
LIGHTING	Available light only

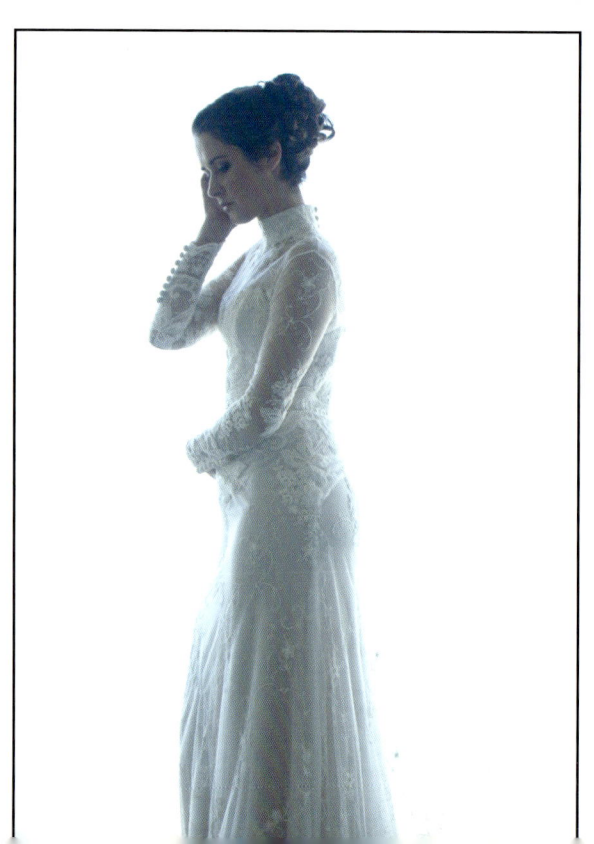

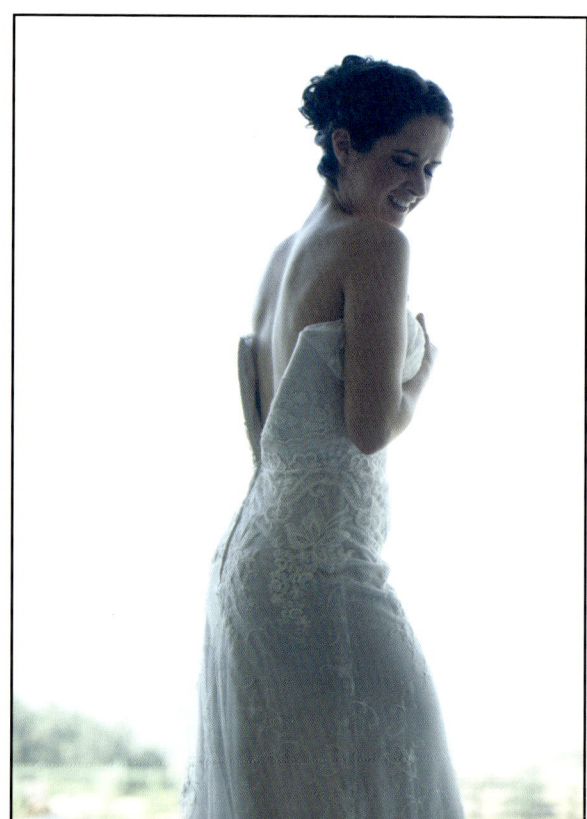

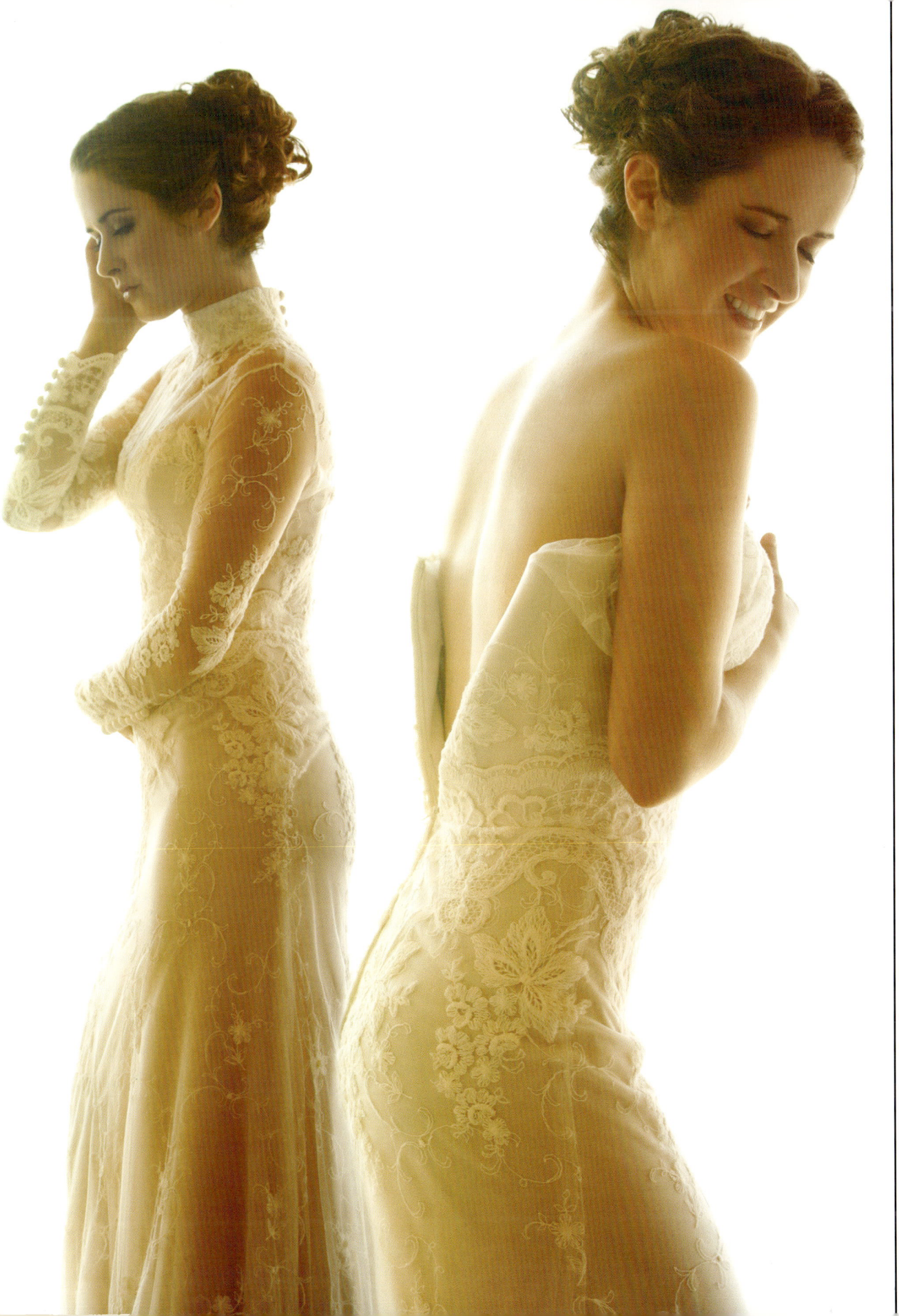

74. STRONG CONTRAST

The Method

As I've mentioned before, I find that contrast in bridal portraits works really well. Sometimes it is an unusual background or location, sometimes it is the lighting that can create the disparity that makes a photograph really stand out. Here, the image is made very striking due to the enormous tonal contrast between the very black background and the bride's bright white dress. This serves to beautifully accentuate the dress in all its glory. In order to create this, I needed to make sure that there was no ambient light behind the bride. Posing her in the doorway to her home, I made sure that the house was completely dark by closing all the curtains and all of the inter-leading doors, and I switched off any lights that were on. This ensured that it went completely black behind her.

Posing the bride in a fairly conventional stance, I asked her to give me quite a bit of sensual body shape in the hip and shoulder areas. I then asked a bridesmaid who was positioned crouched behind the bride to throw her veil into the air behind her. I captured the shot just as the veil billowed around her against the blackness of the doorway.

I modified the lighting by getting my assistant to hold the 5-in-1 reflector in order to bounce light back onto the bride's left side.

Postproduction

As you can see in the supporting image, a little Photoshop work had to be done to get rid of the door frames, as I wanted the background to be completely devoid of detail. I managed to keep the detail in the dress in terms of the exposure, which I felt was important.

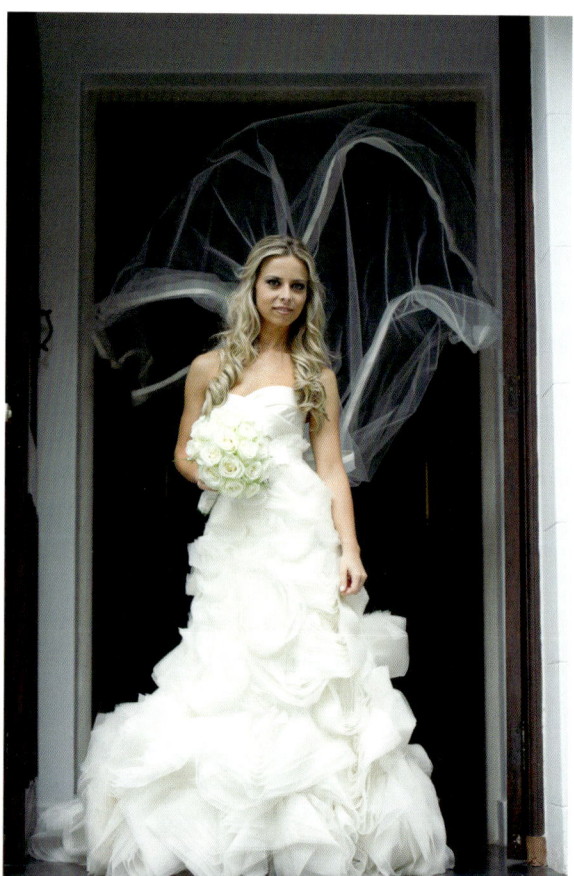

> **QUICK LOOK**
>
> | | |
> |---|---|
> | **CAMERA** | Nikon D3s |
> | **LENS** | Nikkor 70–200mm f/2.8G ED VR II |
> | **MODE** | A |
> | **ISO** | 800 |
> | **SHUTTER** | $^1/_{800}$ |
> | **APERTURE** | f/3.5 |
> | **LIGHTING** | Lastolite collapsible 5-in-1 reflector |

Left: The image, as captured. **Below:** The reflector position.

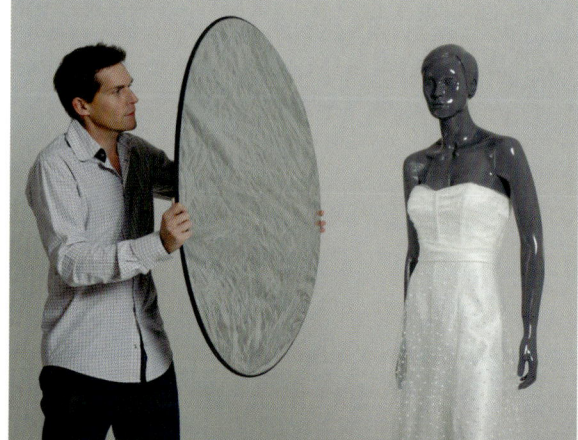

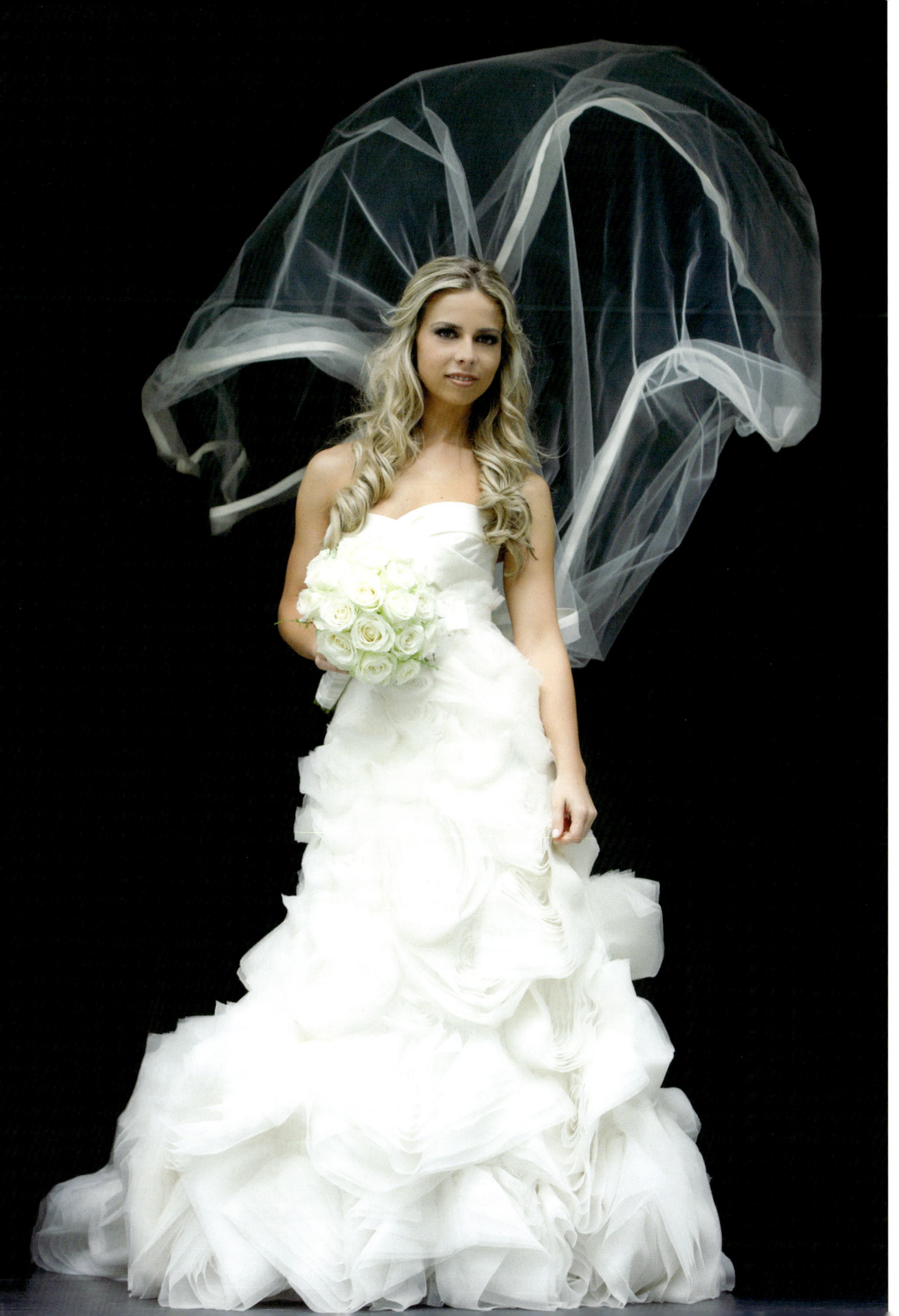

75. COMPOSITIONAL STRATEGIES

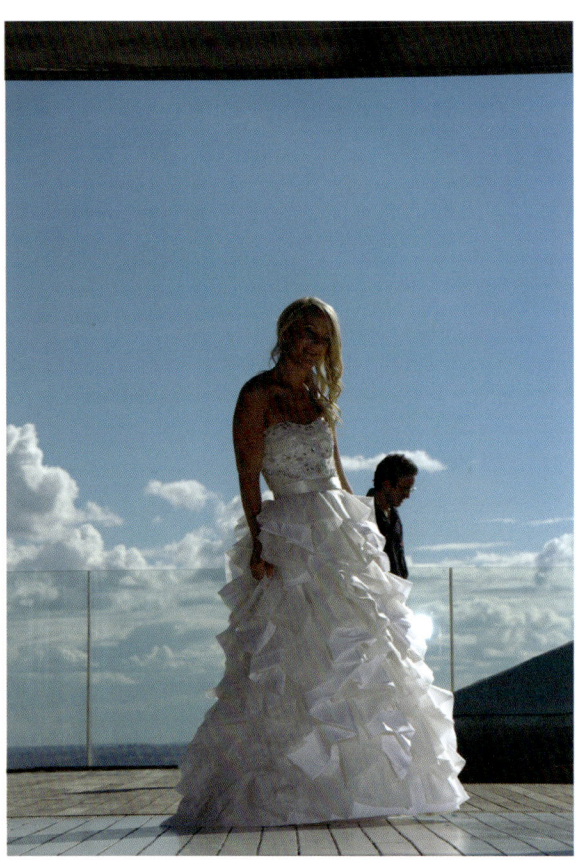

Composition

Here, I used two techniques that have a big impact on composition: dominant (negative) space and the rule of thirds. I positioned my bride in the top right-hand corner of the frame, at the intersection of the imaginary lines. The expanse of the floorboards is dominant, but it doesn't distract from the bride, as there is no busy pattern. In fact, the vertical lines of the floorboards draw the viewer's eyes right to the bride.

Perspective

This angle of view was possible because I lay completely flat on the floor, and my camera was resting along the floorboards, capturing the grooves of the floorboard at the closest-possible range.

Lighting and Exposure

The bride was positioned outdoors in direct sunlight, with her back to the sun. I was inside the venue where we were shooting. I wanted to expose for her face, so I overexposed the image by three stops due to the intense sunlight.

As you can see in the supporting image, one can shoot very different moods in the very same location just by adjusting the lighting.

I manipulated the image using Nik Software's Color Efex Pro.

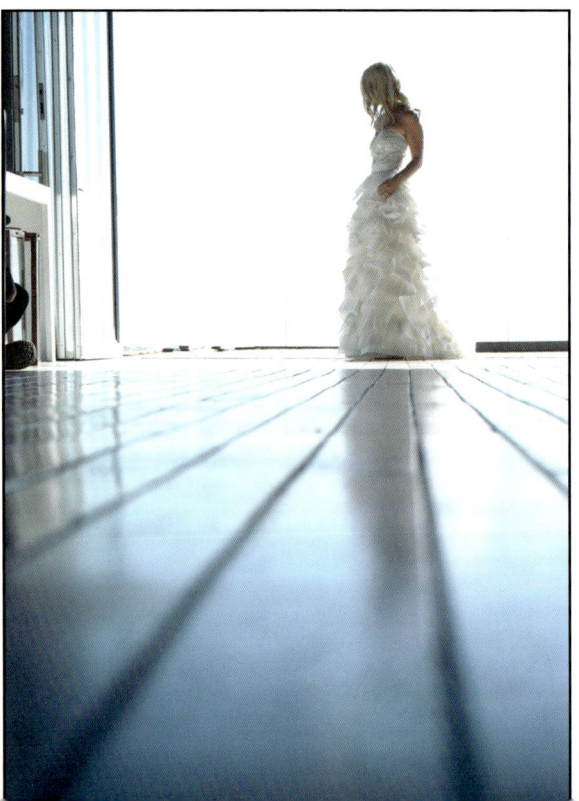

Top: The setting. **Bottom:** The image prior to postproduction.

QUICK LOOK	
CAMERA	Nikon D4
LENS	Nikkor 70–200mm f/2.8G ED VR II
MODE	A
ISO	100
SHUTTER	$^1/_{200}$ +3EV
APERTURE	f/4
LIGHTING	Available light only

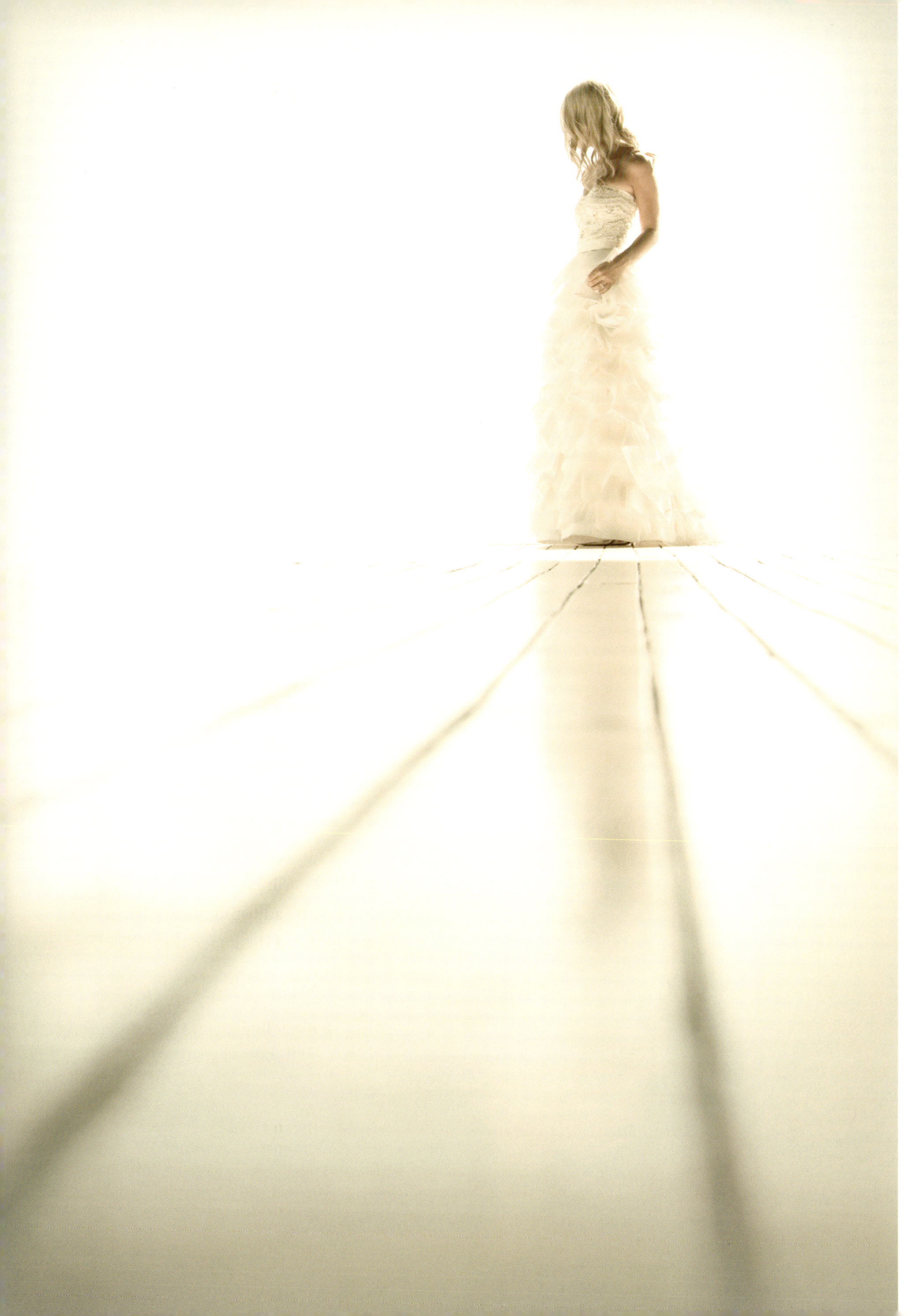

INDEX

OTHER BOOKS FROM
Amherst Media®

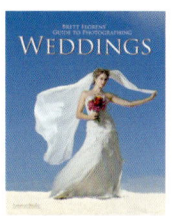

BRETT FLORENS' Guide to Photographing Weddings

Learn the artistic and business strategies Florens uses to remain at the top of his field. *$34.95 list, 8.5x11, 128p, 250 color images, index, order no. 1926.*

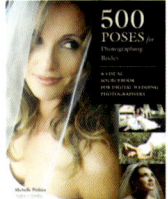

500 Poses for Photographing Brides

Michelle Perkins showcases an array of head-and-shoulders, three-quarter, full-length, and seated and standing poses. *$34.95 list, 8.5x11, 128p, 500 color images, index, order no. 1909.*

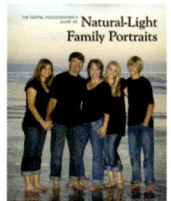

THE DIGITAL PHOTOGRAPHER'S GUIDE TO Natural-Light Family Portraits

Jennifer George teaches you how to use natural light and meaningful locations to create cherished portraits and bigger sales. *$34.95 list, 8.5x11, 128p, 180 color images, index, order no. 1937.*

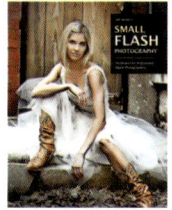

BILL HURTER'S Small Flash Photography

Learn to select and place small flash units, choose proper flash settings and communication, and more. *$34.95 list, 8.5x11, 128p, 180 color photos and diagrams, index, order no. 1936.*

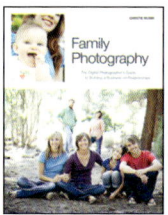

Family Photography

Christie Mumm shows you how to build a business based on client relationships and capture life-cycle milestones, from births, to senior portraits, to weddings. *$34.95 list, 8.5x11, 128p, 220 color images, index, order no. 1941.*

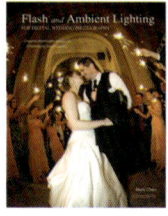

Flash and Ambient Lighting
FOR DIGITAL WEDDING PHOTOGRAPHY

Mark Chen shows you how to master the use of flash and ambient lighting for outstanding wedding images. *$34.95 list, 8.5x11, 128p, 200 color photos and diagrams, index, order no. 1942.*

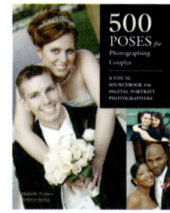

500 Poses for Photographing Couples

Michelle Perkins showcases an array of poses that will give you the creative boost you need to create an evocative, meaningful portrait. *$34.95 list, 8.5x11, 128p, 500 color images, order no. 1943.*

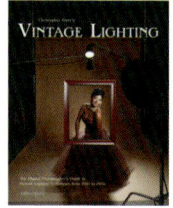

CHRISTOPHER GREY'S Vintage Lighting

Re-create portrait styles popular from 1910 to 1970 or tweak the setups to create modern images with an edge. *$34.95 list, 8.5x11, 128p, 185 color images, 15 diagrams, index, order no. 1945.*

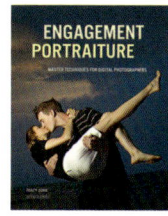

Engagement Portraiture

Tracy Dorr demonstrates how to create masterful engagement portraits and build a marketing and sales approach that maximizes profits. *$34.95 list, 8.5x11, 128p, 200 color images, index, order no. 1946.*

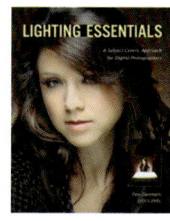

Lighting Essentials

Don Giannatti's subject-centric approach to lighting will teach you how to make confident lighting choices and flawlessly execute images that match your creative vision. *$34.95 list, 8.5x11, 128p, 240 color images, index, order no. 1947.*

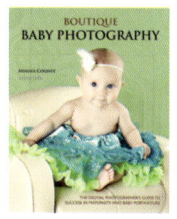

Boutique Baby Photography

Mimika Cooney shows you how to create the ultimate portrait experience—from start to finish—for your higher-end baby and maternity portrait clients. *$34.95 list, 7.5x10, 160p, 200 color images, index, order no. 1952.*

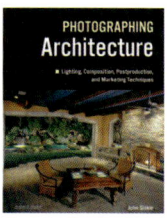

Lighting for Architectural Photography

John Siskin teaches you how to work with strobe and ambient light to capture rich, textural images your clients will love. *$34.95 list, 7.5x10, 160p, 180 color images, index, order no. 1955.*

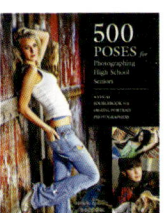

500 Poses for Photographing High School Seniors

Michelle Perkins presents head-and-shoulders, three-quarter, and full-length poses tailored to seniors' eclectic tastes. *$34.95 list, 8.5x11, 128p, 500 color images, order no. 1957.*

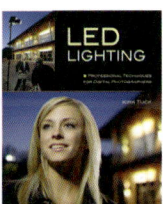

LED Lighting: PROFESSIONAL TECHNIQUES FOR DIGITAL PHOTOGRAPHERS

Kirk Tuck's comprehensive look at LED lighting reveals the ins-and-outs of the technology and shows how to put it to great use. *$34.95 list, 7.5x10, 160p, 380 color images, order no. 1958.*

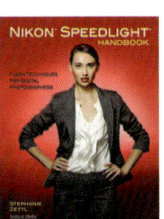

Nikon® Speedlight® Handbook

Stephanie Zettl gets down and dirty with this dynamic lighting system, showing you how to maximize your results in the studio or on location. *$34.95 list, 7.5x10, 160p, 300 color images, order no. 1959.*

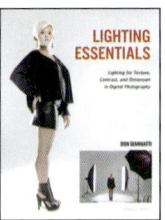

Lighting Essentials: LIGHTING FOR TEXTURE, CONTRAST, AND DIMENSION

Don Giannatti explores lighting to define shape, conceal or emphasize texture, and enhance the feeling of a third dimension. *$34.95 list, 7.5x10, 160p, 220 color images, order no. 1961.*

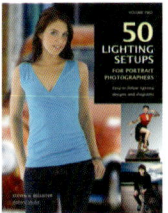

50 Lighting Setups for Portrait Photographers, VOLUME 2

Steven Begleiter provides recipes for portrait success. Concise text, diagrams, and screen shots track the complete creative process. *$34.95 list, 7.5x10, 160p, 250 color images, order no. 1962.*

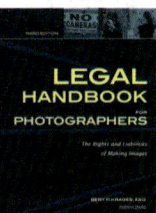

Legal Handbook for Photographers, THIRD EDITION

Acclaimed intellectual-property attorney Bert Krages shows you how to protect your rights when creating and selling your work. *$39.95 list, 7.5x10, 160p, 110 color images, order no. 1965.*

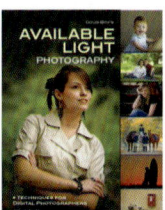

DOUG BOX'S Available Light Photography

Popular photo-educator Doug Box shows you how to capture (and refine) the simple beauty of available light—indoors and out. *$39.95 list, 7.5x10, 160p, 240 color images, order no. 1964.*

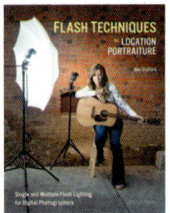

Flash Techniques for Location Portraiture

Alyn Stafford takes flash on the road, showing you how to achieve big results with these small systems. *$34.95 list, 7.5x10, 160p, 220 color images, order no. 1963.*

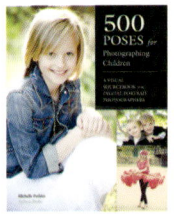

500 Poses for Photographing Children

Michelle Perkins presents head-and-shoulders, three-quarter, and full-length poses to help you capture the magic of childhood. *$39.95 list, 8.5x11, 128p, 500 color images, order no. 1967.*

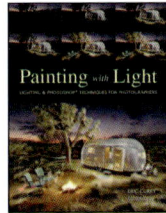

Painting with Light

Eric Curry shows you how to identify optimal scenes and subjects and choose the best light-painting sources for the shape and texture of the surface you're lighting. *$39.95 list, 7.5x10, 160p, 275 color images, index, order no. 1968.*

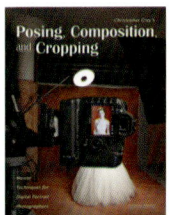

Christopher Grey's Posing, Composition, and Cropping

Make optimal image design choices to produce photographs that flatter your subjects and meet clients' needs. *$39.95 list, 7.5x10, 160p, 330 color images, index, order no. 1969.*

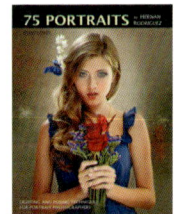

75 Portraits by Hernan Rodriquez

Conceptualize and create stunning shots of men, women, and kids with the high-caliber techniques in this book. *$39.95 list, 7.5x10, 160p, 150 color images, 75 diagrams, index, order no. 1970.*

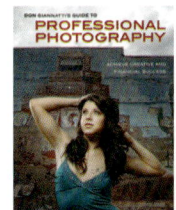

DON GIANNATTI'S Guide to Professional Photography

Perfect your portfolio and get work in the fashion, food, beauty, or editorial markets. Contains insights and images from top pros. *$39.95 list, 7.5x10, 160p, 220 color images, order no. 1971.*

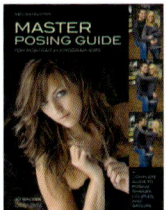

Master Posing Guide for Portrait Photographers, 2nd Ed.

JD Wacker's must-have posing book has been fully updated. You'll learn fail-safe techniques for posing men, women, kids, and groups. *$39.95 list, 7.5x10, 160p, 220 color images, order no. 1972.*

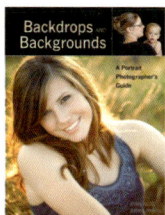

Backdrops and Backgrounds
A PORTRAIT PHOTOGRAPHER'S GUIDE

Ryan Klos' book shows you how to select, light, and modify man-made and natural backdrops to create standout portraits. *$39.95 list, 7.5x10, 160p, 220 color images, order no. 1976.*

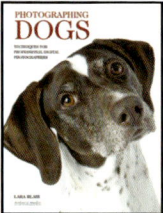

Photographing Dogs

Lara Blair presents strategies for building a thriving dog portraiture studio. You'll learn to attract clients and work with canines in the studio and on location. *$39.95 list, 7.5x10, 160p, 276 color images, order no. 1977.*

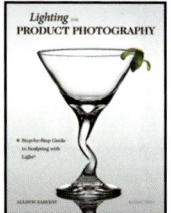

Lighting for Product Photography

Allison Earnest shows you how to select and modify light sources to capture the color, shape, and texture of an array of products. *$39.95 list, 7.5x10, 160p, 195 color images, order no. 1978.*

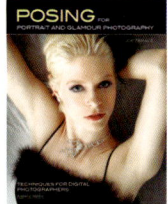

Posing for Portrait and Glamour Photography

Joe Farace provides essential strategies for idealizing portrait subjects and creating flattering, evocative images that sell. *$39.95 list, 7.5x10, 160p, 260 color images, order no. 1979.*

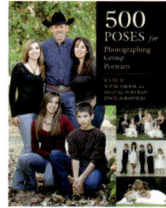

500 Poses for Photographing Groups

Michelle Perkins provides an impressive collection of images that will inspire you to design polished, professional portraits. *$39.95 list, 8.5x11, 128p, 500 color images, order no. 1980.*

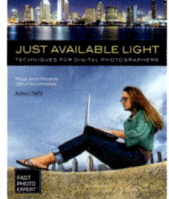

Just Available Light
TECHNIQUES FOR DIGITAL PHOTOGRAPHERS

Rod and Robin Deutschmann show you how to capture high-end images of portrait and still-life subjects. *$24.95 list, 7.5x10, 96p, 220 color images, order no. 1981.*

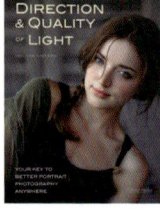

Direction & Quality of Light

Neil Van Niekerk shows you how consciously controlling the direction and quality of light in your portraits can take your work to a whole new level. *$39.95 list, 7.5x10, 160p, 195 color images, order no. 1982.*

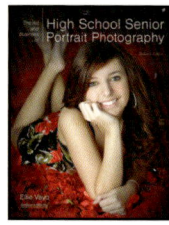

THE ART AND BUSINESS OF HIGH SCHOOL Senior Portrait Photography,
SECOND EDITION

Ellie Vayo provides critical marketing and business tips for all senior portrait photographers. *$39.95 list, 7.5x10, 160p, 200 color images, order no. 1983.*

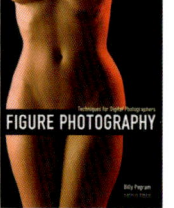

Figure Photography

Billy Pegram provides a comprehensive guide to designing desireable commercial and fine-art figure images. *$39.95 list, 7.5x10, 160p, 300 color images, order no. 1984.*

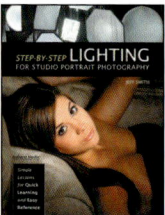

Step-by-Step Lighting for Studio Portrait Photography

Jeff Smith teaches you how to develop a comprehensive lighting strategy that truly sculpts the subject for breathtaking results. *$39.95 list, 7.5x10, 160p, 275 color images, order no. 1985.*